# MACHINE LEARNING

Hayden Van Der Post

**Reactive Publishing**

# CONTENTS

# CHAPTER 1: INTRODUCTION TO MACHINE LEARNING IN FINANCE

Finance is an ideal domain for the application of machine learning. Machine learning, a subset of artificial intelligence, empowers systems to learn from data and improve their performance over time without explicit programming. In the financial sector, this translates to powerful predictive analytics, risk management, fraud detection, and automated trading systems.

Machine learning involves algorithms that parse data, learn from it, and subsequently make a determination or prediction about something in the world. These algorithms are designed to improve their performance as they are exposed to more data. The process typically involves several key steps: data collection, data preprocessing, model training, model evaluation, and model deployment.

- Data Collection: Gathering relevant historical and real-time data.

- Data Preprocessing: Cleaning and preparing the data for analysis.
- Model Training: Using algorithms to learn patterns from the data.
- Model Evaluation: Assessing the model's performance and accuracy.
- Model Deployment: Implementing the model in a real-world setting to make predictions.

Applications and Significance in Finance

The integration of machine learning in finance revolutionizes traditional methodologies, providing significant advancements in various areas:

1. Predictive Analytics:

Predictive analytics involves using historical data to predict future events. In finance, this is particularly useful for predicting stock prices, market trends, and economic indicators. For instance, a well-trained machine learning model can analyze past market behaviors and predict future fluctuations, aiding investors in making informed decisions.

2. Risk Management:

Managing risk is critical in finance. Machine learning models can assess and predict risks with higher accuracy by analyzing vast datasets that include various risk factors. This allows for more dynamic and responsive risk management strategies, reducing potential losses.

3. Fraud Detection:

Fraudulent activities cost the financial industry billions annually. Machine learning algorithms can learn to identify unusual patterns and anomalies in transaction data, flagging potential fraud with greater efficiency than traditional methods. For example, credit card companies often use machine learning to detect and prevent unauthorized transactions.

4. Algorithmic Trading:

Algorithmic trading uses computer programs to make trading decisions at speeds and frequencies that human traders cannot match. Machine learning enhances these programs by enabling them to learn from past trades, adapt to new market conditions, and optimize trading strategies in real-time.

5. Customer Service and Personalization:

In retail banking and investment services, machine learning algorithms can analyze customer data to provide personalized financial advice, detect customer dissatisfaction, and improve customer experience through chatbots and virtual assistants that learn and adapt to user queries.

Practical Examples in Financial Institutions

To illustrate machine learning's significance in finance, consider these practical implementations:

- JPMorgan Chase's COiN: The Contract Intelligence (COiN) platform uses natural language processing, a machine learning subfield, to review and interpret legal documents. This significantly reduces the time required to review complex contracts.

- Goldman Sachs' Marcus: The Marcus platform leverages machine learning for personal loan underwriting, analyzing vast amounts of data to predict creditworthiness with higher accuracy than traditional credit scoring methods.

- Ant Financial's Fraud Detection: Alibaba's financial subsidiary, Ant Financial, employs machine learning to enhance its fraud detection capabilities, analyzing over 3 billion transactions annually to protect its users from fraudulent activities.

Key Concepts and Techniques

Several machine learning techniques are particularly relevant in finance:

- Supervised Learning: Models are trained on labeled data, making it ideal for tasks like loan approval and credit scoring, where historical data with known outcomes is available.
- Unsupervised Learning: Useful for anomaly detection and customer segmentation, where the goal is to identify patterns and structures in unlabeled data.
- Reinforcement Learning: Applicable in areas like portfolio management and algorithmic trading, where the model learns to make decisions through trial and error, optimizing long-term rewards.

While the benefits are substantial, implementing machine learning in finance comes with challenges:

- Data Quality and Quantity: High-quality, extensive datasets are essential for training effective machine learning models. Financial data can be noisy and incomplete, requiring robust preprocessing techniques.

- Interpretability: Financial institutions often require model predictions to be explainable for regulatory compliance and stakeholder trust. Complex models like deep neural networks, though powerful, can lack interpretability.

- Regulatory and Ethical Concerns: Financial applications of machine learning must adhere to strict regulatory standards. Ethical considerations around data privacy and bias also need careful management.

<achine learning is a transformative force in finance, offering enhanced predictive power, improved risk management, and efficient fraud detection, among other benefits. As financial institutions continue to integrate these technologies, the industry is poised for unprecedented innovation and efficiency.

## Historical Perspective and Evolution

Machine learning's integration into the financial sector did not happen overnight. It represents an evolutionary leap from traditional financial modeling, influenced by advances in computing and data science. To appreciate its significance, it is essential to understand the historical context and evolution that has shaped its current state.

### The Genesis: Early Computational Finance

The roots of machine learning in finance can be traced

back to the mid-20th century when the advent of computers began revolutionizing data analysis. The 1950s and 1960s saw the development of early computational finance models, primarily focused on applying statistical techniques to financial problems. During this period, the Efficient Market Hypothesis (EMH) gained prominence, positing that asset prices reflect all available information. This theory spurred interest in quantitative models that could analyze market data to identify patterns and predict future movements.

The Rise of Statistical Models

By the 1970s and 1980s, financial institutions increasingly embraced statistical models for risk assessment and portfolio management. The introduction of the Black-Scholes model in 1973 revolutionized options pricing, providing a mathematical framework that remains influential. This era marked the beginning of quantitative finance, where mathematical models became integral to financial decision-making.

During these decades, the foundation was laid for more sophisticated modeling techniques. Linear regression, logistic regression, and time series analysis became staples in financial analysis, providing tools for predicting stock prices, interest rates, and market trends. However, these models had limitations, notably the assumptions of linearity and normality, which often failed to capture the complexities of financial markets.

The Data Revolution and Advent of Machine Learning

The 1990s heralded a new era with the proliferation of digital data and advancements in computational power. The internet boom generated massive amounts of financial data, offering unprecedented opportunities for analysis. Concurrently, machine learning, a subfield of artificial intelligence, began to mature, driven by breakthroughs in algorithms and computing.

Machine learning diverged from traditional statistical models by focusing on pattern recognition and prediction without explicit programming. Algorithms such as decision trees, neural networks, and support vector machines emerged, capable of handling large datasets and uncovering complex relationships. Financial institutions started experimenting with these techniques, recognizing their potential to enhance predictive accuracy and uncover hidden patterns.

The Dot-Com Bubble and Algorithmic Trading

The late 1990s and early 2000s witnessed the dot-com bubble, a period of speculative investment in internet-based companies. During this time, algorithmic trading gained traction, leveraging machine learning to execute trades at high speeds and frequencies. Pioneers like Renaissance Technologies and its Medallion Fund utilized sophisticated algorithms to achieve extraordinary returns, demonstrating the power of machine learning in finance.

Algorithmic trading systems employed machine learning to analyze market data, identify arbitrage opportunities, and optimize trading strategies. The success of these systems fueled further investment in machine learning research and development, accelerating its adoption across the financial industry.

The Financial Crisis and Risk Management

The 2008 financial crisis underscored the importance of robust risk management and predictive analytics. Traditional models failed to foresee the crisis, highlighting their limitations and the need for more advanced techniques. In response, financial institutions increasingly turned to machine learning for risk assessment and management.

Machine learning models offered several advantages over traditional methods, including the ability to handle non-linear relationships, process vast amounts of data, and adapt to changing market conditions. Techniques such as clustering, anomaly detection, and reinforcement learning became valuable tools for identifying and mitigating risks.

Modern Era: Big Data, Deep Learning, and FinTech

In the past decade, the convergence of big data, cloud computing, and deep learning has propelled machine learning to new heights. Financial institutions now have access to petabytes of data, from transactional records to social media sentiment, enabling more granular and accurate analysis.

Deep learning, a subset of machine learning inspired by the structure and function of the human brain, has shown remarkable success in fields like image and speech recognition. In finance, deep learning models are applied to high-frequency trading, fraud detection, and sentiment analysis. These models can process vast amounts of unstructured data, learning patterns and making highly accurate predictions.

The rise of FinTech companies has further democratized machine learning in finance. Startups like Stripe, Square, and Robinhood leverage machine learning to offer innovative financial services, from payment processing to robo-advisors. These companies challenge traditional financial institutions, fostering a competitive environment that drives technological advancements.

Case Studies: Evolution in Action

To illustrate the evolution of machine learning in finance, consider the following case studies:

- Renaissance Technologies: Founded by mathematician James Simons, Renaissance Technologies is renowned for its use of machine learning in trading. The firm's Medallion Fund employs proprietary algorithms to analyze market data and execute trades, consistently delivering outstanding returns. Their success exemplifies the transformative power of machine learning in finance.

- JPMorgan Chase: The bank's COiN platform automates the review of legal documents using machine learning, significantly reducing processing time. This application demonstrates the versatility of machine learning, extending beyond trading to operational efficiencies.

- Ant Financial: Alibaba's financial arm uses machine learning for credit scoring and risk assessment in its lending platform. By analyzing a wide range of data points, including transaction history and social behavior, Ant Financial can make more accurate lending decisions, highlighting the potential of machine learning in credit risk management.

Challenges

Despite its advancements, machine learning in finance faces several challenges. Ensuring data quality, addressing ethical concerns, and meeting regulatory compliance are ongoing issues. Moreover, the complexity of financial markets means that models must continually adapt to new information and changing conditions.

However, the future of machine learning in finance looks promising. Emerging technologies like quantum computing and blockchain offer new avenues for innovation. Quantum computing, for instance, could exponentially increase computational power, enabling more complex and accurate models. Blockchain, with its transparent and immutable ledger, could enhance data integrity and trust in financial transactions.

the historical evolution of machine learning in finance reflects a journey of continuous innovation and adaptation. From early statistical models to modern deep learning techniques, machine learning has revolutionized financial analysis, risk management, and trading. As technology continues to advance, the synergy between machine learning and finance will undoubtedly lead to even greater achievements, driving the industry towards new frontiers of efficiency and insight.

## Overview of Financial Problems Solved with Machine Learning

### 1. Predictive Analytics and Forecasting

Stock Price Prediction:

Predicting stock prices has long been a coveted goal in finance. Traditional methods relied on linear models and historical data, often falling short due to market complexities. Machine learning, however, employs algorithms like neural networks and support vector machines to analyze vast amounts of data, including historical prices, trading volumes, and even social media sentiment. This multi-faceted approach enables more accurate predictions, allowing traders to make informed decisions and optimize their portfolios.

Example:

```python
import numpy as np
import pandas as pd
from sklearn.model_selection import train_test_split
from sklearn.preprocessing import StandardScaler
from sklearn.svm import SVR
from sklearn.metrics import mean_squared_error

Load data
data = pd.read_csv('historical_stock_prices.csv')

Feature selection
features = data[['Open', 'High', 'Low', 'Volume']]
target = data['Close']

Data preprocessing
X_train, X_test, y_train, y_test = train_test_split(features, target, test_size=0.2, random_state=42)
```

```
scaler = StandardScaler()
X_train = scaler.fit_transform(X_train)
X_test = scaler.transform(X_test)

Model training
model = SVR(kernel='rbf')
model.fit(X_train, y_train)

 Predictions
predictions = model.predict(X_test)

Evaluation
mse = mean_squared_error(y_test, predictions)
print(f"Mean Squared Error: {mse}")
```

2. Risk Management

Credit Scoring:

Credit scoring assesses the likelihood that a borrower will default on a loan. Traditional credit scoring models relied heavily on static criteria like credit history and debt levels. Machine learning introduces a dynamic approach, analyzing a broader range of variables such as transaction history, social behavior, and even real-time financial activities. This leads to more accurate credit scores and better risk assessment.

Fraud Detection:

Fraud detection has been revolutionized by machine learning, offering real-time analysis and pattern recognition. Traditional rule-based systems struggled to keep up with evolving fraud tactics. Machine learning algorithms, such as anomaly detection and clustering, identify unusual patterns and behaviors that may indicate fraudulent activities. These systems continuously learn and adapt, improving their accuracy over time.

Example:

```python
from sklearn.ensemble import IsolationForest
from sklearn.metrics import classification_report

Load data
data = pd.read_csv('transaction_data.csv')

Feature selection
features = data[['amount', 'transaction_type', 'merchant_id']]

Model training
model = IsolationForest(contamination=0.01)
model.fit(features)

Predictions
data['anomaly'] = model.predict(features)

Evaluation
print(classification_report(data['actual_fraud'],
```

```
data['anomaly'] == -1))
```

3. Portfolio Management

Asset Allocation:

Optimizing asset allocation involves selecting the right mix of investments to achieve desired returns while managing risk. Traditional methods like the Mean-Variance Optimization often assume linear relationships and normal distribution of returns, which do not hold in real-world scenarios. Machine learning techniques, such as reinforcement learning, offer more flexible and adaptive approaches. These algorithms learn from market data and dynamically adjust the asset allocation to optimize returns and minimize risk.

Example:

```python
import numpy as np
import pandas as pd
from sklearn.ensemble import RandomForestRegressor

Load data
data = pd.read_csv('asset_returns.csv')

Feature selection
features = data[['asset_1', 'asset_2', 'asset_3']]
target = data['portfolio_return']
```

```
Data preprocessing
X_train, X_test, y_train, y_test = train_test_split(features, target, test_size=0.2, random_state=42)

Model training
model = RandomForestRegressor(n_estimators=100, random_state=42)
model.fit(X_train, y_train)

 Predictions
predictions = model.predict(X_test)

Evaluation
mse = mean_squared_error(y_test, predictions)
print(f"Mean Squared Error: {mse}")
```

4. Customer Segmentation and Personalization

Market Segmentation:

Market segmentation involves dividing a market into distinct groups of consumers with similar needs or characteristics. Traditional segmentation methods relied on demographic data and surveys, which were often static and limited. Machine learning, particularly clustering algorithms like K-Means and DBSCAN, analyzes large datasets to identify natural groupings within the market. This leads to more precise targeting and personalized marketing strategies.

Personalized Financial Services:

Personalization in financial services involves tailoring products and advice to individual customers based on their unique financial situations. Machine learning models analyze a variety of data points, including spending patterns, investment behavior, and life events, to provide personalized recommendations. This enhances customer satisfaction and loyalty.

Example:

```python
from sklearn.cluster import KMeans

import matplotlib.pyplot as plt

Load data

data = pd.read_csv('customer_data.csv')

Feature selection

features = data[['annual_income', 'spending_score']]

Model training

kmeans = KMeans(n_clusters=5, random_state=42)

data['segment'] = kmeans.fit_predict(features)

Visualization

plt.scatter(data['annual_income'], data['spending_score'], c=data['segment'], cmap='viridis')

plt.xlabel('Annual Income')
```

```
plt.ylabel('Spending Score')
plt.title('Customer Segmentation')
plt.show()
```

5. Sentiment Analysis

Financial News Analysis:

Sentiment analysis of financial news and social media provides insights into market sentiment and potential impacts on asset prices. Machine learning models, particularly natural language processing (NLP) techniques, analyze text data to determine the sentiment and its potential effect on the market. This real-time analysis helps traders and analysts anticipate market movements and make informed decisions.

Example:

```python
from sklearn.feature_extraction.text import TfidfVectorizer
from sklearn.linear_model import LogisticRegression

Load data
data = pd.read_csv('financial_news.csv')

Feature selection
vectorizer = TfidfVectorizer(max_features=1000)
X = vectorizer.fit_transform(data['headline'])
y = data['sentiment']
```

```
Model training
model = LogisticRegression()
model.fit(X, y)

Predictions
predictions = model.predict(X)

Evaluation
print(classification_report(y, predictions))
```

Machine learning's impact on solving financial problems is profound and multifaceted. From predictive analytics and risk management to portfolio optimization and personalized financial services, machine learning techniques provide unprecedented accuracy, efficiency, and adaptability. The continuous evolution of algorithms and computational power ensures that machine learning will remain a cornerstone of innovation in the financial industry. As we delve deeper into this book, you'll gain a more comprehensive understanding of how to harness these techniques to address real-world financial challenges and unlock new opportunities.

## Key Concepts and Terminology

### 1. Machine Learning (ML)

Machine learning is a subset of artificial intelligence that enables systems to learn and improve from experience without being explicitly programmed. In the context of finance, machine learning algorithms analyze historical data to identify patterns and make predictions, thereby assisting in decision-making processes. The two primary types of machine learning are supervised and unsupervised learning.

Example:

```python
from sklearn.model_selection import train_test_split
from sklearn.linear_model import LinearRegression
import pandas as pd

Load data
data = pd.read_csv('financial_data.csv')

Feature selection
X = data[['feature1', 'feature2', 'feature3']]
y = data['target']

Data splitting
X_train, X_test, y_train, y_test = train_test_split(X, y, test_size=0.2, random_state=42)

Model training
model = LinearRegression()
model.fit(X_train, y_train)

Predictions
predictions = model.predict(X_test)
```

2. Supervised Learning

Supervised learning involves training a model on a labeled dataset, which means that each training example includes both input data and the corresponding output. Common supervised learning tasks include regression and classification.

- Regression: Predicts continuous outcomes, such as stock prices or interest rates.
- Classification: Categorizes data into discrete classes, such as identifying fraudulent transactions.

Example:

```python
from sklearn.linear_model import LogisticRegression

Classification example: Predicting whether a transaction is fraudulent
model = LogisticRegression()
model.fit(X_train, y_train)
predictions = model.predict(X_test)
```

3. Unsupervised Learning

Unsupervised learning deals with unlabeled data. The goal is to uncover hidden patterns or intrinsic structures within the data. Key unsupervised learning techniques include clustering and dimensionality reduction.

- Clustering: Grouping data points into clusters based on similarities, such as segmenting customers.
- Dimensionality Reduction: Reducing the number of features while preserving essential information, often used for visualization and noise reduction.

Example:

```python
from sklearn.decomposition import PCA

Dimensionality reduction example: Reducing features for visualization
pca = PCA(n_components=2)
X_reduced = pca.fit_transform(X)
```

4. Data Preprocessing

Data preprocessing is a crucial step in machine learning that involves cleaning and transforming raw data to make it suitable for modeling. This process includes handling missing values, encoding categorical variables, and scaling features.

- Feature Scaling: Standardizing the range of independent variables to ensure that each feature contributes equally to the model.
- Normalization: Transforming features to a common scale, usually between 0 and 1.

Example:

```python
from sklearn.preprocessing import StandardScaler

Feature scaling example
scaler = StandardScaler()
X_train_scaled = scaler.fit_transform(X_train)
X_test_scaled = scaler.transform(X_test)
```

5. Model Evaluation

Evaluating the performance of a machine learning model is essential to ensure its accuracy and reliability. Common evaluation metrics vary depending on the type of task (regression or classification).

- Mean Squared Error (MSE): Measures the average squared difference between actual and predicted values in regression tasks.
- Accuracy: The proportion of correct predictions in classification tasks.
- Precision and Recall: Precision is the ratio of true positive predictions to the total predicted positives, while recall is the ratio of true positives to all actual positives.

Example:

```python
```

```
from sklearn.metrics import mean_squared_error, accuracy_score

Regression evaluation example
mse = mean_squared_error(y_test, predictions)
print(f"Mean Squared Error: {mse}")

Classification evaluation example
accuracy = accuracy_score(y_test, predictions)
print(f"Accuracy: {accuracy}")
```

6. Overfitting and Underfitting

These concepts describe the performance of machine learning models:

- Overfitting: When a model learns the training data too well, including noise and outliers, resulting in poor generalization to new data.
- Underfitting: When a model is too simple to capture the underlying patterns in the data, leading to poor performance on both training and new data.

Balancing these is crucial for building robust models. Techniques such as cross-validation, regularization, and ensemble methods help mitigate these issues.

Example:

```python
```

```
from sklearn.model_selection import cross_val_score

Cross-validation to detect overfitting/underfitting
scores = cross_val_score(model, X, y, cv=5)
print(f"Cross-Validation Scores: {scores}")
```

7. Hyperparameter Tuning

Hyperparameters are the configuration settings used to optimize the performance of a machine learning model. Unlike model parameters, which are learned during training, hyperparameters are set before the training process. Techniques such as grid search and random search are commonly used for hyperparameter tuning.

Example:

```python
from sklearn.model_selection import GridSearchCV

Hyperparameter tuning example using GridSearchCV
param_grid = {'C': [0.1, 1, 10], 'kernel': ['linear', 'rbf']}
grid_search = GridSearchCV(SVR(), param_grid, cv=5)
grid_search.fit(X_train, y_train)
print(f"Best Parameters: {grid_search.best_params_}")
```

8. Feature Engineering

Feature engineering involves creating new features or modifying existing ones to improve model performance. This process requires domain knowledge and creativity to identify the most relevant features that capture the underlying patterns in the data.

Example:

```python
Creating new feature example: Calculating moving average of stock prices
data['moving_average'] =
data['Close'].rolling(window=5).mean()
```

9. Ensemble Learning

Ensemble learning combines multiple models to improve overall performance. By aggregating the predictions of individual models, ensemble methods such as Random Forests and Gradient Boosting can achieve better accuracy and robustness compared to a single model.

Example:

```python
from sklearn.ensemble import RandomForestClassifier

Ensemble learning example using Random Forests
model = RandomForestClassifier(n_estimators=100,
random_state=42)
```

```
model.fit(X_train, y_train)
predictions = model.predict(X_test)
```

10. Cross-Validation

Cross-validation is a technique for assessing how well a model will generalize to an independent dataset. It involves partitioning the data into subsets, training the model on some subsets, and validating it on the remaining subsets. This process is repeated multiple times to ensure the model's robustness.

Example:

```python
from sklearn.model_selection import KFold

Cross-validation example using KFold
kf = KFold(n_splits=5, shuffle=True, random_state=42)
for train_index, test_index in kf.split(X):
    X_train, X_test = X[train_index], X[test_index]
    y_train, y_test = y[train_index], y[test_index]
    model.fit(X_train, y_train)
    predictions = model.predict(X_test)
    mse = mean_squared_error(y_test, predictions)
    print(f"Fold MSE: {mse}")
```

Understanding these key concepts and terminology is

fundamental to successfully applying machine learning in finance. As you progress through this book, these principles will serve as the foundational building blocks for more advanced topics and practical implementations. Machine learning's transformative potential in finance rests on a thorough comprehension of these core ideas, enabling you to harness its power for innovative and effective solutions in the financial industry.

## Types of Machine Learning Algorithms

Machine learning algorithms serve as the cornerstone for developing predictive models, identifying patterns, and making data-driven decisions. These algorithms can be broadly categorized into supervised, unsupervised, semi-supervised, reinforcement, and ensemble learning methods. Each category has its unique characteristics and applications, making it essential to understand their strengths and limitations to leverage them effectively in financial contexts.

### Supervised Learning Algorithms

Supervised learning algorithms are designed to learn from labeled data, where each training example consists of an input-output pair. They aim to predict the output based on new input data. Supervised learning is further divided into regression and classification tasks.

1. Linear Regression:

Linear regression is used for predicting a continuous target variable based on one or more input features. It assumes a linear relationship between the input features and the target variable. In finance, it is commonly used for predicting stock prices, interest rates, and other continuous metrics.

Example:

```python
from sklearn.linear_model import LinearRegression
import pandas as pd

 Load data
data = pd.read_csv('financial_data.csv')

 Feature selection
X = data[['feature1', 'feature2']]
y = data['target']

 Model training
model = LinearRegression()
model.fit(X, y)

 Predictions
predictions = model.predict(X)
```

2. Logistic Regression:

Despite its name, logistic regression is used for classification tasks. It estimates the probability of a binary outcome based on one or more input features. In finance, logistic regression is often applied to identify fraudulent transactions or to perform credit scoring.

Example:

```python
from sklearn.linear_model import LogisticRegression

Classification example: Predicting whether a transaction is fraudulent
model = LogisticRegression()
model.fit(X, y)
predictions = model.predict(X)
```

3. Decision Trees:

Decision trees split the data into subsets based on the value of input features. Each node represents a decision point, leading to a final prediction at the leaf nodes. They can handle both regression and classification tasks and are known for their interpretability.

Example:

```python
from sklearn.tree import DecisionTreeClassifier

Classification example: Predicting risk category of an investment
model = DecisionTreeClassifier()
model.fit(X, y)
predictions = model.predict(X)
```

4. Support Vector Machines (SVM):

SVMs are powerful for classification and regression tasks. They work by finding the optimal hyperplane that separates different classes in the feature space. SVMs are particularly useful for high-dimensional data.

Example:

```python
from sklearn.svm import SVC

Classification example: Categorizing investments into high and low risk
model = SVC(kernel='linear')
model.fit(X, y)
predictions = model.predict(X)
```

Unsupervised Learning Algorithms

Unsupervised learning algorithms analyze data without labeled outcomes, aiming to uncover hidden patterns or intrinsic structures. These algorithms are particularly useful in exploratory data analysis.

1. K-Means Clustering:

K-means clustering partitions the data into K distinct clusters based on feature similarity. It is widely used in market segmentation, customer profiling, and identifying similar investment opportunities.

Example:

```python
from sklearn.cluster import KMeans

Clustering example: Segmenting clients based on transaction behavior
kmeans = KMeans(n_clusters=3)
kmeans.fit(X)
labels = kmeans.labels_
```

2. Principal Component Analysis (PCA):

PCA is a dimensionality reduction technique that transforms high-dimensional data into a lower-dimensional space while preserving most of the variance. It is often used in finance for portfolio management and risk analysis.

Example:

```python
from sklearn.decomposition import PCA

Dimensionality reduction example: Reducing features for portfolio analysis
pca = PCA(n_components=2)
X_reduced = pca.fit_transform(X)
```

3. Hierarchical Clustering:

Hierarchical clustering builds a tree-like structure of nested clusters. It is useful for identifying hierarchical relationships within the data, such as grouping financial instruments based on their characteristics.

Example:

```python
from scipy.cluster.hierarchy import linkage, dendrogram
import matplotlib.pyplot as plt

 Hierarchical clustering example: Visualizing relationships between stocks
Z = linkage(X, method='ward')
dendrogram(Z)
plt.show()
```

Semi-Supervised Learning

Semi-supervised learning combines both labeled and unlabeled data for training. This approach is particularly beneficial when labeled data is scarce but unlabeled data is abundant. In finance, semi-supervised learning can enhance predictive models by leveraging additional data points without incurring high labeling costs.

Example:

```python
from sklearn.semi_supervised import LabelSpreading

Semi-supervised learning example: Enhancing credit scoring model
model = LabelSpreading()
model.fit(X, y)
predictions = model.predict(X)
```

Reinforcement Learning

Reinforcement learning involves training agents to make a sequence of decisions by rewarding desirable actions and penalizing undesirable ones. This approach is gaining traction in finance for algorithmic trading, portfolio management, and optimizing investment strategies.

Example:

```python
import numpy as np

Example: Q-Learning for simple trading strategy
def q_learning(env, num_episodes, learning_rate, discount_factor, epsilon):
    q_table = np.zeros((env.observation_space.n, env.action_space.n))

    for episode in range(num_episodes):
```

```
        state = env.reset()
        done = False

        while not done:
            if np.random.rand() < epsilon:
                action = env.action_space.sample()
            else:
                action = np.argmax(q_table[state])

            next_state, reward, done, _ = env.step(action)
            q_table[state, action] = q_table[state, action] + learning_rate * (reward + discount_factor * np.max(q_table[next_state]) - q_table[state, action])
            state = next_state

    return q_table
```

Ensemble Learning

Ensemble learning algorithms combine multiple base models to improve overall performance. By aggregating the predictions of individual models, ensemble methods such as Random Forests and Gradient Boosting achieve higher accuracy and robustness.

1. Random Forests:

Random forests are an ensemble of decision trees trained on different subsets of the data. They reduce overfitting and improve predictive performance by averaging the results of multiple trees.

Example:

```python
from sklearn.ensemble import RandomForestClassifier

 Ensemble learning example using Random Forests
model = RandomForestClassifier(n_estimators=100, random_state=42)
model.fit(X, y)
predictions = model.predict(X)
```

2. Gradient Boosting Machines (GBM):

GBMs build an ensemble of sequential models, where each model corrects the errors of its predecessor. They are powerful for both regression and classification tasks, offering high predictive accuracy.

Example:

```python
from sklearn.ensemble import GradientBoostingClassifier

 Gradient Boosting example: Predicting loan default probability
model = GradientBoostingClassifier(n_estimators=100, learning_rate=0.1, random_state=42)
model.fit(X, y)
predictions = model.predict(X)
```

```

Understanding the various types of machine learning algorithms and their applications in finance is crucial for developing robust and accurate predictive models. Each algorithm has its strengths and is suited for specific tasks, making it essential to choose the right method based on the problem at hand. As you master these algorithms, you'll be better equipped to tackle complex financial challenges and drive innovative solutions.

Supervised vs Unsupervised Learning

Supervised learning algorithms are designed to learn from labeled data. In other words, the training dataset includes both the input features and the corresponding output labels. The goal is to learn a mapping from inputs to outputs that can be used to predict the outputs for new, unseen inputs. This paradigm is particularly powerful for tasks where historical data with known outcomes is available.

Regression and Classification

Supervised learning tasks can be broadly categorized into regression and classification. Regression involves predicting a continuous target variable, while classification deals with assigning inputs into predefined categories.

1. Regression in Finance:

- Linear Regression: Linear regression predicts a continuous target variable based on linear relationships between the input features and the target. In finance, it's often used to forecast stock prices, interest rates, or economic indicators.
```

Example:

```python
from sklearn.linear_model import LinearRegression
import pandas as pd

 Load financial data
data = pd.read_csv('financial_data.csv')
X = data[['feature1', 'feature2']]
y = data['target']

 Initialize and train model
model = LinearRegression()
model.fit(X, y)

 Make predictions
predictions = model.predict(X)
```

2. Classification in Finance:

- Logistic Regression: Despite its name, logistic regression is used for binary classification tasks. It predicts the probability that a given input belongs to a particular class. In finance, it's used for credit scoring, fraud detection, and predicting default risk.

Example:

```python
from sklearn.linear_model import LogisticRegression
```

```
 Classification example: Fraud detection
model = LogisticRegression()
model.fit(X, y)
predictions = model.predict(X)
```

- Support Vector Machines (SVM): SVMs are robust classifiers that find the optimal hyperplane separating different classes in the feature space. They are effective in high-dimensional spaces and are used in finance for risk categorization and anomaly detection.

Example:

```python
from sklearn.svm import SVC

 Classification example: Risk categorization
model = SVC(kernel='linear')
model.fit(X, y)
predictions = model.predict(X)
```

- Decision Trees and Random Forests: Decision trees split the data into subsets based on feature values, while random forests combine multiple decision trees to improve accuracy and robustness. These methods are used for predicting financial market trends and investment risk.

Example:

```python
from sklearn.tree import DecisionTreeClassifier
from sklearn.ensemble import RandomForestClassifier

 Decision tree example
tree_model = DecisionTreeClassifier()
tree_model.fit(X, y)
tree_predictions = tree_model.predict(X)

 Random forest example
forest_model = RandomForestClassifier(n_estimators=100)
forest_model.fit(X, y)
forest_predictions = forest_model.predict(X)
```

Unsupervised Learning

Unsupervised learning algorithms, on the other hand, are used to analyze and interpret data that does not have labeled outcomes. The aim is to uncover hidden patterns, structures, or relationships within the data. This approach is invaluable for exploratory data analysis and deriving insights from complex datasets.

Clustering and Dimensionality Reduction

Unsupervised learning methods can be broadly categorized into clustering and dimensionality reduction techniques.

1. Clustering in Finance:

- K-Means Clustering: K-means partitions the data into K distinct clusters based on feature similarity. It's commonly used for market segmentation, customer profiling, and identifying investment opportunities.

Example:

```python
from sklearn.cluster import KMeans

 Clustering example: Market segmentation
kmeans = KMeans(n_clusters=3)
kmeans.fit(X)
labels = kmeans.labels_
```

- Hierarchical Clustering: Builds a tree-like structure of nested clusters, useful for visualizing hierarchical relationships within financial data, such as grouping stocks or assets based on their characteristics.

Example:

```python
from scipy.cluster.hierarchy import linkage, dendrogram
import matplotlib.pyplot as plt

 Hierarchical clustering example: Asset grouping
Z = linkage(X, method='ward')
dendrogram(Z)
plt.show()
```

2. Dimensionality Reduction in Finance:

- Principal Component Analysis (PCA): PCA reduces the dimensionality of the data while preserving most of the variance. It's widely used in portfolio management to identify key factors driving returns and risk.

Example:

```python
from sklearn.decomposition import PCA

PCA example: Portfolio analysis
pca = PCA(n_components=2)
X_reduced = pca.fit_transform(X)
```

- t-Distributed Stochastic Neighbor Embedding (t-SNE): t-SNE is a non-linear dimensionality reduction technique used for visualizing high-dimensional data. It's useful for identifying patterns in financial data that are not apparent in the original feature space.

Example:

```python
from sklearn.manifold import TSNE

 t-SNE example: Visualizing trading patterns
tsne = TSNE(n_components=2)
X_embedded = tsne.fit_transform(X)
```

Comparing Supervised and Unsupervised Learning

Objective: The primary objective of supervised learning is to make accurate predictions based on past data, whereas unsupervised learning aims to discover hidden structures from the data.

Data Requirement: Supervised learning requires labeled datasets, meaning that each input is associated with an output label. Unsupervised learning, however, works with unlabeled data, relying on the inherent structure of the data itself.

Applications in Finance:

- Supervised Learning: Primarily used for predictive modeling, such as forecasting stock prices, credit scoring, and fraud detection. Its ability to learn from past data makes it ideal for making informed predictions about future events.
- Unsupervised Learning: Often used for exploratory analysis and pattern recognition, such as market segmentation, portfolio diversification, and anomaly detection. It helps in understanding the underlying structure of financial data without prior knowledge of the outcomes.

Advantages and Limitations:

- Supervised Learning: Provides more straightforward and interpretable results, especially when the relationship between inputs and outputs is well understood. However, it requires a large amount of labeled data, which can be costly and time-consuming to obtain.
- Unsupervised Learning: Excels in discovering hidden patterns and structures, making it useful in exploratory data analysis. Nevertheless, the results can be less interpretable,

and the lack of labels can make it challenging to validate the findings.

Practical Considerations

When choosing between supervised and unsupervised learning techniques in finance, several factors must be considered:

- Data Availability: The availability of labeled data often dictates whether supervised learning is feasible. When labeled data is scarce or expensive to obtain, unsupervised learning can provide valuable insights.
- Problem Nature: The specific nature of the financial problem at hand will influence the choice of algorithm. Predictive tasks benefit from supervised learning, while exploratory analysis and pattern recognition are best suited for unsupervised methods.
- Model Complexity: Supervised learning models can become complex and overfit to the training data, requiring techniques like cross-validation and regularization. Unsupervised learning models, while simpler, may require more sophisticated interpretation of the results.

Overview of Scikit-Learn

Scikit-Learn offers a robust and user-friendly interface for implementing a variety of machine learning models. Its modularity ensures that it can be seamlessly integrated into diverse workflows, making it an indispensable tool for financial analysts and data scientists. Here's a breakdown of its primary features:

1. Ease of Use: Scikit-Learn is designed with simplicity and consistency in mind. The API follows a unified interface for different models, making it accessible even for beginners. This consistency facilitates quick learning and easier transitions between different algorithms.

2. Comprehensive Algorithm Coverage: The library includes a wide range of machine learning algorithms, supporting tasks such as classification, regression, clustering, dimensionality reduction, and model selection. This extensive coverage makes it suitable for various financial applications, from predicting stock prices to detecting anomalies.

3. Integration with Python Ecosystem: Scikit-Learn integrates seamlessly with other popular Python libraries like NumPy, SciPy, pandas, and Matplotlib. This integration enhances its capabilities, allowing users to leverage the strengths of multiple libraries simultaneously.

4. Preprocessing Tools: The library provides numerous utilities for preprocessing data, including scaling, normalization, and imputation of missing values. These tools are crucial for preparing financial data, which often comes with its own set of challenges, such as noise and missing entries.

5. Model Evaluation and Selection: Scikit-Learn offers various tools for model evaluation and selection, including cross-validation, grid search, and metrics for assessing the performance of models. These features are essential for ensuring that the models are both accurate and reliable.

6. Community and Documentation: Scikit-Learn boasts a large and active community, alongside extensive documentation

and tutorials. This support network aids users in troubleshooting issues and staying updated with the latest developments.

Design Philosophy

Scikit-Learn's design philosophy revolves around three key principles: simplicity, efficiency, and reusability. These principles are reflected in its API design and overall architecture.

1. Simplicity: The API is designed to be easy to use, with a consistent interface for all machine learning models. This means that once you learn how to use one model, you can easily apply that knowledge to others. For instance, the `fit`, `predict`, and `transform` methods are common across different estimators, ensuring a smooth learning curve.

2. Efficiency: The library is built on top of efficient numerical libraries like NumPy and SciPy, ensuring that operations are performed quickly and effectively. This efficiency is critical when dealing with large financial datasets.

3. Reusability: Scikit-Learn follows the principle of reusability by providing reusable components that can be easily combined to create complex workflows. This modularity is beneficial in financial modeling, where different preprocessing steps, models, and evaluation techniques need to be combined seamlessly.

Practical Applications in Finance

Scikit-Learn's versatility enables its application across a wide array of financial tasks. Here, we illustrate some practical applications of Scikit-Learn in the finance domain:

1. Predictive Modeling:

- Stock Price Prediction: Linear regression models from Scikit-Learn can be used to predict future stock prices based on historical data and relevant financial indicators.

- Credit Scoring: Classification models like logistic regression and random forests can assess the creditworthiness of applicants by analyzing historical loan data and demographic information.

Example:

```python
from sklearn.linear_model import LinearRegression
import pandas as pd

 Load financial data
data = pd.read_csv('stock_data.csv')
X = data[['previous_day_price', 'trading_volume']]
y = data['current_day_price']

 Initialize and train model
model = LinearRegression()
model.fit(X, y)

 Make predictions
predictions = model.predict(X)
```

2. Risk Management:

- Fraud Detection: Anomaly detection algorithms can identify unusual patterns in transaction data, flagging potential fraudulent activities.

- Portfolio Optimization: Clustering techniques can group similar stocks, assisting in the construction of diversified portfolios to minimize risk.

Example:

```python
from sklearn.ensemble import IsolationForest

 Load transaction data
data = pd.read_csv('transaction_data.csv')
X = data[['amount', 'transaction_time']]

 Initialize and train model
model = IsolationForest(contamination=0.01)
model.fit(X)

 Detect anomalies
anomalies = model.predict(X) == -1
```

3. Market Segmentation:

- Customer Profiling: Clustering algorithms like K-means can segment customers based on their behavior and preferences, helping in targeted marketing and personalized financial services.

- Investor Segmentation: Dimensionality reduction techniques can identify key factors that differentiate investor groups, facilitating tailored investment strategies.

Example:

```python
from sklearn.cluster import KMeans

 Load customer data
data = pd.read_csv('customer_data.csv')
X = data[['age', 'investment_amount', 'risk_tolerance']]

 Initialize and train model
kmeans = KMeans(n_clusters=3)
kmeans.fit(X)

 Assign cluster labels
labels = kmeans.labels_
```

Getting Started with Scikit-Learn

To harness the power of Scikit-Learn, one must first set up the environment. This involves installing the library and understanding its basic data structures and API conventions.

1. Installation: Scikit-Learn can be installed using pip, the Python package installer, or conda, the package manager for Anaconda distribution. Here's how to install it:

```bash
pip install scikit-learn
```

Or, with conda:

```bash
conda install scikit-learn
```

2. Basic Data Structures: Scikit-Learn primarily works with NumPy arrays and pandas DataFrames. Understanding how to manipulate these data structures is crucial for effective use of the library.

3. API Conventions: Scikit-Learn's API conventions revolve around the Estimator interface, which includes methods like `fit`, `predict`, and `transform`. These methods provide a consistent way to interact with different machine learning models.

- Estimator: Any object that learns from data, essentially any model in Scikit-Learn.
- Predictor: An Estimator that can make predictions, such as classifiers and regressors.
- Transformer: An Estimator that can transform data, such as preprocessors.

Example:

```python
```

```
from sklearn.preprocessing import StandardScaler
from sklearn.linear_model import LogisticRegression

 Load and preprocess data
scaler = StandardScaler()
X_scaled = scaler.fit_transform(X)

 Initialize and train model
model = LogisticRegression()
model.fit(X_scaled, y)

 Make predictions
predictions = model.predict(X_scaled)
```

Scikit-Learn's strengths lie in its simplicity, versatility, and efficiency. Its comprehensive range of algorithms and tools, coupled with a user-friendly interface, make it an invaluable asset for financial analysts and data scientists. By mastering Scikit-Learn, you can unlock the potential of machine learning to tackle complex financial challenges, driving innovation and success in your endeavors.

Why Data Preprocessing Matters

It's crucial to understand why data preprocessing holds such immense importance in financial contexts:

1. Data Quality: Financial data, sourced from transactions, stock exchanges, and other financial entities, often contains inaccuracies, inconsistencies, and missing entries.

Preprocessing steps like cleaning and imputation are necessary to enhance data quality, ensuring that models are trained on reliable information.

2. Feature Relevance: Not all available features contribute equally to the predictive power of a model. Feature selection and extraction techniques help identify and create relevant features that improve model performance and interpretability.

3. Normalization and Scaling: Financial datasets often consist of variables with differing scales. Without normalization, models may become biased towards features with larger scales. Scaling techniques standardize the data, ensuring that each feature contributes equally to the model.

4. Noise Reduction: Financial data is notoriously noisy due to market fluctuations and external influences. Preprocessing techniques like smoothing can reduce noise, helping models to focus on underlying patterns rather than random variations.

5. Handling Missing Data: Missing data can pose significant challenges in financial datasets. Imputation techniques allow for the estimation and replacement of missing values, maintaining the integrity of the dataset.

6. Enhancing Model Training: Properly preprocessed data leads to more effective training of machine learning models, improving their ability to generalize and predict accurately on new, unseen data.

Key Preprocessing Techniques

Let's explore essential data preprocessing techniques,

demonstrated with practical examples using Scikit-Learn.

Data Cleaning

The first step in preprocessing is cleaning the data, which includes removing duplicates, correcting inconsistencies, and addressing outliers. For instance, in a dataset containing stock prices, erroneous entries or duplicate records can skew model predictions. Here's how to clean such a dataset:

Example:

```python
import pandas as pd

Load the dataset
data = pd.read_csv('financial_data.csv')

Remove duplicates
data = data.drop_duplicates()

Handle missing values by removing rows with missing entries
cleaned_data = data.dropna()
```

Handling Missing Values

In financial datasets, missing values are common and need to be addressed to avoid biases in model training. Scikit-Learn's `SimpleImputer` can be used to fill missing values with a specified strategy, such as mean, median, or most frequent value.

Example:

```python
from sklearn.impute import SimpleImputer

Load the dataset
data = pd.read_csv('financial_data.csv')

Initialize the imputer with a strategy (e.g., mean)
imputer = SimpleImputer(strategy='mean')

Fit and transform the data to fill missing values
imputed_data = imputer.fit_transform(data)
```

Feature Scaling and Normalization

Scaling ensures that all features contribute equally to the model. Techniques like Standard Scaling and Min-Max Scaling standardize feature ranges, crucial in financial modeling where features can have vastly different scales.

Example:

```python
from sklearn.preprocessing import StandardScaler

Load the dataset
data = pd.read_csv('financial_data.csv')

Initialize the scaler
```

```
scaler = StandardScaler()

Fit and transform the data
scaled_data = scaler.fit_transform(data)
```

Encoding Categorical Variables

Financial datasets often include categorical variables, such as stock tickers or transaction types, which need to be converted into numerical formats. Scikit-Learn's `OneHotEncoder` can be used for this purpose.

Example:

```python
from sklearn.preprocessing import OneHotEncoder

Load the dataset
data = pd.read_csv('financial_data.csv')

Initialize the encoder
encoder = OneHotEncoder()

Fit and transform the data
encoded_data = encoder.fit_transform(data[['stock_ticker']])
```

Feature Engineering

Feature engineering involves creating new features from

existing data to better capture underlying patterns. For example, generating features like moving averages or volatility measures from raw stock price data can enhance model performance.

Example:

```python
import numpy as np

Load the dataset
data = pd.read_csv('stock_prices.csv')

Calculate moving averages
data['moving_average'] =
data['price'].rolling(window=5).mean()

Calculate volatility
data['volatility'] = data['price'].rolling(window=5).std()
```

Dimensionality Reduction

High-dimensional data can lead to overfitting. Techniques like Principal Component Analysis (PCA) reduce dimensionality while preserving essential information, improving model efficiency and performance.

Example:

```python
from sklearn.decomposition import PCA
```

Load the dataset

data = pd.read_csv('financial_data.csv')

Initialize PCA with the number of components

pca = PCA(n_components=2)

Fit and transform the data

reduced_data = pca.fit_transform(data)

```

Practical Example: Preprocessing Financial Data

To illustrate the importance and application of these techniques, consider a practical scenario involving the preprocessing of a financial dataset containing historical stock prices, trading volumes, and other relevant indicators.

Example:

```python
import pandas as pd

from sklearn.impute import SimpleImputer

from sklearn.preprocessing import StandardScaler

from sklearn.decomposition import PCA

Load the dataset

data = pd.read_csv('historical_stock_data.csv')

Data Cleaning

data = data.drop_duplicates()
```
```

```
data = data.dropna()

Impute missing values
imputer = SimpleImputer(strategy='mean')
imputed_data = imputer.fit_transform(data[['price', 'volume']])

Feature Scaling
scaler = StandardScaler()
scaled_data = scaler.fit_transform(imputed_data)

Feature Engineering
data['moving_average'] = data['price'].rolling(window=5).mean()
data['volatility'] = data['price'].rolling(window=5).std()

Dimensionality Reduction
pca = PCA(n_components=2)
reduced_data = pca.fit_transform(scaled_data)

Combine preprocessed features
preprocessed_data = pd.DataFrame(reduced_data, columns=['principal_component_1', 'principal_component_2'])
preprocessed_data['moving_average'] = data['moving_average']
preprocessed_data['volatility'] = data['volatility']

print(preprocessed_data.head())
```

Data preprocessing is not merely a preliminary step but a foundational pillar of financial modeling. By cleaning, scaling, and transforming data, financial analysts can ensure that their models are trained on high-quality, relevant information, leading to more accurate and insightful predictions. Mastering these preprocessing techniques with Scikit-Learn equips you with the tools necessary to tackle the complexities of financial data and unlock the full potential of machine learning in finance.

Prerequisites and Recommended Resources

1. Basic Financial Knowledge

Before diving into machine learning applications in finance, it's essential to have a grounding in fundamental financial concepts. Understanding financial markets, instruments, and basic economic principles is indispensable. Concepts such as portfolio management, risk assessment, and financial derivatives (options, futures) should be familiar to you. This knowledge will allow you to contextualize machine learning models within real-world financial scenarios.

2. Programming Skills - Python

Python is the lingua franca of machine learning and finance. Familiarity with Python programming is a prerequisite. You should be comfortable with basic programming constructs such as loops, conditionals, functions, and classes. Additionally, an understanding of libraries such as NumPy, Pandas, Matplotlib, and Scikit-Learn is crucial. Python's simplicity, combined with its powerful libraries, makes it the preferred language for implementing machine learning models.

3. Mathematics and Statistics

Machine learning is deeply rooted in mathematical principles. A solid understanding of linear algebra, calculus, probability, and statistics is necessary. Key topics include matrix operations, differentiation and integration, probability distributions, hypothesis testing, and statistical significance. These mathematical foundations will help you comprehend the inner workings of machine learning algorithms and their applications in finance.

4. Machine Learning Fundamentals

While this book aims to provide a comprehensive guide, having a basic understanding of machine learning principles will be advantageous. Concepts such as supervised and unsupervised learning, regression, classification, clustering, and model evaluation metrics should be understood.

Recommended Resources

To build the requisite knowledge and skills, the following resources are recommended:

1. Books and Literature

- *"Python for Data Analysis"* by Wes McKinney: This book is a comprehensive introduction to using Python for data analysis, focusing on the Pandas library. It provides practical examples and is an excellent starting point for those new to Python and data manipulation.

- *"Introduction to Statistical Learning"* by Gareth James, Daniela Witten, Trevor Hastie, and Robert Tibshirani: This book offers an accessible introduction to statistical learning techniques, with applications in R. The concepts are easily transferable to Python.

- *"Machine Learning: A Probabilistic Perspective"* by Kevin P. Murphy: For a deeper dive into the probabilistic foundations of machine learning, this book is a must-read. It covers a wide range of topics with a focus on understanding the underlying principles.

2. Online Courses and Tutorials

- *Coursera's "Machine Learning" by Andrew Ng*: This is a foundational course that provides an excellent introduction to machine learning concepts and techniques. Although it uses MATLAB, the concepts can be implemented in Python.

- *edX's "Introduction to Computational Finance and Financial Econometrics" by MIT*: A course that bridges finance and data science, offering insights into computational techniques used in financial analysis.

- *DataCamp's Python Courses*: DataCamp offers numerous courses focusing on Python for data science, including introductions to NumPy, Pandas, and Scikit-Learn. These courses are interactive and provide hands-on practice.

3. Python Libraries Documentation

- *NumPy*: The official [NumPy documentation](https://numpy.org/doc/stable/) provides comprehensive guides and references for numerical computations in Python.

- *Pandas*: The [Pandas documentation](https://pandas.pydata.org/pandas-docs/stable/) is an invaluable resource for data manipulation and analysis.

- *Scikit-Learn*: The [Scikit-Learn documentation](https://scikit-learn.org/stable/) offers an extensive overview of machine learning algorithms and their implementation in Python.

4. Financial Data Sources

- *Yahoo Finance*: A reliable source for historical and real-time financial data, accessible via APIs.

- *Quandl*: Provides a vast array of financial, economic, and alternative data, suitable for machine learning projects in finance.

- *Bloomberg Terminal*: For professional-grade financial data and analytics, the Bloomberg Terminal is unmatched, though it may be less accessible due to cost constraints.

5. Communities and Forums

- *Kaggle*: An online community of data scientists and machine learning practitioners. Kaggle offers datasets, competitions, and a platform for sharing code and solutions.

- *Stack Overflow*: A go-to resource for programming-related queries, where you can find answers to specific coding issues and participate in discussions.

- *QuantConnect*: A community and platform focusing on algorithmic trading and financial machine learning.

6. Software and Tools

- *Jupyter Notebooks*: An interactive environment for writing and running Python code, ideal for machine learning experiments and data analysis.

- *Anaconda Distribution*: A comprehensive package that includes Python, Jupyter Notebooks, and many essential libraries, simplifying the setup process.

- *Integrated Development Environments (IDEs)*: Tools like PyCharm, VS Code, and Spyder can enhance your coding efficiency and project management.

# CHAPTER 2: GETTING STARTED WITH SCIKIT-LEARN

Ensure you have Python installed on your system. Python 3.6 or later is recommended for compatibility with the latest versions of Scikit-Learn and other libraries. Additionally, it is advisable to use a virtual environment to manage dependencies and avoid conflicts with other projects.

Step-by-Step Installation Guide

1. Setting Up a Virtual Environment

Creating a virtual environment is a best practice when working on Python projects. It isolates your project's dependencies, making it easier to manage and avoiding conflicts with other projects.

Open your terminal (or command prompt) and navigate to the directory where you want to create your virtual environment. Execute the following commands:

```bash
Install virtualenv if you haven't already
pip install virtualenv

Create a virtual environment named 'finance_ml'
virtualenv finance_ml

Activate the virtual environment
On Windows
finance_ml\Scripts\activate

On macOS/Linux
source finance_ml/bin/activate
```

After activation, your terminal prompt will change to indicate that you are working within the virtual environment.

2. Installing Scikit-Learn

With the virtual environment set up, you can now install Scikit-Learn. The preferred method is using `pip`, Python's package installer. Execute the following command:

```bash
pip install scikit-learn
```

This command will download and install the latest version of

Scikit-Learn along with its dependencies.

3. Installing Required Libraries

Machine learning projects often require several auxiliary libraries for data manipulation, visualization, and numerical computations. Installing these libraries ensures you have all the necessary tools at your disposal.

```bash
pip install numpy pandas matplotlib seaborn
```

Here is a brief overview of these libraries:

- NumPy: Provides support for large, multi-dimensional arrays and matrices, along with a collection of mathematical functions to operate on these arrays.
- Pandas: A powerful data manipulation and analysis library that provides data structures like DataFrames for handling structured data.
- Matplotlib: A plotting library that allows you to create static, animated, and interactive visualizations in Python.
- Seaborn: Built on top of Matplotlib, Seaborn provides a high-level interface for drawing attractive and informative statistical graphics.

4. Verifying the Installation

After installing the libraries, it's crucial to verify that they are correctly installed and functioning. Create a Python script named `verify_installation.py` and add the following code:

```python
import numpy as np
import pandas as pd
import matplotlib.pyplot as plt
import seaborn as sns
import sklearn

print("NumPy version:", np.__version__)
print("Pandas version:", pd.__version__)
print("Matplotlib version:", plt.__version__)
print("Seaborn version:", sns.__version__)
print("Scikit-Learn version:", sklearn.__version__)
```

Run the script using the following command:

```bash
python verify_installation.py
```

You should see the versions of the installed libraries printed in the terminal, confirming that the installation was successful.

Additional Tools and Resources

1. Jupyter Notebooks

Jupyter Notebooks provide an interactive environment for

writing and running Python code, making them ideal for data analysis and machine learning experiments. To install Jupyter Notebooks, execute the following command:

```bash
pip install jupyter
```

You can launch Jupyter Notebooks by running:

```bash
jupyter notebook
```

This command will open a new tab in your default web browser, where you can create and manage notebooks.

2. Anaconda Distribution

An alternative to installing libraries individually is using the Anaconda distribution, which includes Python along with many useful libraries and tools for data science. It simplifies the installation process and ensures compatibility among different packages.

Download Anaconda from [the official website](https://www.anaconda.com/products/distribution) and follow the installation instructions for your operating system.

Once installed, you can create a new environment with Scikit-Learn and other libraries using the following commands:

```bash
Create a new environment named 'finance_ml'
conda create --name finance_ml python=3.8

Activate the new environment
conda activate finance_ml

Install Scikit-Learn and other libraries
conda install scikit-learn numpy pandas matplotlib seaborn jupyter
```

3. Integrated Development Environments (IDEs)

Using an IDE can significantly enhance your coding efficiency and project management. Popular IDEs for Python include:

- PyCharm: A powerful IDE specifically designed for Python development, offering features like code completion, debugging, and version control integration.
- VS Code: A versatile code editor with support for Python through extensions. It provides features like IntelliSense, debugging, and integrated terminal.
- Spyder: An IDE tailored for scientific computing and data analysis, with a user-friendly interface and built-in IPython console.

Download and install the IDE of your choice, and configure it to work with your virtual environment or Anaconda environment.

Following this guide, you will have a robust setup with Scikit-Learn and other essential libraries, ready to tackle machine learning projects in finance. This foundation sets the stage for exploring and implementing advanced techniques, transforming financial data into actionable insights. As you progress through the subsequent chapters, this setup will serve as your toolkit for unlocking the potential of machine learning in the dynamic and complex world of finance.

## Understanding the Scikit-Learn API Structure

Once you've successfully set up your environment and installed Scikit-Learn along with the essential libraries, the next step is to understand the structure of the Scikit-Learn API. This understanding is paramount for efficiently leveraging Scikit-Learn for various machine learning tasks in finance. The API's design is intuitive yet powerful, making it accessible for beginners while offering depth for advanced users.

Scikit-Learn's API is built around a few core components that form the backbone of its functionality. These components include datasets, estimators, transformers, and pipelines. Understanding these core components will enable you to navigate and utilize the library effectively.

### 1. Datasets

Datasets are fundamental to any machine learning application. Scikit-Learn provides utilities for loading and generating datasets, catering to both real-world data and synthetic data for testing and experimentation. Here's a brief overview:

- Toy Datasets: Scikit-Learn includes several small datasets, such as `iris` and `digits`, that are useful for learning and experimentation.

- Real-World Datasets: The library also offers access to larger, real-world datasets like the Boston housing price dataset and the diabetes dataset.

- Synthetic Datasets: For testing and validation purposes, you can generate synthetic datasets using functions like `make_classification`, `make_regression`, and `make_blobs`.

Example:

```python
from sklearn.datasets import load_iris, make_classification

Load a toy dataset
iris = load_iris()
X, y = iris.data, iris.target

 Generate a synthetic dataset
X_synthetic, y_synthetic = make_classification(n_samples=100, n_features=20, n_informative=2, n_redundant=10, random_state=42)
```

2. Estimators

Estimators are objects in Scikit-Learn that implement machine learning algorithms. They can be broadly classified into supervised and unsupervised learning estimators. The main methods associated with estimators are `fit`, `predict`, and `score`.

- Supervised Learning Estimators: These include regression and classification algorithms such as `LinearRegression`, `LogisticRegression`, `DecisionTreeClassifier`, and `RandomForestClassifier`.
- Unsupervised Learning Estimators: These include clustering and dimensionality reduction algorithms such as `KMeans`, `PCA`, and `DBSCAN`.

Example:

```python
from sklearn.linear_model import LinearRegression

from sklearn.cluster import KMeans

Supervised learning estimator
model = LinearRegression()
model.fit(X, y)
predictions = model.predict(X)

Unsupervised learning estimator
kmeans = KMeans(n_clusters=3, random_state=42)
kmeans.fit(X_synthetic)
clusters = kmeans.predict(X_synthetic)
```

3. Transformers

Transformers are used to preprocess data before feeding it into an estimator. They handle tasks such as scaling, normalization, and feature extraction. The main methods associated with transformers are `fit` and `transform`. Some transformers also provide an `inverse_transform` method to revert the data to its original form.

- StandardScaler: Standardizes features by removing the mean and scaling to unit variance.
- MinMaxScaler: Scales features to a given range, typically between 0 and 1.
- PCA (Principal Component Analysis): Reduces the dimensionality of data while retaining most of the variance.

Example:

```python
from sklearn.preprocessing import StandardScaler
from sklearn.decomposition import PCA

Standardize data
scaler = StandardScaler()
X_scaled = scaler.fit_transform(X)

Apply PCA
pca = PCA(n_components=2)
X_pca = pca.fit_transform(X_scaled)
```

4. Pipelines

Pipelines are powerful tools in Scikit-Learn that allow you to chain together multiple processing steps, ensuring that your data transformations and model training occur in a seamless and reproducible manner. This is especially useful in complex workflows where maintaining a clean and organized code structure is crucial.

Example:

```python
from sklearn.pipeline import Pipeline
from sklearn.preprocessing import StandardScaler
from sklearn.linear_model import LogisticRegression

Define a pipeline
pipeline = Pipeline([
    ('scaler', StandardScaler()),
    ('classifier', LogisticRegression())
])

Fit the pipeline
pipeline.fit(X, y)

Make predictions
pipeline_predictions = pipeline.predict(X)
```

## Understanding the Estimator Interface

The estimator interface in Scikit-Learn adheres to a consistent and predictable pattern, making it easier to learn and apply different machine learning algorithms. The key methods in this interface are:

- fit(X, y=None): Trains the estimator on the given data. The `X` parameter represents the feature matrix, while `y` is the target vector (for supervised learning).
- predict(X): Makes predictions on new data.
- transform(X): Applies data transformation (used by transformers).
- fit_transform(X, y=None): A combination of `fit` and `transform` methods.
- score(X, y): Evaluates the performance of the estimator.

Example:

```python
from sklearn.ensemble import RandomForestClassifier

Create an instance of the estimator
rf = RandomForestClassifier(n_estimators=100, random_state=42)

Fit the model
rf.fit(X, y)

Make predictions
```

rf_predictions = rf.predict(X)

Evaluate the model

accuracy = rf.score(X, y)

print(f'Accuracy: {accuracy}')

```
```

## Advanced API Features

While the core components and methods form the foundation of the Scikit-Learn API, several advanced features enhance its functionality and flexibility.

1. Grid Search and Random Search

Hyperparameter tuning is a critical aspect of machine learning model development. Scikit-Learn provides `GridSearchCV` and `RandomizedSearchCV` for systematic and randomized search over hyperparameter space.

Example:

```python
from sklearn.model_selection import GridSearchCV

Define the parameter grid
param_grid = {
    'n_estimators': [50, 100, 200],
    'max_depth': [None, 10, 20, 30]
}
```

```
Create a grid search instance
grid_search = GridSearchCV(estimator=rf, param_grid=param_grid, cv=5, scoring='accuracy')

Fit the grid search
grid_search.fit(X, y)

Best parameters and score
best_params = grid_search.best_params_
best_score = grid_search.best_score_
print(f'Best Parameters: {best_params}')
print(f'Best Score: {best_score}')
```

2. Custom Transformers

In addition to built-in transformers, you can create custom transformers by implementing the `fit` and `transform` methods. This allows for greater flexibility in preprocessing and feature engineering.

Example:

```python
from sklearn.base import BaseEstimator, TransformerMixin

class CustomTransformer(BaseEstimator, TransformerMixin):
    def fit(self, X, y=None):
```

```
        return self

    def transform(self, X):
         Custom transformation logic
        X_transformed = X 2  Example: squaring the features
        return X_transformed

Use the custom transformer in a pipeline
custom_pipeline = Pipeline([
    ('custom_transformer', CustomTransformer()),
    ('classifier', LogisticRegression())
])

Fit the pipeline
custom_pipeline.fit(X, y)
```

3. Model Persistence

Saving and loading models is essential for deploying machine learning solutions. Scikit-Learn supports model persistence using Python's `joblib` library, enabling you to save trained models to disk and load them later for inference.

Example:

```python
import joblib

Save the model
```

joblib.dump(rf, 'random_forest_model.pkl')

Load the model

loaded_rf = joblib.load('random_forest_model.pkl')

Make predictions with the loaded model

loaded_predictions = loaded_rf.predict(X)

```

Understanding the Scikit-Learn API structure empowers you to harness its full potential for machine learning applications in finance. From datasets and estimators to transformers and pipelines, the API offers a cohesive and powerful framework that simplifies the development and deployment of machine learning models. As you continue through this book, this foundational knowledge will serve as a crucial asset, enabling you to build sophisticated models that drive actionable insights and innovative solutions in the financial domain.

Basic Data Structures in Scikit-Learn

As we unravel the layers of Scikit-Learn, it's imperative to grasp the fundamental data structures that underpin its functionality. These data structures play a pivotal role in organizing and manipulating the data used in your machine learning models. By understanding these core components, you will be better equipped to harness the full potential of Scikit-Learn for various financial applications.

Scikit-Learn's data manipulation lies the Numpy array. Numpy arrays are powerful, flexible, and efficient structures for handling numerical data. They provide the foundation upon
```

which many Scikit-Learn functions operate. Whether you're dealing with feature matrices or target vectors, Numpy arrays offer the performance and versatility required for complex data processing tasks.

Example:

```python
import numpy as np

Creating a Numpy array
data = np.array([[1.2, 3.5, 5.1], [4.3, 2.1, 6.8], [7.5, 1.3, 9.4]])
print(data)
```

In the example above, a simple Numpy array is created, showcasing its ease of use and the compact representation of numerical data.

Pandas DataFrames: Enhanced Data Handling

While Numpy arrays are efficient, Pandas DataFrames offer additional functionality by incorporating tabular data structures with labeled axes (rows and columns). This makes DataFrames particularly useful for handling and analyzing structured data, which is common in financial datasets.

Example:

```python
import pandas as pd
```

```
Creating a Pandas DataFrame
data = {'Feature1': [1.2, 4.3, 7.5], 'Feature2': [3.5, 2.1, 1.3], 'Feature3': [5.1, 6.8, 9.4]}
df = pd.DataFrame(data)
print(df)
```

The above code snippet demonstrates the creation of a Pandas DataFrame from a dictionary, making it easier to work with labeled data and perform operations such as aggregation, filtering, and joining.

Scikit-Learn's Built-in Dataset Objects

Scikit-Learn provides several built-in dataset objects that are designed to streamline the workflow of loading and using datasets. These objects typically come with attributes such as `data` (features) and `target` (labels), along with metadata that describes the dataset.

Example:

```python
from sklearn.datasets import load_iris

Loading a built-in dataset
iris = load_iris()
print(iris.data[:5])  Display the first 5 records of the feature matrix
print(iris.target[:5])  Display the first 5 labels
```

```
```

In this example, the Iris dataset is loaded, giving access to both the feature matrix and the target vector. This built-in dataset is ideal for learning and experimentation.

Feature Matrix and Target Array

The feature matrix and target array are central to any machine learning model. The feature matrix, often represented as `X`, contains the input data, while the target array, denoted as `y`, holds the corresponding labels or target values. Both structures are typically represented as Numpy arrays or Pandas DataFrames.

Example:

```python
Feature matrix (X) and target array (y)
X = iris.data
y = iris.target

print(X.shape)  Output: (150, 4)
print(y.shape)  Output: (150,)
```

Here, `X` is a 2D array (feature matrix) with 150 samples and 4 features, while `y` is a 1D array (target array) with 150 labels.

Bunch Objects: Flexible Data Containers

Many of Scikit-Learn's datasets are returned as Bunch objects, which are flexible containers similar to dictionaries. They allow you to access their elements using both dot notation and key indexing, making them convenient for handling dataset attributes.

Example:

```python
Accessing elements of a Bunch object
print(iris['data'][:5])  Using key indexing
print(iris.data[:5])  Using dot notation
```

The Bunch object in the example above showcases its flexibility, enabling easy access to dataset attributes through multiple methods.

Sparse Matrices: Efficient Representation of Sparse Data

Sparse matrices are crucial when dealing with data that contains a large number of zero entries. Scikit-Learn provides support for sparse matrices through the `scipy.sparse` module, enabling efficient storage and computation.

Example:

```python
from scipy.sparse import csr_matrix
```

```
Creating a sparse matrix
dense_data = np.array([[0, 0, 1], [0, 2, 0], [3, 0, 0]])
sparse_data = csr_matrix(dense_data)
print(sparse_data)
```

In this example, a dense matrix with many zero entries is converted into a sparse matrix, demonstrating the efficiency gains in storage and computation.

Custom Data Structures: Extending Scikit-Learn

While Scikit-Learn's built-in data structures cover a wide range of use cases, there may be scenarios where custom data structures are required. You can extend Scikit-Learn's functionality by implementing custom transformers, estimators, and data containers.

Example:

```python
from sklearn.base import BaseEstimator, TransformerMixin

class CustomTransformer(BaseEstimator, TransformerMixin):
    def fit(self, X, y=None):
        return self

    def transform(self, X):
        Custom transformation logic
```

X_transformed = X 2 Example: squaring the features

return X_transformed

Using the custom transformer

custom_transformer = CustomTransformer()

X_transformed = custom_transformer.fit_transform(X)

print(X_transformed[:5])

```

The custom transformer in the example above illustrates how you can create and utilize specialized data structures that cater to specific needs, enhancing the flexibility and power of your machine learning pipeline.

Data Splitters: Managing Training and Test Data

Effectively splitting data into training and test sets is vital for building robust and unbiased models. Scikit-Learn provides several utilities for this purpose, such as `train_test_split` and cross-validation splitters.

Example:

```python
from sklearn.model_selection import train_test_split

Splitting data into training and test sets

X_train, X_test, y_train, y_test = train_test_split(X, y, test_size=0.2, random_state=42)

print(X_train.shape, X_test.shape)

```
```

The `train_test_split` function in the example demonstrates how to partition data, ensuring that models are trained and evaluated on separate datasets to avoid overfitting and assess generalization performance.

With a detailed understanding of these basic data structures in Scikit-Learn, you are now equipped to handle a wide array of data manipulation tasks essential for financial machine learning. This foundational knowledge lays the groundwork for building sophisticated models and pipelines that drive actionable insights and innovative solutions in the financial domain. As you progress through this book, these data structures will become indispensable tools in your machine learning toolkit.

Dataset Loading Strategies in Finance

Financial datasets come in various forms, including stock prices, trading volumes, economic indicators, company financial statements, and alternative data such as sentiment analysis from news articles. Each type of data serves a unique purpose and requires different handling strategies.

Example Financial Data Formats:

- CSV Files: Commonly used for historical stock prices, economic indicators, and other tabular data.
- JSON/XML: Frequently employed for more complex data structures, such as hierarchical financial reports.
- SQL Databases: Utilized for storing large volumes of

transactional data, providing efficient querying capabilities.

- APIs: Often the source of real-time data, including live stock prices, market indices, and news feeds.

Loading Data from CSV Files

Comma-separated values (CSV) files are one of the most common formats for financial data due to their simplicity and compatibility with various tools. Using Pandas, loading data from CSV files is straightforward.

Example:

```python
import pandas as pd

Loading a CSV file
df = pd.read_csv('historical_stock_prices.csv')
print(df.head())
```

In the example above, the `read_csv` function from Pandas is used to load historical stock prices from a CSV file into a DataFrame. This DataFrame can then be manipulated and analyzed as needed.

Handling Large CSV Files

Large CSV files can pose challenges due to memory constraints. Efficient loading strategies include chunking and using specific data types to reduce memory usage.

Example:

```python
Loading a large CSV file in chunks
chunk_size = 10000
chunks = pd.read_csv('large_historical_data.csv', chunksize=chunk_size)
for chunk in chunks:
    Process each chunk
    print(chunk.head())
```

By specifying a `chunksize`, the CSV file is read in smaller, more manageable chunks, allowing for efficient processing of large datasets.

Loading Data from SQL Databases

Financial institutions often store data in SQL databases due to their robustness and efficiency in handling large datasets. Utilizing SQL queries to load specific subsets of data can optimize performance.

Example:

```python
import pandas as pd
import sqlite3
```

```
Connecting to a SQLite database
conn = sqlite3.connect('financial_data.db')

Loading data using an SQL query
query = "SELECT * FROM stock_prices WHERE date >= '2022-01-01'"
df = pd.read_sql_query(query, conn)
print(df.head())
```

The example demonstrates how to connect to a SQLite database and execute a query to load only the relevant data, ensuring efficient use of resources.

Real-time Data Loading via APIs

APIs provide access to real-time financial data, which is crucial for applications such as algorithmic trading and market monitoring. Libraries like `requests` in Python facilitate API interactions.

Example:

```python
import requests

API endpoint for real-time stock price
url = 'https://api.example.com/stock_price'
params = {'symbol': 'AAPL'}
```

```
Fetching data from the API
response = requests.get(url, params=params)
data = response.json()
print(data)
```

In this example, an API call is made to fetch the real-time stock price of Apple Inc. The response is in JSON format, which can then be parsed and integrated into your analysis.

Handling JSON and XML Data

Financial data in JSON or XML formats often requires parsing before use. These formats are common in APIs and complex data structures such as hierarchical financial reports.

Example:

```python
import json

Loading a JSON file
with open('financial_data.json') as f:
    data = json.load(f)

print(data)
```

Dataset Loading from Web Scraping

Web scraping is a technique to extract data from websites, often used when APIs are not available. Libraries like `BeautifulSoup` and `Selenium` can be employed for web scraping tasks.

Example:

```python
import requests
from bs4 import BeautifulSoup

URL of the website to scrape
url = 'https://example.com/financial_reports'

Fetching the web page
response = requests.get(url)
soup = BeautifulSoup(response.text, 'html.parser')

Extracting data
tables = soup.find_all('table')
for table in tables:
    print(table)
```

The example showcases how to fetch and parse a web page to extract financial data tables using `BeautifulSoup`.

Integrating Multiple Data Sources

Combining data from multiple sources can provide a comprehensive view and enhance the robustness of your models. Techniques such as data merging and joining are essential for this purpose.

Example:

```python
Merging two DataFrames
df1 = pd.read_csv('economic_indicators.csv')
df2 = pd.read_csv('stock_prices.csv')

merged_df = pd.merge(df1, df2, on='date')
print(merged_df.head())
```

In this example, economic indicators and stock prices are merged on the `date` column, creating a comprehensive dataset for analysis.

Optimizing Data Loading

Optimizing data loading involves techniques such as selective loading, using efficient data structures, and leveraging parallel processing. The goal is to minimize memory usage and maximize speed.

Example:

```python
```

Using specific data types to reduce memory usage

df = pd.read_csv('financial_data.csv', dtype={'column1': 'float32', 'column2': 'int32'})

print(df.info())

```
```

Using specific data types can significantly reduce the memory footprint, making it easier to work with large datasets.

---

Mastering dataset loading strategies in finance is crucial for building efficient and reliable machine learning models. By leveraging the techniques discussed, you can ensure that your data is well-organized, easily accessible, and ready for rigorous analysis. This foundation will allow you to tackle more advanced topics and develop sophisticated models that drive actionable insights and innovative solutions in the financial domain.

0.16.5 Training vs Test Datasets

Understanding the Concept

At the core of machine learning, particularly in finance, lies the division of available data into two key segments: the training dataset and the test dataset. The training dataset is utilized to 'teach' the model, enabling it to learn patterns and relationships within the data. Conversely, the test dataset is used to evaluate the model's performance, assessing its ability to generalize to new, unseen data.

1. Training Dataset: This subset of the data is used to fit the machine learning model. It includes a significant portion of the entire dataset and is crucial for the development phase of your model.
2. Test Dataset: This subset is kept separate from the training process and is used exclusively to evaluate the model's performance. It helps in determining how well the model can predict or classify new data that it has not encountered before.

Importance in Financial Modelling

In financial applications, the distinction between training and test datasets is critical due to the high stakes involved. Accurate predictions can lead to substantial profits, while poor predictions can result in significant losses. Properly partitioning the data ensures that the model is robust and reliable.

Case in Point: Consider a quantitative analyst working on a stock price prediction model. By dividing historical stock price data into training and test datasets, the analyst can train the model on one part and validate its performance on another. This approach helps in identifying overfitting, where a model performs exceptionally well on training data but fails to generalize to new data.

Best Practices for Splitting Data

The process of splitting data into training and test sets should be done thoughtfully to ensure a fair evaluation of the model. Here are some best practices:

1. Random Splitting: Randomly splitting the data can help in creating unbiased training and test sets. This method works well when you have a large, homogeneous dataset.

Example:

```python
from sklearn.model_selection import train_test_split

df = pd.read_csv('financial_data.csv')
train_df, test_df = train_test_split(df, test_size=0.2, random_state=42)
```

In the example above, we use the `train_test_split` function from Scikit-Learn to randomly split the dataset into training (80%) and test (20%) sets.

2. Time-based Splitting: In financial datasets, where data is sequential, a time-based split is often more appropriate. This method respects the temporal order of the data, ensuring that the model is trained on past data and tested on future data.

Example:

```python
Assuming the dataset is already sorted by date
n = len(df)
train_df = df[:int(n*0.8)]
test_df = df[int(n*0.8):]
```

```
```

This approach ensures that the training set contains older data, while the test set consists of more recent data, mimicking real-world scenario forecasting.

3. Stratified Splitting: When dealing with classification problems, ensuring that both training and test datasets have similar class distributions is crucial. Stratified splitting maintains the proportion of classes in both sets.

Example:

```python
from sklearn.model_selection import train_test_split

df = pd.read_csv('credit_scoring_data.csv')
X = df.drop('target', axis=1)
y = df['target']
X_train, X_test, y_train, y_test = train_test_split(X, y, test_size=0.2, stratify=y, random_state=42)
```

Here, `stratify=y` ensures that the class distribution in the target variable `y` remains consistent across the training and test sets.

Practical Implementation

Let's walk through a complete example, where we load a financial dataset, preprocess it, and split it into training and test sets.

Example: Predicting Stock Prices

1. Loading and Preprocessing Data

```python
import pandas as pd
from sklearn.preprocessing import StandardScaler

 Loading the dataset
df = pd.read_csv('historical_stock_prices.csv')
df['date'] = pd.to_datetime(df['date'])
df.set_index('date', inplace=True)

 Feature engineering
df['returns'] = df['close'].pct_change()
df.dropna(inplace=True)

 Selecting features and target
X = df[['returns']]
y = df['close'].shift(-1).dropna()
X = X[:-1]  Aligning features and target
```

2. Splitting Data

```python
from sklearn.model_selection import train_test_split
```

X_train, X_test, y_train, y_test = train_test_split(X, y, test_size=0.2, random_state=42, shuffle=False)
```

Here, we ensure that the data is not shuffled, respecting the temporal order.

3. Scaling Data

```python
scaler = StandardScaler()
X_train_scaled = scaler.fit_transform(X_train)
X_test_scaled = scaler.transform(X_test)
```

Scaling the features ensures that the model's performance is not biased by the magnitude of the different features.

4. Training a Model

```python
from sklearn.linear_model import LinearRegression

model = LinearRegression()
model.fit(X_train_scaled, y_train)
```

5. Evaluating the Model
```

```python
from sklearn.metrics import mean_squared_error

y_pred = model.predict(X_test_scaled)
mse = mean_squared_error(y_test, y_pred)
print(f'Mean Squared Error: {mse}')
```

The evaluation metric, in this case, the Mean Squared Error (MSE), provides insight into the model's predictive accuracy on the test set.

---

By adhering to best practices and employing appropriate splitting strategies, you can ensure that your financial machine learning models are both robust and reliable. The distinction between training and test datasets is not merely a procedural step but a cornerstone of sound model evaluation. Mastering this aspect will empower you to build models that withstand the rigorous demands of real-world financial environments, ultimately driving more accurate and actionable insights.

## 0.17.6 Creating and Using Synthetic Datasets

In the landscape of financial machine learning, the availability and quality of data are paramount. However, obtaining sufficient high-quality data can often be challenging due to factors like privacy concerns, regulatory issues, and the sheer cost of acquiring proprietary datasets. This is where synthetic data comes into play. Synthetic datasets are artificially generated data that can mimic the statistical properties of real-world data without compromising confidentiality or incurring high costs.

## The Need for Synthetic Data in Finance

Synthetic data serves multiple purposes within financial machine learning:

1. Addressing Data Scarcity: In many situations, historical financial data might be limited, particularly for new markets or emerging financial instruments. Synthetic data can help fill these gaps, providing a larger dataset for training robust models.
2. Enhancing Model Performance: By creating diverse and comprehensive datasets, synthetic data can help in training models that generalize better, thereby improving their performance on unseen data.
3. Testing and Validation: Synthetic datasets can be used to rigorously test models under various hypothetical scenarios, aiding in model validation and robustness assessments.
4. Privacy Preservation: Synthetic data allows analysts and researchers to work with data that retains the statistical properties of real data without exposing sensitive information, thus ensuring privacy and compliance with regulations.

## Techniques for Generating Synthetic Data

Several methods exist for generating synthetic data, each with its unique advantages and applications:

1. Random Sampling: This method involves generating random data points within the range of observed values. While simple, it may not capture complex relationships within the data.

Example:

```python
import numpy as np

 Generate random returns data
synthetic_returns = np.random.normal(loc=0, scale=0.01, size=1000)
```

2. Bootstrapping: Bootstrapping samples data points with replacement from the original dataset, creating a new dataset that maintains the statistical properties of the original.

Example:

```python
import pandas as pd

 Load real financial data
df = pd.read_csv('financial_data.csv')

 Generate synthetic data using bootstrapping
synthetic_data = df.sample(n=1000, replace=True,
```

random_state=42)
```

3. Generating Time Series Data: For time-series data, methods like Autoregressive Integrated Moving Average (ARIMA) models can generate synthetic sequences that follow similar patterns as the original data.

Example:

```python
from statsmodels.tsa.arima.model import ARIMA

 Fit ARIMA model on real data
model = ARIMA(df['returns'], order=(1, 1, 1))
model_fit = model.fit()

 Generate synthetic time series data
synthetic_series = model_fit.simulate(nsamples=1000)
```

4. Generative Adversarial Networks (GANs): GANs are a powerful method for generating synthetic data. They consist of two neural networks—a generator and a discriminator—that compete against each other, producing highly realistic synthetic data.

Example:

```python
import numpy as np

```
from keras.models import Sequential
from keras.layers import Dense, LeakyReLU, BatchNormalization, Reshape, Flatten
from keras.optimizers import Adam

 Generator model
generator = Sequential()
generator.add(Dense(128, input_shape=(100,)))
generator.add(LeakyReLU(alpha=0.2))
generator.add(BatchNormalization(momentum=0.8))
generator.add(Dense(256))
generator.add(LeakyReLU(alpha=0.2))
generator.add(BatchNormalization(momentum=0.8))
generator.add(Dense(512))
generator.add(LeakyReLU(alpha=0.2))
generator.add(BatchNormalization(momentum=0.8))
generator.add(Dense(np.prod((28,28,1)), activation='tanh'))
generator.add(Reshape((28,28,1)))

 Discriminator model
discriminator = Sequential()
discriminator.add(Flatten(input_shape=(28,28,1)))
discriminator.add(Dense(512))
discriminator.add(LeakyReLU(alpha=0.2))
discriminator.add(Dense(256))
discriminator.add(LeakyReLU(alpha=0.2))
discriminator.add(Dense(1, activation='sigmoid'))
discriminator.compile(loss='binary_crossentropy',
```

```
optimizer=Adam(0.0002, 0.5), metrics=['accuracy'])

    GAN model
   discriminator.trainable = False
   gan = Sequential([generator, discriminator])
   gan.compile(loss='binary_crossentropy',
optimizer=Adam(0.0002, 0.5))

    Training GAN
   def train_gan(gan, dataset, epochs, batch_size, latent_dim):
      half_batch = int(batch_size / 2)
      for epoch in range(epochs):
          Train Discriminator
         idx = np.random.randint(0, dataset.shape[0],
half_batch)
         real_imgs = dataset[idx]
         noise = np.random.normal(0, 1, (half_batch,
latent_dim))
         fake_imgs = generator.predict(noise)
         d_loss_real = discriminator.train_on_batch(real_imgs,
np.ones((half_batch, 1)))
         d_loss_fake =
discriminator.train_on_batch(fake_imgs,
np.zeros((half_batch, 1)))
         d_loss = 0.5 * np.add(d_loss_real, d_loss_fake)

          Train Generator
         noise = np.random.normal(0, 1, (batch_size,
latent_dim))
```

```
        valid_y = np.array([1] * batch_size)
        g_loss = gan.train_on_batch(noise, valid_y)

        print(f"{epoch} [D loss: {d_loss[0]} | D accuracy: {100*d_loss[1]}] [G loss: {g_loss}]")

  Assuming dataset is normalized financial data
 train_gan(gan, df.values, epochs=10000, batch_size=32, latent_dim=100)
```

Practical Considerations

While synthetic data offers numerous advantages, there are several practical considerations to keep in mind:

1. Statistical Consistency: Ensure that synthetic data maintains the same statistical properties as the real data. This includes mean, variance, and any distributional characteristics.
2. Model Validation: Validate your model using both synthetic and real data to ensure that it performs well under various conditions.
3. Ethical Use: Be mindful of the ethical implications of using synthetic data, particularly in scenarios where decisions have significant financial or social impact.

Example: Using Synthetic Data for Credit Scoring

Let's walk through a practical example where we generate synthetic data for a credit scoring model.

1. Generating Synthetic Data

```python
from sklearn.datasets import make_classification

 Generate synthetic dataset
X, y = make_classification(n_samples=1000, n_features=20, n_informative=15, n_classes=2, random_state=42)

 Convert to DataFrame for easier manipulation
synthetic_df = pd.DataFrame(X, columns=[f'feature_{i}' for i in range(20)])
synthetic_df['target'] = y
```

2. Splitting Data

```python
X = synthetic_df.drop('target', axis=1)
y = synthetic_df['target']

X_train, X_test, y_train, y_test = train_test_split(X, y, test_size=0.2, random_state=42)
```

3. Training a Model

```python
from sklearn.ensemble import RandomForestClassifier
```

```
model = RandomForestClassifier()
model.fit(X_train, y_train)
```

4. Evaluating the Model

```python
from sklearn.metrics import accuracy_score

y_pred = model.predict(X_test)
accuracy = accuracy_score(y_test, y_pred)
print(f'Accuracy: {accuracy}')
```

By using synthetic data, we can build and test a credit scoring model without relying on sensitive or proprietary data. This approach not only preserves privacy but also allows for extensive experimentation and model validation.

---

In summary, synthetic datasets are invaluable tools in financial machine learning. They address data scarcity, enhance model performance, facilitate rigorous testing, and ensure privacy. By mastering the techniques of generating and using synthetic data, you can significantly bolster your financial models, making them more robust, accurate, and reliable. As you incorporate these practices into your workflow, you'll find yourself better equipped to tackle the complexities of financial data and drive meaningful insights.

### 0.18.7 Feature Scaling and Normalization

In machine learning, feature scaling and normalization are two indispensable techniques that wield significant influence on the performance and efficiency of your models. In finance, where data is often multifaceted and varied in scale, these preprocessing steps become even more critical. The aim is to bring all features onto a similar scale or distribution, allowing algorithms to converge more quickly and perform optimally. Understanding and implementing these techniques can be the difference between a mediocre model and an outstanding one.

Understanding Feature Scaling

Feature scaling refers to the process of transforming the data so that the features are on a similar scale. This is particularly crucial for algorithms that rely on distance metrics, such as K-Nearest Neighbors (KNN), Support Vector Machines (SVM), and gradient descent-based methods like linear and logistic regression.

There are several methods to achieve feature scaling, but two of the most common are Min-Max Scaling and Standardization.

Min-Max Scaling

Min-Max Scaling transforms the features to lie within a specific range, typically [0, 1]. This method is simple and preserves the relationships between data points.

Here's an example using Python and Scikit-Learn:

```python
from sklearn.preprocessing import MinMaxScaler
import numpy as np

Sample financial data (e.g., stock prices, trading volumes)
data = np.array([
    [200, 1000],
    [150, 750],
    [300, 1500],
    [250, 1200]
])

Initialize the scaler
scaler = MinMaxScaler()

Fit and transform the data
scaled_data = scaler.fit_transform(data)

print(scaled_data)
```

In this example, stock prices and trading volumes are scaled to fall within the range of 0 to 1. This helps the model treat both features with equal importance.

Standardization

Standardization transforms the data to have a mean of 0 and a standard deviation of 1. Unlike Min-Max Scaling, Standardization does not bound the data to a specific range, but rather rescales it based on the distribution of values.

Here's how you can standardize data using Scikit-Learn:

```python
from sklearn.preprocessing import StandardScaler

Sample financial data (e.g., stock prices, trading volumes)
data = np.array([
    [200, 1000],
    [150, 750],
    [300, 1500],
    [250, 1200]
])

Initialize the scaler
scaler = StandardScaler()

Fit and transform the data
standardized_data = scaler.fit_transform(data)

print(standardized_data)
```

Standardization is particularly useful for techniques that assume a Gaussian distribution in the data, such as Linear Discriminant Analysis (LDA) or Logistic Regression.

The Importance of Normalization

Normalization is another preprocessing technique that adjusts the length of the feature vectors. It's particularly useful in scenarios where the direction of the vector is more important than its magnitude, such as cosine similarity measures in text data.

Normalization can be performed using the L2 norm, which scales the feature vector to have a Euclidean length of 1. In financial contexts, normalization helps in transforming the data for better interpretability and precision in distance-based algorithms.

Here's an example of normalization using Scikit-Learn:

```python
from sklearn.preprocessing import Normalizer

Sample financial data (e.g., stock prices, trading volumes)
data = np.array([
    [200, 1000],
    [150, 750],
    [300, 1500],
    [250, 1200]
])
```

```
Initialize the normalizer
normalizer = Normalizer()

Fit and transform the data
normalized_data = normalizer.fit_transform(data)

print(normalized_data)
```

Normalization ensures that all feature vectors have a unit norm, which can be particularly advantageous in high-dimensional spaces.

Practical Considerations in Financial Data

When dealing with financial data, it’s essential to consider the inherent properties and distribution of the features. Financial data often exhibits skewness and heavy tails, which may necessitate additional preprocessing steps such as log transformation before scaling or normalization.

Additionally, it's important to apply scaling or normalization consistently across both the training and testing datasets to ensure that the model generalizes well.

Example: Impact on Model Performance

To illustrate the impact of feature scaling and normalization on model performance, let’s consider a simple linear regression model predicting stock prices based on trading volume and other features.

Without Scaling:

```python
from sklearn.linear_model import LinearRegression
from sklearn.model_selection import train_test_split
from sklearn.metrics import mean_squared_error

Sample financial data
data = np.array([
    [200, 1000, 1],
    [150, 750, 0],
    [300, 1500, 1],
    [250, 1200, 1]
])
target = np.array([300, 200, 500, 450])

Split the data
X_train, X_test, y_train, y_test = train_test_split(data, target, test_size=0.2, random_state=42)

Initialize and train the model
model = LinearRegression()
model.fit(X_train, y_train)

 Predict and evaluate
predictions = model.predict(X_test)
mse = mean_squared_error(y_test, predictions)
print(f'Mean Squared Error without scaling: {mse}')
```

With Scaling:

```python
Apply Min-Max Scaling
scaler = MinMaxScaler()
X_train_scaled = scaler.fit_transform(X_train)
X_test_scaled = scaler.transform(X_test)

Initialize and train the model
model = LinearRegression()
model.fit(X_train_scaled, y_train)

 Predict and evaluate
predictions = model.predict(X_test_scaled)
mse_scaled = mean_squared_error(y_test, predictions)
print(f'Mean Squared Error with scaling: {mse_scaled}')
```

By comparing the Mean Squared Error (MSE) from both cases, you can observe the tangible benefits of feature scaling on model performance.

feature scaling and normalization are foundational steps in the data preprocessing pipeline, particularly for financial applications. These techniques ensure that your machine learning models receive data they can effectively learn from, leading to more accurate and reliable predictions. As you progress through machine learning in finance, mastering these preprocessing steps will significantly enhance your model-building capabilities.

## 0.19.8 Data Splitting Techniques

In the journey of building robust machine learning models, one of the pivotal steps is splitting the data into training and testing subsets. This step is crucial because it allows us to evaluate the model's performance on unseen data, thereby giving us a measure of its generalization capability. In the financial world, where models often handle time-sensitive and volatile data, effective data splitting techniques can significantly enhance the reliability and accuracy of predictions.

### The Importance of Data Splitting

Splitting the data helps in mitigating overfitting, which occurs when a model performs exceedingly well on the training data but fails to generalize to new, unseen data. By reserving a portion of the data for testing, we can simulate how the model will behave in real-world scenarios. This is particularly important in finance, where predictive models are often used for high-stakes decision-making, such as stock price forecasting, credit scoring, and risk management.

### Common Data Splitting Techniques

Several techniques can be employed to split data, each with its advantages and specific use cases. Here, we will explore some of the most commonly used methods in the context of financial data.

1. Train-Test Split

The most straightforward technique is the train-test split, where the dataset is divided into two parts: a training set and a testing set. The typical ratio used is 80%-20% or 70%-30%, depending on the size of the dataset.

```python
from sklearn.model_selection import train_test_split
import numpy as np

Sample financial data (e.g., stock prices, trading volumes, market indicators)
data = np.array([
    [200, 1000, 1],
    [150, 750, 0],
    [300, 1500, 1],
    [250, 1200, 1],
    [220, 1100, 0],
    [180, 900, 1]
])
target = np.array([300, 200, 500, 450, 320, 280])

Split the data
X_train, X_test, y_train, y_test = train_test_split(data, target, test_size=0.2, random_state=42)

print("Training set:", X_train)
print("Testing set:", X_test)
```

This method ensures that the model is trained on a substantial portion of the data while being evaluated on a separate subset, providing an unbiased assessment of its performance.

2. Cross-Validation

Cross-validation is a more sophisticated technique that involves splitting the data into multiple folds. The model is trained and tested multiple times, each time using a different fold as the testing set and the remaining folds as the training set. This provides a more comprehensive evaluation of the model's performance.

The most common type of cross-validation is k-fold cross-validation, where the dataset is divided into k folds. The model is trained k times, each time using a different fold as the testing set.

```python
from sklearn.model_selection import KFold
from sklearn.linear_model import LinearRegression
from sklearn.metrics import mean_squared_error

Sample financial data
data = np.array([
    [200, 1000, 1],
    [150, 750, 0],
    [300, 1500, 1],
    [250, 1200, 1],
```

```
    [220, 1100, 0],
    [180, 900, 1]
])
target = np.array([300, 200, 500, 450, 320, 280])

Initialize k-fold cross-validation
kf = KFold(n_splits=3, shuffle=True, random_state=42)

mse_scores = []

Perform k-fold cross-validation
for train_index, test_index in kf.split(data):
    X_train, X_test = data[train_index], data[test_index]
    y_train, y_test = target[train_index], target[test_index]

    model = LinearRegression()
    model.fit(X_train, y_train)
    predictions = model.predict(X_test)
    mse = mean_squared_error(y_test, predictions)
    mse_scores.append(mse)

print("Mean Squared Errors for each fold:", mse_scores)
print("Average MSE:", np.mean(mse_scores))
```

Cross-validation is particularly beneficial in financial applications, where datasets may be limited or where each data point is valuable. By using the entire dataset for both training and testing across different iterations, we obtain a more reliable measure of model performance.

3. Time Series Split

For financial data, which often involves time series, a traditional train-test split might not be appropriate due to the temporal dependencies in the data. In such cases, a time series split is more suitable. This technique respects the temporal order of the data, ensuring that the training set always precedes the testing set.

```python
from sklearn.model_selection import TimeSeriesSplit

Sample time series data (e.g., daily stock prices)
data = np.array([
    [200, 1000],
    [150, 750],
    [300, 1500],
    [250, 1200],
    [220, 1100],
    [180, 900]
])
target = np.array([300, 200, 500, 450, 320, 280])

Initialize time series split
tscv = TimeSeriesSplit(n_splits=3)

for train_index, test_index in tscv.split(data):
    X_train, X_test = data[train_index], data[test_index]
```

```
    y_train, y_test = target[train_index], target[test_index]

    model = LinearRegression()
    model.fit(X_train, y_train)
    predictions = model.predict(X_test)
    mse = mean_squared_error(y_test, predictions)
    print(f'Train indices: {train_index}, Test indices: {test_index}, MSE: {mse}')
```

Time series split is critical in scenarios such as forecasting future stock prices or economic indicators, where preserving the chronological order of data is essential for maintaining the integrity of predictions.

Best Practices

1. Shuffle Before Splitting: For non-time-series data, shuffling before splitting can help in ensuring that the training and testing sets are representative of the overall dataset.
2. Consistent Preprocessing: Ensure that any preprocessing steps, such as scaling or normalization, are applied consistently across both the training and testing sets to prevent data leakage.
3. Use Ensemble Methods: Combining multiple splitting techniques can enhance the robustness of model evaluation. For instance, using cross-validation on top of a train-test split can provide deeper insights.

Example: Evaluating a Model

To demonstrate the importance of effective data splitting, let's walk through an example where we evaluate a model's performance using different splitting techniques.

```python
from sklearn.datasets import make_regression
from sklearn.ensemble import RandomForestRegressor
from sklearn.metrics import mean_squared_error

Generate synthetic financial data
X, y = make_regression(n_samples=1000, n_features=20, noise=0.1, random_state=42)

Train-test split
X_train, X_test, y_train, y_test = train_test_split(X, y, test_size=0.2, random_state=42)
model = RandomForestRegressor()
model.fit(X_train, y_train)
predictions = model.predict(X_test)
mse_train_test = mean_squared_error(y_test, predictions)

K-fold cross-validation
kf = KFold(n_splits=5, shuffle=True, random_state=42)
mse_scores_kfold = []
for train_index, test_index in kf.split(X):
    X_train, X_test = X[train_index], X[test_index]
    y_train, y_test = y[train_index], y[test_index]
    model.fit(X_train, y_train)
```

```
    predictions = model.predict(X_test)
    mse_scores_kfold.append(mean_squared_error(y_test, predictions))

mse_kfold_avg = np.mean(mse_scores_kfold)

print(f'Mean Squared Error (Train-Test Split): {mse_train_test}')
print(f'Mean Squared Error (K-Fold Cross-Validation): {mse_kfold_avg}')
```

Comparing the Mean Squared Errors from train-test split and k-fold cross-validation, we can assess the consistency and reliability of the model. Typically, k-fold cross-validation provides a more comprehensive evaluation, reducing the risk of overfitting and offering a better estimate of the model's performance on unseen data.

Understanding and effectively implementing data splitting techniques is foundational for building reliable and accurate financial models. Each technique has its unique advantages and is suited for different scenarios. As you continue to develop and fine-tune your models, these splitting strategies will serve as essential tools in your machine learning arsenal, ensuring that your models are both robust and ready for real-world deployment.

## Introduction to Model Validation Methods

Model validation is a crucial step in the machine learning pipeline, ensuring that our models are not only accurate but also generalizable. This process involves evaluating the performance of a model on a separate dataset that it has not seen during training, thereby providing a realistic measure of how the model is likely to perform on new data. In the world of finance, where models are often applied to high-stakes decisions, robust model validation is indispensable.

The Significance of Model Validation

In financial applications, the accuracy and reliability of predictions can have substantial impacts, from risk management to trading strategies. Without proper validation, a model that performs well on training data might fail catastrophically in real-world scenarios due to overfitting. Overfitting occurs when a model captures noise or patterns specific to the training data, rather than underlying trends that generalize to new data.

Common Model Validation Techniques

1. Holdout Method

The holdout method is the simplest form of validation, where the dataset is split into two parts: a training set and a testing set. Typically, 70-80% of the data is used for training, and the remaining 20-30% is reserved for testing.

```python
from sklearn.model_selection import train_test_split
from sklearn.linear_model import LogisticRegression
from sklearn.metrics import accuracy_score
```

```
Sample financial data (e.g., credit scores, loan defaults)
data = np.array([
    [750, 1],
    [600, 0],
    [800, 1],
    [550, 0],
    [700, 1],
    [650, 0]
])
target = np.array([1, 0, 1, 0, 1, 0])

Split the data
X_train, X_test, y_train, y_test = train_test_split(data, target,
test_size=0.2, random_state=42)

Train the model
model = LogisticRegression()
model.fit(X_train, y_train)

 Test the model
predictions = model.predict(X_test)
accuracy = accuracy_score(y_test, predictions)

print("Holdout Method Accuracy:", accuracy)
```

While the holdout method is straightforward, its main drawback is that it does not provide a comprehensive evaluation of the model, as it relies on a single train-test split.

2. K-Fold Cross-Validation

K-fold cross-validation is a more sophisticated method that addresses the limitations of the holdout method. The dataset is divided into k equally sized folds. The model is trained and tested k times, each time using a different fold as the testing set and the remaining folds as the training set. The final performance metric is the average of the performance across all k iterations.

```python
from sklearn.model_selection import KFold
from sklearn.tree import DecisionTreeClassifier
from sklearn.metrics import accuracy_score

Sample financial data
data = np.array([
    [750, 1],
    [600, 0],
    [800, 1],
    [550, 0],
    [700, 1],
    [650, 0]
])
target = np.array([1, 0, 1, 0, 1, 0])

Initialize k-fold cross-validation
kf = KFold(n_splits=3, shuffle=True, random_state=42)
```

```
accuracy_scores = []

Perform k-fold cross-validation
for train_index, test_index in kf.split(data):
    X_train, X_test = data[train_index], data[test_index]
    y_train, y_test = target[train_index], target[test_index]

    model = DecisionTreeClassifier()
    model.fit(X_train, y_train)
    predictions = model.predict(X_test)
    accuracy = accuracy_score(y_test, predictions)
    accuracy_scores.append(accuracy)

print("K-Fold Cross-Validation Accuracy Scores:", accuracy_scores)
print("Average Accuracy:", np.mean(accuracy_scores))
```

K-fold cross-validation is particularly beneficial for financial datasets, which may be limited in size. By utilizing the entire dataset for both training and testing across different iterations, it provides a more reliable measure of model performance.

3. Leave-One-Out Cross-Validation (LOOCV)

LOOCV is a special case of k-fold cross-validation where k equals the number of data points in the dataset. Each data point is used once as the testing set while the remaining data points form the training set. LOOCV can be computationally expensive but provides an unbiased estimate of model performance, especially useful for small datasets.

```python
from sklearn.model_selection import LeaveOneOut
from sklearn.svm import SVC
from sklearn.metrics import accuracy_score

Sample financial data
data = np.array([
    [750, 1],
    [600, 0],
    [800, 1],
    [550, 0],
    [700, 1],
    [650, 0]
])
target = np.array([1, 0, 1, 0, 1, 0])

Initialize leave-one-out cross-validation
loo = LeaveOneOut()

accuracy_scores = []

Perform leave-one-out cross-validation
for train_index, test_index in loo.split(data):
    X_train, X_test = data[train_index], data[test_index]
    y_train, y_test = target[train_index], target[test_index]
```

```
    model = SVC()
    model.fit(X_train, y_train)
    predictions = model.predict(X_test)
    accuracy = accuracy_score(y_test, predictions)
    accuracy_scores.append(accuracy)

print("Leave-One-Out Cross-Validation Accuracy Scores:", accuracy_scores)
print("Average Accuracy:", np.mean(accuracy_scores))
```

Despite its computational intensity, LOOCV is valuable in scenarios where maximizing the use of limited data is critical.

4. Time Series Cross-Validation

For time series data, traditional cross-validation methods like k-fold are not suitable due to the temporal dependencies in the data. Time series cross-validation respects the chronological order of data. One common approach is walk-forward validation, where the model is trained on a growing window of data and tested on the next time step.

```python
from sklearn.model_selection import TimeSeriesSplit
from sklearn.ensemble import RandomForestRegressor
from sklearn.metrics import mean_squared_error

Sample time series data (e.g., daily stock prices)
```

```
data = np.array([
    [200, 1000],
    [150, 750],
    [300, 1500],
    [250, 1200],
    [220, 1100],
    [180, 900]
])
target = np.array([300, 200, 500, 450, 320, 280])

Initialize time series split
tscv = TimeSeriesSplit(n_splits=3)

mse_scores = []

Perform time series cross-validation
for train_index, test_index in tscv.split(data):
    X_train, X_test = data[train_index], data[test_index]
    y_train, y_test = target[train_index], target[test_index]

    model = RandomForestRegressor()
    model.fit(X_train, y_train)
    predictions = model.predict(X_test)
    mse = mean_squared_error(y_test, predictions)
    mse_scores.append(mse)

print("Time Series Cross-Validation MSE Scores:", mse_scores)
print("Average MSE:", np.mean(mse_scores))
```

Time series cross-validation is essential for financial applications like stock price forecasting or economic trend analysis, where preserving the sequence of observations is critical.

Best Practices for Model Validation

1. Consistency in Preprocessing: Ensure that any preprocessing steps, such as scaling or normalization, are consistently applied to both the training and testing sets to prevent data leakage.
2. Stratified Sampling: For classification problems, use stratified sampling to ensure that the training and testing sets have similar class distributions, which is particularly important for imbalanced datasets.
3. Multiple Runs: Perform multiple validation runs with different random seeds to get a more robust estimate of model performance.

Example: Evaluating a Model with Different Validation Techniques

Let's walk through an example where we evaluate a model's performance using different validation techniques.

```python
from sklearn.datasets import make_classification
from sklearn.linear_model import LogisticRegression
from sklearn.metrics import accuracy_score
```

Generate synthetic financial data

X, y = make_classification(n_samples=1000, n_features=20, n_classes=2, random_state=42)

Holdout Method

X_train, X_test, y_train, y_test = train_test_split(X, y, test_size=0.2, random_state=42)

model = LogisticRegression()

model.fit(X_train, y_train)

predictions = model.predict(X_test)

accuracy_holdout = accuracy_score(y_test, predictions)

K-Fold Cross-Validation

kf = KFold(n_splits=5, shuffle=True, random_state=42)

accuracy_scores_kfold = []

for train_index, test_index in kf.split(X):

    X_train, X_test = X[train_index], X[test_index]

    y_train, y_test = y[train_index], y[test_index]

    model.fit(X_train, y_train)

    predictions = model.predict(X_test)

    accuracy_scores_kfold.append(accuracy_score(y_test, predictions))

Time Series Cross-Validation

tscv = TimeSeriesSplit(n_splits=5)

accuracy_scores_tscv = []

for train_index, test_index in tscv.split(X):

    X_train, X_test = X[train_index], X[test_index]

```
    y_train, y_test = y[train_index], y[test_index]
    model.fit(X_train, y_train)
    predictions = model.predict(X_test)
    accuracy_scores_tscv.append(accuracy_score(y_test, predictions))

print(f'Holdout Method Accuracy: {accuracy_holdout}')
print(f'K-Fold Cross-Validation Accuracy: {np.mean(accuracy_scores_kfold)}')
print(f'Time Series Cross-Validation Accuracy: {np.mean(accuracy_scores_tscv)}')
```

Comparing the accuracy scores obtained from different validation techniques, we can assess the consistency and reliability of the model. Typically, k-fold cross-validation provides a more comprehensive evaluation, while time series cross-validation is crucial for temporal data.

Robust model validation is foundational for building reliable and accurate financial models. Each technique has its unique advantages and is suited for different scenarios. As you continue to develop and fine-tune your models, these validation strategies will ensure that your predictions are not only accurate but also generalizable to real-world financial data.

## Hands-on Example: First Steps with Financial Datasets

### Loading Financial Data

The cornerstone of any machine learning project is data. We will start by loading a sample financial dataset using the popular Python library, pandas. For this example, we'll use a dataset containing historical stock prices, which can be downloaded from various sources like Yahoo Finance or Quandl.

```python
import pandas as pd

Load dataset
url = 'https://example.com/historical_stock_prices.csv'
stock_data = pd.read_csv(url, parse_dates=['Date'])

Display the first few rows of the dataset
print(stock_data.head())
```

Here, we load the dataset and parse the 'Date' column as datetime objects, which is crucial for any time series analysis.

Exploring and Preprocessing the Data

Once loaded, we need to explore and preprocess the data to prepare it for modeling. This involves checking for missing values, handling outliers, and creating new features if necessary.

```python
Check for missing values
```

```
print(stock_data.isnull().sum())

Fill or drop missing values
stock_data.fillna(method='ffill', inplace=True)

Basic statistics
print(stock_data.describe())

Create new features: Daily Returns
stock_data['Daily_Return'] = stock_data['Close'].pct_change()

print(stock_data.head())
```

By filling missing values using forward fill and calculating daily returns, we enhance our dataset's robustness and relevance for predictive modeling.

Splitting the Data

Next, we split the data into training and testing sets. It's important to maintain the temporal order of the data, especially in financial applications, to avoid look-ahead bias.

```python
from sklearn.model_selection import train_test_split

Split the data
train_size = int(len(stock_data) * 0.8)
train_data = stock_data[:train_size]
```

```
test_data = stock_data[train_size:]

print(f"Training data size: {len(train_data)}")
print(f"Testing data size: {len(test_data)}")
```

Here, we split the dataset into an 80/20 ratio, ensuring that our testing data is future data relative to the training data.

Feature Scaling

Feature scaling is a critical step, particularly for algorithms sensitive to the scale of data, such as Support Vector Machines and Neural Networks. We will use StandardScaler from Scikit-Learn to scale our features.

```python
from sklearn.preprocessing import StandardScaler

Initialize the scaler
scaler = StandardScaler()

Fit and transform the training data
train_features = train_data[['Open', 'High', 'Low', 'Close', 'Volume']]
train_scaled = scaler.fit_transform(train_features)

Transform the test data
test_features = test_data[['Open', 'High', 'Low', 'Close', 'Volume']]
```

```
test_scaled = scaler.transform(test_features)

print(train_scaled[:5])
print(test_scaled[:5])
```

By scaling our features, we ensure that all variables contribute equally to the model training process.

Training a Basic Model

For our first model, let's use a simple linear regression to predict the closing price of the stock based on the other features. Linear regression is a great starting point due to its simplicity and interpretability.

```python
from sklearn.linear_model import LinearRegression
from sklearn.metrics import mean_squared_error

Initialize the model
model = LinearRegression()

Train the model
X_train = train_scaled
y_train = train_data['Close'][1:]    Aligning with pct_change which causes one NaN
model.fit(X_train[:-1], y_train)

Make predictions on the test set
```

```
X_test = test_scaled
y_test = test_data['Close']
predictions = model.predict(X_test)

Evaluate the model
mse = mean_squared_error(y_test, predictions)
print(f"Mean Squared Error: {mse}")
```

This preliminary model gives us a baseline understanding of the relationship between our features and the target variable.

Visualizing the Results

Visualizations help in interpreting the model's performance and understanding the results. We will plot the actual vs predicted closing prices to assess our model.

```python
import matplotlib.pyplot as plt

Plot actual vs predicted closing prices
plt.figure(figsize=(14, 7))
plt.plot(test_data['Date'], y_test, label='Actual Closing Prices')
plt.plot(test_data['Date'], predictions, label='Predicted Closing Prices')
plt.xlabel('Date')
plt.ylabel('Closing Price')
plt.title('Actual vs Predicted Closing Prices')
```

```
plt.legend()
plt.show()
```

This plot will help us visually inspect how well our model's predictions align with the actual data over time.

Next Steps

While this example provides a solid foundation, it's merely the beginning. As we progress through the book, we will explore more complex models, advanced feature engineering, and sophisticated validation techniques to enhance our predictive capabilities in financial data analysis.

# CHAPTER 3: SUPERVISED LEARNING TECHNIQUES

Linear regression aims to model the relationship between a dependent variable and one or more independent variables by fitting a linear equation to observed data. The equation of a simple linear regression model can be expressed as:

$$y = \beta_0 + \beta_1 x_1 + \epsilon$$

Where:

- $y$ is the dependent variable (e.g., stock price),

- $x_1$ is the independent variable (e.g., trading volume),

- $\beta_0$ and $\beta_1$ are coefficients that represent the intercept and slope of the line, respectively,

- $\epsilon$ is the error term.

For multiple linear regression, which involves more than one independent variable, the equation extends to:

$$ y = \beta_0 + \beta_1 x_1 + \beta_2 x_2 + \ldots + \beta_n x_n + \epsilon $$

Where $x_2, x_3, \ldots, x_n$ are additional independent variables.

The goal of linear regression is to find the values of $\beta_0, \beta_1, \ldots, \beta_n$ that minimize the sum of squared residuals, providing the best fit line through the data points.

Implementing Linear Regression with Scikit-Learn

To understand the practical aspects of linear regression, let's implement it using Scikit-Learn. We'll use a financial dataset containing stock prices and trading volumes.

First, load the necessary libraries and the dataset:

```python
import pandas as pd
from sklearn.linear_model import LinearRegression
from sklearn.model_selection import train_test_split
from sklearn.metrics import mean_squared_error
import matplotlib.pyplot as plt

Load dataset
url = 'https://example.com/historical_stock_prices.csv'
stock_data = pd.read_csv(url, parse_dates=['Date'])
```

```
Display the first few rows of the dataset
print(stock_data.head())
```

Preparing the Data

Before fitting a linear regression model, preprocess the data. This includes handling missing values, creating new features, and splitting the data into training and testing sets.

```python
Fill or drop missing values
stock_data.fillna(method='ffill', inplace=True)

Create new features: Daily Returns and Moving Averages
stock_data['Daily_Return'] = stock_data['Close'].pct_change()
stock_data['50_MA'] = stock_data['Close'].rolling(window=50).mean()
stock_data['200_MA'] = stock_data['Close'].rolling(window=200).mean()

Drop any remaining NaN values after feature creation
stock_data.dropna(inplace=True)

Split the data into training and testing sets
train_data, test_data = train_test_split(stock_data, test_size=0.2, shuffle=False)

Extract features and target variable
```

```
X_train = train_data[['Volume', '50_MA', '200_MA']]
y_train = train_data['Close']
X_test = test_data[['Volume', '50_MA', '200_MA']]
y_test = test_data['Close']
```

Fitting the Linear Regression Model

With the data prepared, fit the linear regression model:

```python
Initialize the model
model = LinearRegression()

 Train the model
model.fit(X_train, y_train)

 Make predictions on the test set
predictions = model.predict(X_test)

Evaluate the model
mse = mean_squared_error(y_test, predictions)
print(f"Mean Squared Error: {mse}")
```

Visualizing the Results

Visualizing the actual vs. predicted stock prices helps in assessing model performance:

```python
Plot actual vs predicted closing prices
plt.figure(figsize=(14, 7))
plt.plot(test_data['Date'], y_test, label='Actual Closing Prices')
plt.plot(test_data['Date'], predictions, label='Predicted Closing Prices')
plt.xlabel('Date')
plt.ylabel('Closing Price')
plt.title('Actual vs Predicted Closing Prices')
plt.legend()
plt.show()
```

Practical Applications in Finance

Linear regression has numerous applications in finance, including but not limited to:

1. Stock Price Prediction:

- Predicting future stock prices based on historical data and other predictors such as trading volume and moving averages. While linear regression may not capture all the complexities of stock price movements, it provides a baseline model that can be enhanced with more sophisticated techniques.

2. Risk Management:

- Estimating the beta coefficient of a stock, which measures its volatility relative to the market. The Capital Asset Pricing Model (CAPM) uses linear regression to relate the returns of an asset to the returns of the market, aiding in portfolio management and risk assessment.

3. Credit Risk Modeling:

- Predicting the likelihood of default by analyzing the relationship between borrowers' financial attributes and their default rates. Linear regression helps in identifying key predictors and assessing their impact on credit risk.

4. Portfolio Optimization:

- Determining the optimal asset allocation by modeling the relationship between asset returns and various economic factors. Linear regression assists in forecasting future returns and assessing the risk-reward profile of different portfolios.

Advanced Techniques and Considerations

While linear regression provides valuable insights, it's essential to be aware of its limitations and consider advanced techniques for enhanced accuracy:

- Multicollinearity: Highly correlated independent variables can distort the model. Techniques like Principal Component Analysis (PCA) or Ridge Regression help in mitigating this issue.

- Heteroscedasticity: Unequal variance of residuals can impact model reliability. Transforming variables or using weighted least squares regression addresses this problem.

- Non-linearity: Financial data often exhibit non-linear patterns. Polynomial regression or non-linear models like Decision Trees and Neural Networks capture these complexities better.

Linear regression remains a foundational tool in financial analysis, offering a straightforward yet effective way to model relationships and make predictions. By understanding its principles and applying it judiciously, financial analysts can unlock significant insights and drive informed decision-making. As we progress through the book, we will build upon this foundation, exploring more sophisticated models and techniques to tackle the diverse challenges in financial data analysis.

## 3.2 Logistic Regression for Classification Problems

### Understanding Logistic Regression

Logistic regression estimates the probability that a given input point belongs to a certain class. The model transforms the linear combination of input features using the logistic function (also known as the sigmoid function), which maps any real-valued number into a value between 0 and 1.

The logistic function is defined as:

$$ \sigma(z) = \frac{1}{1 + e^{-z}} $$

Where:

- $\sigma(z)$ is the logistic function,
- $z$ is the linear combination of input features.

In the context of logistic regression, $z$ is given by:

$$z = \beta_0 + \beta_1 x_1 + \beta_2 x_2 + \ldots + \beta_n x_n$$

Where:

- $x_1, x_2, \ldots, x_n$ are the input features,
- $\beta_0, \beta_1, \ldots, \beta_n$ are the coefficients to be estimated.

The output of the logistic function, $\sigma(z)$, represents the probability that the input point belongs to the positive class. For binary classification, we can define a threshold (usually 0.5) to make the final class prediction.

Implementing Logistic Regression with Scikit-Learn

Let's implement logistic regression using Scikit-Learn to predict whether a stock will go up or down based on historical financial data.

First, load the necessary libraries and the dataset:

```python
import pandas as pd
from sklearn.model_selection import train_test_split
from sklearn.linear_model import LogisticRegression
from sklearn.metrics import accuracy_score, confusion_matrix, classification_report

Load dataset
url = 'https://example.com/stock_movement.csv'
```

```
data = pd.read_csv(url, parse_dates=['Date'])

Display the first few rows of the dataset
print(data.head())
```

Preparing the Data

Data preprocessing is crucial for the effectiveness of the model. This includes handling missing values, creating new features, and splitting the data into training and testing sets.

```python
Fill or drop missing values
data.fillna(method='ffill', inplace=True)

Create new features: Daily Returns and Moving Averages
data['Daily_Return'] = data['Close'].pct_change()
data['50_MA'] = data['Close'].rolling(window=50).mean()
data['200_MA'] = data['Close'].rolling(window=200).mean()

Generate the target variable: 1 if stock goes up, 0 if it goes down
data['Target'] = (data['Close'].shift(-1) > data['Close']).astype(int)

Drop any remaining NaN values after feature creation
data.dropna(inplace=True)

Split the data into training and testing sets
train_data, test_data = train_test_split(data, test_size=0.2,
```

```
shuffle=False)

Extract features and target variable
X_train = train_data[['Volume', '50_MA', '200_MA']]
y_train = train_data['Target']
X_test = test_data[['Volume', '50_MA', '200_MA']]
y_test = test_data['Target']
```

Fitting the Logistic Regression Model

With the data prepared, fit the logistic regression model:

```python
Initialize the model
model = LogisticRegression()

 Train the model
model.fit(X_train, y_train)

 Make predictions on the test set
predictions = model.predict(X_test)

Evaluate the model
accuracy = accuracy_score(y_test, predictions)
print(f"Accuracy: {accuracy}")

conf_matrix = confusion_matrix(y_test, predictions)
print(f"Confusion Matrix:\n{conf_matrix}")
```

```
class_report = classification_report(y_test, predictions)
print(f"Classification Report:\n{class_report}")
```

Practical Applications in Finance

Logistic regression has several critical applications in the financial sector:

1. Credit Default Prediction:

- Predicting whether a borrower will default on a loan is a classic application of logistic regression. By analyzing historical borrower data, such as credit scores, income levels, and past payment behavior, logistic regression models can estimate the probability of default, aiding in risk assessment and decision-making.

2. Fraud Detection:

- Financial institutions use logistic regression to identify fraudulent transactions. By examining transaction attributes such as the amount, location, and time, the model can flag unusual patterns that deviate from a user's typical behavior, triggering alerts for further investigation.

3. Market Movement Prediction:

- As illustrated in our example, logistic regression can predict stock price movements. By leveraging historical data and technical indicators, traders can make informed decisions about buying or selling stocks, potentially enhancing their trading strategies.

4. Customer Churn Analysis:

- Companies use logistic regression to predict whether a customer is likely to stop using a service. By analyzing customer attributes, usage patterns, and engagement metrics, the model can help businesses take proactive measures to retain valuable customers.

Advanced Techniques and Considerations

While logistic regression is powerful, it has limitations that can be addressed with advanced techniques:

- Feature Engineering: Creating meaningful features is paramount to model performance. Domain knowledge in finance can guide the creation of features that capture relevant information, such as volatility measures or sentiment indicators.
- Regularization: L1 (Lasso) and L2 (Ridge) regularization techniques help prevent overfitting by penalizing large coefficients. This is especially important when dealing with high-dimensional data.
- Class Imbalance: Financial datasets often have imbalanced classes (e.g., few instances of fraud compared to non-fraud). Techniques such as SMOTE (Synthetic Minority Over-sampling Technique) or adjusting class weights can help address this imbalance.
- Model Evaluation: Beyond accuracy, metrics like precision, recall, and the F1-score provide a more comprehensive evaluation of model performance, especially in imbalanced datasets.

Logistic regression remains a robust and interpretable method for tackling various classification problems in finance. By understanding its principles, effectively preprocessing data, and considering advanced techniques, financial analysts can harness the power of logistic regression to derive meaningful insights and make data-driven decisions. As we continue, we will explore other sophisticated models and techniques that complement and enhance the capabilities of logistic regression in financial analysis.

## 3.3 Decision Trees: Theory and Implementation

### Understanding Decision Trees

At their core, decision trees are a type of binary tree structure used to make decisions based on the input features. Each internal node represents a "decision" based on a feature, each branch represents the outcome of the decision, and each leaf node represents a class label (for classification) or a continuous value (for regression).

The tree-building process involves recursively splitting the dataset into subsets based on the feature that minimizes a specified criterion, such as Gini impurity or entropy for classification, and mean squared error (MSE) for regression.

### Gini Impurity and Entropy

For classification tasks, two common criteria are used to evaluate splits:

1. Gini Impurity:

$$
Gini(p) = 1 - \sum_{i=1}^{C} p_i^2
$$

where $p_i$ is the proportion of samples belonging to class $i$.

2. Entropy:

$$
Entropy(p) = - \sum_{i=1}^{C} p_i \log(p_i)
$$

where $p_i$ is the probability of class $i$.

Both criteria aim to measure the "impurity" or disorder within a dataset, with the goal of selecting splits that reduce this impurity.

### Mean Squared Error

For regression tasks, the criterion is typically the mean squared error (MSE):

$$
MSE = \frac{1}{N} \sum_{i=1}^{N} (y_i - \hat{y}_i)^2
$$

where $y_i$ is the actual value and $\hat{y}_i$ is the predicted value.

### Implementing Decision Trees with Scikit-Learn

Let's implement a decision tree using Scikit-Learn to classify whether a credit card transaction is fraudulent based on various features.

First, load the necessary libraries and the dataset:

```python
import pandas as pd
from sklearn.model_selection import train_test_split
from sklearn.tree import DecisionTreeClassifier
from sklearn.metrics import accuracy_score, confusion_matrix, classification_report
import matplotlib.pyplot as plt
from sklearn.tree import plot_tree

Load dataset
url = 'https://example.com/creditcard_fraud.csv'
data = pd.read_csv(url)

Display the first few rows of the dataset
print(data.head())
```

Preparing the Data

Data preprocessing is crucial for the effectiveness of the model. This includes handling missing values, creating new features, and splitting the data into training and testing sets.

```python
Handle missing values
data.fillna(method='ffill', inplace=True)

Split the data into training and testing sets
X = data.drop(columns=['Fraud'])
y = data['Fraud']

X_train, X_test, y_train, y_test = train_test_split(X, y, test_size=0.2, random_state=42)
```

Fitting the Decision Tree Model

With the data prepared, fit the decision tree model:

```python
Initialize the model
model = DecisionTreeClassifier(criterion='gini', max_depth=5, random_state=42)

 Train the model
model.fit(X_train, y_train)

 Make predictions on the test set
predictions = model.predict(X_test)

Evaluate the model
accuracy = accuracy_score(y_test, predictions)
```

```
print(f"Accuracy: {accuracy}")

conf_matrix = confusion_matrix(y_test, predictions)
print(f"Confusion Matrix:\n{conf_matrix}")

class_report = classification_report(y_test, predictions)
print(f"Classification Report:\n{class_report}")

Plot the decision tree
plt.figure(figsize=(20,10))
plot_tree(model, filled=True, feature_names=X.columns, class_names=['Not Fraud', 'Fraud'], rounded=True)
plt.show()
```

Practical Applications in Finance

Decision trees have several vital applications in the financial sector:

1. Credit Scoring:

- Decision trees can be used to evaluate the creditworthiness of loan applicants. By analyzing various features such as income, employment history, and past credit behavior, the model can classify applicants into different risk categories, aiding in the decision-making process for granting loans.

2. Fraud Detection:

- Financial institutions often use decision trees to detect fraudulent transactions. By examining transaction characteristics such as amount, frequency, and location, the model can identify patterns indicative of fraud, helping to prevent financial losses.

3. Investment Decisions:

- Decision trees can assist in making investment decisions by analyzing historical market data and other relevant features. The model can predict the potential return of different investment options, guiding investors in selecting the most promising opportunities.

4. Customer Segmentation:

- Companies use decision trees to segment customers based on various attributes such as spending behavior and preferences. This segmentation allows businesses to tailor their marketing strategies and offer personalized services, enhancing customer satisfaction and loyalty.

Advanced Techniques and Considerations

While decision trees are powerful, they can be prone to overfitting and may not always capture complex relationships in the data. Here are some advanced techniques and considerations:

- Pruning: Pruning helps reduce the size of the tree by removing branches that have little importance. This technique can be pre-pruning (setting a maximum depth) or post-pruning (removing branches after the tree is built).
- Ensemble Methods: Combining multiple decision trees using techniques like Random Forests or Gradient Boosting can improve model performance and robustness by reducing variance and bias.
- Feature Importance: Decision trees provide a measure

of feature importance, indicating which features are most influential in making predictions. This insight can be valuable for understanding the underlying factors driving financial outcomes.

- Handling Imbalanced Data: Financial datasets often have imbalanced classes. Techniques such as resampling, adjusting class weights, or using ensemble methods can help address this issue and improve model performance.

- Hyperparameter Tuning: Optimizing hyperparameters such as the maximum depth, minimum samples per leaf, and the splitting criterion can significantly enhance the model's performance.

Decision trees remain a powerful and interpretable method for tackling various classification and regression problems in finance. By understanding their principles, effectively preprocessing data, and considering advanced techniques, financial analysts can harness the power of decision trees to derive meaningful insights and make data-driven decisions. As we continue, we will explore other sophisticated models and techniques that complement and enhance the capabilities of decision trees in financial analysis.

## 3.4 Random Forests: Ensemble Methods in Practice

### Understanding Random Forests

Random Forests are an ensemble learning method primarily used for classification and regression tasks. They operate by constructing a multitude of decision trees during training and outputting the mode of the classes (classification) or the mean prediction (regression) of the individual trees. This aggregation process helps in reducing the variance of the model and improving overall accuracy.

Bagging and Bootstrap Aggregation

The core idea behind Random Forests is bagging, or bootstrap aggregation. This technique involves:

1. Bootstrap Sampling: Randomly sampling, with replacement, from the training dataset to create multiple subsets. Each subset is used to train an individual decision tree.
2. Aggregating Predictions: Combining the predictions of all the decision trees. For classification tasks, this typically involves a majority vote, while for regression tasks, it involves averaging the predictions.

By training multiple trees on different subsets of the data, Random Forests help in reducing the likelihood of overfitting, a common issue with single decision trees.

Feature Randomness

In addition to bagging, Random Forests introduce another layer of randomness by selecting a random subset of features for each split in the decision trees. This feature randomness ensures that the trees are not overly correlated, further enhancing the model's robustness and generalization capability.

Implementing Random Forests with Scikit-Learn

To illustrate the implementation of Random Forests, let's consider a practical example where we predict loan defaults based on historical financial data.

First, we start by loading the necessary libraries and the dataset:

```python
import pandas as pd
from sklearn.model_selection import train_test_split
from sklearn.ensemble import RandomForestClassifier
from sklearn.metrics import accuracy_score, confusion_matrix, classification_report

Load dataset
url = 'https://example.com/loan_defaults.csv'
data = pd.read_csv(url)

Display the first few rows of the dataset
print(data.head())
```

Preparing the Data

As with any machine learning model, data preprocessing is essential. This involves handling missing values, encoding categorical variables, and splitting the data into training and testing sets:

```python
```

```
Handle missing values
data.fillna(method='ffill', inplace=True)

Encode categorical variables
data = pd.get_dummies(data)

Split the data into features and target variable
X = data.drop(columns=['Default'])
y = data['Default']

Split the data into training and testing sets
X_train, X_test, y_train, y_test = train_test_split(X, y, test_size=0.2, random_state=42)
```

Training the Random Forest Model

Next, we initialize and train the Random Forest model:

```python
Initialize the Random Forest model
model = RandomForestClassifier(n_estimators=100, max_depth=10, random_state=42)

 Train the model
model.fit(X_train, y_train)

 Make predictions on the test set
predictions = model.predict(X_test)
```

```
Evaluate the model
accuracy = accuracy_score(y_test, predictions)
print(f"Accuracy: {accuracy}")

conf_matrix = confusion_matrix(y_test, predictions)
print(f"Confusion Matrix:\n{conf_matrix}")

class_report = classification_report(y_test, predictions)
print(f"Classification Report:\n{class_report}")
```

Practical Applications in Finance

Random Forests have numerous applications in the financial sector, offering insights and predictions that drive better decision-making:

1. Credit Scoring:

- By analyzing historical loan repayment data, Random Forests can predict the likelihood of a borrower defaulting on a loan. This helps financial institutions assess credit risk more accurately and make informed lending decisions.

2. Fraud Detection:

- Random Forests can detect fraudulent transactions by identifying patterns and anomalies in transaction data. This capability is crucial for preventing financial fraud and safeguarding customer accounts.

3. Stock Price Prediction:

- Financial analysts use Random Forests to predict stock price movements based on historical price data, trading volumes, and other market indicators. These predictions assist in developing trading strategies and managing investment portfolios.

4. Customer Segmentation:

- Financial institutions segment customers based on their behavior, preferences, and demographics using Random Forests. This segmentation enables personalized marketing campaigns and targeted product offerings, enhancing customer satisfaction and loyalty.

Advanced Techniques and Considerations

While Random Forests are highly effective, there are several advanced techniques and considerations to further improve their performance:

- Hyperparameter Tuning:

- Adjusting hyperparameters such as the number of trees (n_estimators), maximum depth (max_depth), and minimum samples per leaf (min_samples_leaf) can significantly enhance model performance. Scikit-Learn's `GridSearchCV` or `RandomizedSearchCV` can help automate this process.

- Feature Importance:

- Random Forests provide a measure of feature importance, indicating the relative contribution of each feature to the prediction. This insight can be valuable for feature selection and understanding the factors driving financial outcomes.

- Handling Imbalanced Data:

- Financial datasets often have imbalanced classes. Techniques such as oversampling minority classes, undersampling majority classes, or using balanced class weights can help address this issue and improve model performance.

- Out-of-Bag (OO Error:

- OOB error provides an unbiased estimate of the model's performance without the need for a separate validation set. It is calculated using the data not included in the bootstrap samples for each tree, offering a more efficient evaluation method.

Example: Hyperparameter Tuning with GridSearchCV

Let's enhance our Random Forest model by tuning its hyperparameters using `GridSearchCV`:

```python
from sklearn.model_selection import GridSearchCV

Define the parameter grid
param_grid = {
    'n_estimators': [50, 100, 200],
    'max_depth': [None, 10, 20, 30],
    'min_samples_split': [2, 5, 10],
    'min_samples_leaf': [1, 2, 4]
}

Initialize the GridSearchCV
grid_search = GridSearchCV(estimator=model,
```

```
param_grid=param_grid, cv=3, n_jobs=-1, verbose=2)

Fit the grid search to the data
grid_search.fit(X_train, y_train)

 Output the best parameters
print(f"Best Parameters: {grid_search.best_params_}")

Evaluate the best model
best_model = grid_search.best_estimator_
predictions = best_model.predict(X_test)

accuracy = accuracy_score(y_test, predictions)
print(f"Accuracy: {accuracy}")

conf_matrix = confusion_matrix(y_test, predictions)
print(f"Confusion Matrix:\n{conf_matrix}")

class_report = classification_report(y_test, predictions)
print(f"Classification Report:\n{class_report}")
```

By leveraging Random Forests and their ensemble methodology, financial analysts can tackle a diverse range of predictive tasks with improved accuracy and robustness. Understanding their theoretical foundation, mastering their implementation in Scikit-Learn, and applying advanced techniques are crucial steps in harnessing the full potential of Random Forests in financial analytics.

## 3.5 Support Vector Machines for Financial Data

In the ever-evolving landscape of finance, data churns like the waves of the Pacific, and within this sea of information lie patterns waiting to be harnessed. Support Vector Machines (SVMs) are among the most potent tools for untangling these patterns. Their power lies not only in their robustness but also in their versatility, making them a favorite for many financial analysts. Let's dive into the theory, implementation, and application of SVMs in the financial arena.

### The Theory Behind Support Vector Machines

a Support Vector Machine is a supervised learning model designed for classification and regression tasks. The fundamental premise is to find the hyperplane that best separates data points of different classes in an N-dimensional space. If the data is not linearly separable, SVMs employ a technique known as the kernel trick to transform the data into a higher-dimensional space where a hyperplane can be used effectively.

Imagine you are tasked with distinguishing between profitable and non-profitable investments based on historical data. The SVM works by positioning a hyperplane in such a way that the margin between the closest data points of each class (known as support vectors) is maximized. This separation ensures the model's robustness to future, unseen data.

### Mathematical Formulation

For classification, the primal optimization problem of an SVM can be written as:

\[ \min_{\mathbf{w}, b, \xi} \frac{1}{2} \|\mathbf{w}\|^2 + C \sum_{i=1}^N \xi_i \]

subject to:

\geq 1 - \xi_i, \]
\[ \xi_i \geq 0, \]

where:

- \(\mathbf{w}\) is the normal vector to the hyperplane,
- \(b\) is the offset,
- \(y_i\) are the class labels,
- \(\xi_i\) are slack variables for handling misclassification,
- \(C\) is a regularization parameter controlling the trade-off between maximizing the margin and minimizing classification error.

Implementing SVMs with Scikit-Learn

Scikit-Learn provides an intuitive API for implementing SVMs. Let's walk through a practical example using financial data to classify credit risk.

First, we need to import the necessary libraries and load our dataset:

```python
import pandas as pd
from sklearn.model_selection import train_test_split
```

```python
from sklearn.preprocessing import StandardScaler
from sklearn.svm import SVC
from sklearn.metrics import classification_report

Load dataset (assuming a CSV file with appropriate data)
data = pd.read_csv('credit_risk_data.csv')

Features and labels
X = data.drop('Risk', axis=1)
y = data['Risk']

Split the data into training and testing sets
X_train, X_test, y_train, y_test = train_test_split(X, y, test_size=0.2, random_state=42)

Standardize the features
scaler = StandardScaler()
X_train = scaler.fit_transform(X_train)
X_test = scaler.transform(X_test)
```

With our data prepared, we can now instantiate and train the SVM model:

```python
Initialize the SVM classifier with a linear kernel
svm = SVC(kernel='linear', C=1.0)

Train the SVM model on the training data
```

svm.fit(X_train, y_train)
```

After training the model, it's crucial to evaluate its performance using the test data:

```python
Make predictions on the test set
y_pred = svm.predict(X_test)

Evaluate the model
print(classification_report(y_test, y_pred))
```

The classification report will provide insights into the precision, recall, F1-score, and support for each class, offering a comprehensive evaluation of the SVM's performance.

Applications in Finance

Support Vector Machines excel in various financial applications:

1. Credit Risk Assessment: By classifying borrowers into different risk categories, SVMs help financial institutions mitigate potential losses.
2. Fraud Detection: SVMs can distinguish between legitimate and fraudulent transactions, protecting businesses from financial fraud.
3. Stock Market Prediction: While challenging, SVMs can be applied to classify stocks into high or low return
```

categories based on historical performance and other financial indicators.

4. Customer Segmentation: Financial service providers can use SVMs to segment customers based on their financial behaviors, allowing for tailored marketing strategies.

Hyperparameter Tuning

The performance of an SVM can be significantly influenced by its hyperparameters, primarily the choice of kernel and the regularization parameter $C$. Scikit-Learn's `GridSearchCV` can be employed for hyperparameter tuning:

```python
from sklearn.model_selection import GridSearchCV

Define the parameter grid
param_grid = {
    'C': [0.1, 1, 10, 100],
    'kernel': ['linear', 'rbf', 'poly'],
    'gamma': ['scale', 'auto']
}

Initialize GridSearchCV
grid_search = GridSearchCV(SVC(), param_grid, cv=5, scoring='accuracy')

Fit the model
grid_search.fit(X_train, y_train)
```

```
Best parameters
print("Best parameters found: ", grid_search.best_params_)
```

Support Vector Machines stand as a robust and versatile tool in the financial analyst's toolkit. Their ability to handle high-dimensional data and their flexibility through kernel methods make them particularly suited for the complex and varied nature of financial data. By mastering SVMs, you equip yourself with a powerful method for tackling classification challenges in finance, driving both innovation and precision in your analyses.

## K-Nearest Neighbors: Simplicity and Effectiveness

Navigating the labyrinth of financial data, one often seeks methods that balance simplicity with effectiveness. K-Nearest Neighbors (K-NN) stands out in this regard, offering a straightforward yet powerful approach to classification and regression problems. The elegance of K-NN lies in its intuitive mechanism and the profound insights it can yield, particularly in the financial sector.

### The Essence of K-Nearest Neighbors

K-Nearest Neighbors is a non-parametric, lazy learning algorithm. Non-parametric means it makes no strong assumptions about the underlying data distribution—an advantageous trait given the often unpredictable nature of financial markets. Lazy learning indicates that K-NN doesn't construct a model during the training phase; instead, it stores the training dataset and defers computation until making predictions.

Imagine a scenario where you need to predict whether a new investment will be profitable or not based on historical performance. K-NN approaches this by identifying the 'k' most similar historical investments (the nearest neighbors) and using their outcomes to make predictions. Here, the similarity is typically measured using distance metrics such as Euclidean distance.

Mathematical Foundation

The distance metric is central to K-NN's functionality. For two points $\mathbf{x}$ and $\mathbf{y}$ in an N-dimensional space, the Euclidean distance is defined as:

$$d(\mathbf{x}, \mathbf{y}) = \sqrt{\sum_{i=1}^{N} (x_i - y_i)^2}$$

Once the distances are calculated, the algorithm proceeds as follows:

1. Identify the Nearest Neighbors: Sort the distances and select the 'k' smallest ones.
2. Vote for Classification: For classification tasks, the class label is determined by the majority vote among the 'k' neighbors.
3. Average for Regression: For regression tasks, the prediction is the average of the target values of the 'k' neighbors.

Implementing K-NN with Scikit-Learn

Scikit-Learn provides a seamless interface for implementing

K-NN. Let's walk through a practical example where we classify stocks into high or low return categories based on historical financial metrics.

First, import the necessary libraries and load the dataset:

```python
import pandas as pd
from sklearn.model_selection import train_test_split
from sklearn.preprocessing import StandardScaler
from sklearn.neighbors import KNeighborsClassifier
from sklearn.metrics import classification_report

Load dataset (assuming a CSV file with historical stock data)
data = pd.read_csv('stock_data.csv')

Features and labels
X = data.drop('ReturnCategory', axis=1)
y = data['ReturnCategory']

Split the data into training and testing sets
X_train, X_test, y_train, y_test = train_test_split(X, y, test_size=0.2, random_state=42)

Standardize the features
scaler = StandardScaler()
X_train = scaler.fit_transform(X_train)
X_test = scaler.transform(X_test)
```

With the data preprocessed, we can initialize and train the K-NN classifier:

```python
Initialize the K-NN classifier
knn = KNeighborsClassifier(n_neighbors=5)

Train the K-NN model on the training data
knn.fit(X_train, y_train)
```

After training, evaluate the model's performance:

```python
Make predictions on the test set
y_pred = knn.predict(X_test)

Evaluate the model
print(classification_report(y_test, y_pred))
```

The classification report provides a detailed breakdown of the model's precision, recall, F1-score, and support for each class, offering insight into the K-NN's effectiveness.

Applications in Finance

K-NN's simplicity belies its broad applicability in finance:

1. Stock Classification: By grouping stocks into categories based on historical performance metrics, K-NN aids in portfolio diversification.

2. Credit Scoring: Banks and financial institutions use K-NN to classify loan applicants into different risk categories, thereby mitigating defaults.

3. Fraud Detection: K-NN can detect anomalous transactions by comparing them to known legitimate transactions.

4. Customer Segmentation: Financial service providers can segment customers based on their financial behaviors, allowing for personalized services and targeted marketing campaigns.

Hyperparameter Tuning

The primary hyperparameter in K-NN is 'k,' the number of nearest neighbors considered. Selecting an optimal 'k' is crucial; a small 'k' can lead to noisy predictions, while a large 'k' may overlook local patterns. Scikit-Learn's `GridSearchCV` can assist in finding the best 'k':

```python
from sklearn.model_selection import GridSearchCV

Define the parameter grid
param_grid = {'n_neighbors': [3, 5, 7, 9, 11]}

Initialize GridSearchCV
grid_search = GridSearchCV(KNeighborsClassifier(), param_grid, cv=5, scoring='accuracy')
```

```
Fit the model
grid_search.fit(X_train, y_train)

Best parameters
print("Best parameters found: ", grid_search.best_params_)
```

Advantages and Limitations

K-NN holds several advantages:

- Intuitive and Easy to Understand: The algorithm's simplicity makes it easy to implement and interpret.
- No Assumptions about Data Distribution: K-NN's non-parametric nature is a boon in the unpredictable financial domain.

However, K-NN isn't without limitations:

- Computationally Intensive: K-NN can be slow for large datasets since it requires calculating the distance to every training point during prediction.
- Sensitive to Irrelevant Features: Feature selection and scaling are critical as irrelevant or differently scaled features can skew the distance calculations.

K-Nearest Neighbors remains a valuable tool in the financial analyst's arsenal, offering a blend of simplicity and effectiveness. Its ability to handle diverse financial tasks, from stock classification to fraud detection, underscores its versatility. By mastering K-NN, you gain a method that transforms raw data into actionable insights, driving informed and strategic financial decisions.

## Gradient Boosting Machines

At its heart, Gradient Boosting is an ensemble method—a collection of weaker models, often decision trees, that combine to form a stronger predictive model. Unlike simple averaging (as seen in Random Forests), GBMs build models sequentially, with each new model attempting to correct errors made by the previous ones. This iterative refinement leads to a robust, highly accurate model.

The process can be broken down into several steps:

1. Initialization: Start with a base model, typically predicting the mean of the target variable.
2. Compute Residuals: Calculate the residuals, which are the differences between the actual values and the predictions.
3. Fit a New Model: Fit a new model to the residuals.
4. Update Predictions: Adjust the predictions by adding the new model's predictions, scaled by a learning rate.
5. Repeat: Iterate this process for a specified number of iterations or until convergence.

Mathematically, the model at iteration $m$ can be expressed as:

$$F_m(x) = F_{m-1}(x) + \gamma \cdot h_m(x)$$

where $\gamma$ is the learning rate, and $h_m(x)$ is the new model fitted to the residuals.

### Mathematical Foundation

The optimization in Gradient Boosting involves minimizing

a loss function $L$ through gradient descent. For a given dataset $(x_i, y_i)$, the objective is to minimize:

$$ \sum_{i=1}^n L(y_i, F_m(x_i)) $$

The gradient boosting algorithm modifies this by adding a new model $h_m$ that approximates the negative gradient of the loss function with respect to the predictions of the ensemble:

$$ h_m(x) \approx - \left[ \frac{\partial L(y_i, F(x_i))}{\partial F(x_i)} \right] $$

By iteratively adding these gradient steps, the model gradually corrects its errors and improves its performance.

Implementing GBMs with Scikit-Learn

Scikit-Learn makes it straightforward to implement GBMs through its `GradientBoostingClassifier` and `GradientBoostingRegressor` classes. Let's walk through a practical example where we predict the credit risk of loan applicants.

First, import the necessary libraries and load the dataset:

```python
import pandas as pd
from sklearn.model_selection import train_test_split
from sklearn.preprocessing import StandardScaler
from sklearn.ensemble import GradientBoostingClassifier
```

```
from sklearn.metrics import classification_report

Load dataset (assuming a CSV file with credit risk data)
data = pd.read_csv('credit_risk_data.csv')

Features and labels
X = data.drop('RiskCategory', axis=1)
y = data['RiskCategory']

Split the data into training and testing sets
X_train, X_test, y_train, y_test = train_test_split(X, y, test_size=0.2, random_state=42)

Standardize the features
scaler = StandardScaler()
X_train = scaler.fit_transform(X_train)
X_test = scaler.transform(X_test)
```

With the data preprocessed, we can initialize and train the GBM classifier:

```python
Initialize the Gradient Boosting Classifier
gbm = GradientBoostingClassifier(n_estimators=100, learning_rate=0.1, max_depth=3, random_state=42)

Train the GBM model on the training data
gbm.fit(X_train, y_train)
```

After training, evaluate the model's performance:

```python
Make predictions on the test set
y_pred = gbm.predict(X_test)

Evaluate the model
print(classification_report(y_test, y_pred))
```

The classification report provides a detailed breakdown of the model's precision, recall, F1-score, and support for each class, offering insight into the GBM's effectiveness.

Applications in Finance

GBMs have a plethora of applications in the financial industry:

1. Credit Scoring: By predicting the likelihood of default, GBMs help in making informed lending decisions.
2. Stock Price Prediction: GBMs can model the complex relationships between historical stock prices and market indicators to forecast future prices.
3. Fraud Detection: GBMs excel in identifying fraudulent activities by learning patterns that deviate from normal behavior.
4. Risk Management: Financial institutions use GBMs to predict various risk factors, aiding in strategic planning and decision-making.

Hyperparameter Tuning

Optimizing a GBM involves tuning several hyperparameters. The key ones include:

- n_estimators: Number of boosting stages (trees) to be run.
- learning_rate: Shrinkage parameter applied to each tree's contribution.
- max_depth: Depth of the individual trees.
- min_samples_split: Minimum number of samples required to split an internal node.
- min_samples_leaf: Minimum number of samples required to be at a leaf node.

Using `GridSearchCV` in Scikit-Learn, we can automate the search for optimal hyperparameters:

```python
from sklearn.model_selection import GridSearchCV

Define the parameter grid
param_grid = {
    'n_estimators': [100, 200, 300],
    'learning_rate': [0.01, 0.05, 0.1],
    'max_depth': [3, 4, 5],
    'min_samples_split': [2, 5, 10],
    'min_samples_leaf': [1, 2, 4]
}

Initialize GridSearchCV
```

```
grid_search = GridSearchCV(GradientBoostingClassifier(), param_grid, cv=5, scoring='accuracy')

Fit the model
grid_search.fit(X_train, y_train)

Best parameters
print("Best parameters found: ", grid_search.best_params_)
```

Advantages and Limitations

Advantages:

- High Predictive Accuracy: GBMs often outperform other models due to their ability to correct previous errors iteratively.
- Flexibility: They can handle various types of data, including numerical, categorical, and missing values.
- Feature Importance: GBMs provide insights into the importance of each feature, aiding in feature selection and model interpretation.

Limitations:

- Computationally Intensive: Training GBMs can be time-consuming and require significant computational resources.
- Overfitting: Without careful tuning, GBMs can overfit, especially with small datasets or high tree depths.
- Complexity: The model's complexity can make it difficult to interpret compared to simpler models.

Gradient Boosting Machines represent a pinnacle of predictive modeling in finance, offering both power and precision. Their iterative refinement process allows for robust handling of complex financial data, making them indispensable in tasks ranging from credit scoring to risk management. By mastering GBMs, financial analysts can elevate their predictive analytics, driving strategic decisions and fostering innovation in the competitive landscape of finance.

Mean Absolute Error (MAE)

Mean Absolute Error (MAE) is a straightforward metric that quantifies the average absolute differences between predicted values and actual values. It is particularly useful for understanding the model's prediction error in the same units as the target variable.

$$\text{MAE} = \frac{1}{n} \sum_{i=1}^{n} | y_i - \hat{y}_i |$$

where:

- $n$ is the number of observations.
- $y_i$ represents the actual values.
- $\hat{y}_i$ denotes the predicted values.

Application in Finance:

MAE is advantageous when predicting stock prices, as it provides a clear, interpretable measure of average prediction error.

Mean Squared Error (MSE) and Root Mean Squared Error (RMSE)

Mean Squared Error (MSE) and its square root, Root

Mean Squared Error (RMSE), are fundamental metrics that emphasize larger errors due to their quadratic nature. MSE is defined as:

$$\text{MSE} = \frac{1}{n} \sum_{i=1}^{n} (y_i - \hat{y}_i)^2$$

RMSE, being the square root of MSE, reverts the error measure back to the original units of the target variable:

$$\text{RMSE} = \sqrt{\text{MSE}}$$

Application in Finance:

RMSE is often used when the financial model's primary concern is penalizing large errors more heavily, such as in the prediction of market volatility or risk measures.

$R^2$ Score (Coefficient of Determination)

The $R^2$ score, or coefficient of determination, measures the proportion of variance in the dependent variable that is predictable from the independent variables. It provides a goodness-of-fit measure:

$$R^2 = 1 - \frac{SS_{\text{res}}}{SS_{\text{tot}}}$$

where:

- $SS_{\text{res}}$ is the sum of squared residuals.
- $SS_{\text{tot}}$ is the total sum of squares.

Application in Finance:

$R^2$ is valuable for models such as those forecasting economic indicators or financial indices, where understanding the variance explained by the predictors is crucial.

Mean Absolute Percentage Error (MAPE)

Mean Absolute Percentage Error (MAPE) expresses the prediction accuracy as a percentage, providing a relative measure of error:

$$\text{MAPE} = \frac{1}{n} \sum_{i=1}^{n} \left| \frac{y_i - \hat{y}_i}{y_i} \right| \times 100$$

Application in Finance:

MAPE is particularly useful in scenarios where understanding the percentage error is meaningful, like in forecasting company earnings or budgeting future expenses.

Adjusted $R^2$

Adjusted $R^2$ adjusts the $R^2$ value based on the number of predictors in the model, accounting for model complexity and preventing overfitting:

$$\text{Adjusted} \, R^2 = 1 - \left(1 - R^2\right) \frac{n - 1}{n - k - 1}$$

where:

- $n$ is the number of observations.
- $k$ is the number of predictors.

Application in Finance:

Adjusted $R^2$ is essential in financial models with numerous predictors, ensuring that the addition of new variables genuinely improves model performance.

Mean Bias Deviation (MBD)

Mean Bias Deviation (MBD) evaluates the average bias in predictions, indicating whether the model consistently overestimates or underestimates the target:

$$\text{MBD} = \frac{1}{n} \sum_{i=1}^{n} (\hat{y}_i - y_i)$$

Application in Finance:

MBD is useful in risk management and financial forecasting to detect and correct systematic prediction biases.

Symmetric Mean Absolute Percentage Error (sMAPE)

Symmetric Mean Absolute Percentage Error (sMAPE) is a variation of MAPE that treats overestimations and underestimations symmetrically:

$$\text{sMAPE} = \frac{1}{n} \sum_{i=1}^{n} \frac{| y_i - \hat{y}_i |}{(| y_i | + | \hat{y}_i |)/2} \times 100$$

Application in Finance:

sMAPE is valuable for financial time series predictions where symmetrical error treatment is necessary, such as in forex and commodity price forecasts.

Implementing Performance Metrics with Python

Let's implement these performance metrics using Python and Scikit-Learn, focusing on a financial dataset predicting stock prices.

```python
from sklearn.metrics import mean_absolute_error, mean_squared_error, r2_score

Assuming y_true and y_pred are arrays of actual and predicted values
y_true = [100, 150, 200, 250, 300]
y_pred = [110, 140, 205, 240, 310]

Mean Absolute Error
mae = mean_absolute_error(y_true, y_pred)
print(f"Mean Absolute Error (MAE): {mae}")

Mean Squared Error and Root Mean Squared Error
mse = mean_squared_error(y_true, y_pred)
rmse = mse  0.5
print(f"Mean Squared Error (MSE): {mse}")
print(f"Root Mean Squared Error (RMSE): {rmse}")

R-squared Score
r2 = r2_score(y_true, y_pred)
print(f"R-squared (R2): {r2}")

Mean Absolute Percentage Error
mape = np.mean(np.abs((np.array(y_true) -
```

```
np.array(y_pred)) / np.array(y_true))) * 100
print(f"Mean Absolute Percentage Error (MAPE): {mape} %")

Adjusted R-squared
n = len(y_true)
k = 1  Assuming one predictor for simplicity
adjusted_r2 = 1 - (1 - r2) * (n - 1) / (n - k - 1)
print(f"Adjusted R-squared: {adjusted_r2}")

Mean Bias Deviation
mbd = np.mean(np.array(y_pred) - np.array(y_true))
print(f"Mean Bias Deviation (MBD): {mbd}")

Symmetric Mean Absolute Percentage Error
sMAPE = np.mean(2.0 * np.abs(np.array(y_pred) - np.array(y_true)) / (np.abs(np.array(y_true)) + np.abs(np.array(y_pred)))) * 100
print(f"Symmetric Mean Absolute Percentage Error (sMAPE): {sMAPE} %")
```

Choosing the Right Metric

Selecting the appropriate performance metric depends on the specific financial task at hand:

- MAE and MSE/ RMSE are ideal for general prediction tasks where understanding the magnitude of errors is crucial.

- $R^2$ and Adjusted $R^2$ are suited for models requiring an explanation of variance and model complexity.

- MAPE and sMAPE are beneficial for understanding relative

prediction errors.

- MBD helps uncover systematic biases in financial forecasts.

Assessing the performance of regression models is as critical as building them. Performance metrics such as MAE, MSE, RMSE, $R^2$, MAPE, Adjusted $R^2$, MBD, and sMAPE provide a comprehensive toolkit for evaluating financial models. By meticulously analyzing these metrics, financial analysts can ensure their models not only perform well but also offer reliable and actionable insights. This thorough evaluation process is fundamental to making informed financial decisions and maintaining a competitive edge.

Performance Metrics for Classification Tasks

Accuracy is the most straightforward performance metric, representing the proportion of correctly predicted instances out of the total instances:

$$\text{Accuracy} = \frac{TP + TN}{TP + TN + FP + FN}$$

where:

- $TP$ (True Positives) are correctly predicted positive instances.
- $TN$ (True Negatives) are correctly predicted negative instances.
- $FP$ (False Positives) are incorrectly predicted positive instances.
- $FN$ (False Negatives) are incorrectly predicted negative instances.

Application in Finance:

Accuracy is a starting point for evaluating models like credit scoring systems, where the goal is to correctly classify borrowers as either low-risk or high-risk.

Precision and Recall

Precision and recall provide a deeper understanding of the model's performance, particularly in imbalanced datasets where one class significantly outweighs the other.

- Precision measures the proportion of true positive predictions among all positive predictions:

$$\text{Precision} = \frac{TP}{TP + FP}$$

- Recall (Sensitivity or True Positive Rate) measures the proportion of true positive predictions among all actual positives:

$$\text{Recall} = \frac{TP}{TP + FN}$$

Application in Finance:

Precision is critical in fraud detection, where the cost of false positives is high. Recall is pivotal in identifying fraudulent transactions, ensuring that all potential fraud cases are flagged.

F1 Score

The F1 Score is the harmonic mean of precision and recall, providing a single metric that balances both concerns:

$$\text{F1 Score} = 2 \times \frac{\text{Precision} \times \text{Recall}}{\text{Precision} + \text{Recall}}$$

Application in Finance:

The F1 Score is valuable in applications like credit default prediction, where both precision and recall are important to minimize the risk of misclassifying borrowers.

Area Under the ROC Curve (AUC-ROC)

The AUC-ROC is a comprehensive metric that evaluates the performance of a classification model across all threshold levels. The ROC (Receiver Operating Characteristic) curve plots the True Positive Rate (Recall) against the False Positive Rate (1 – Specificity).

$$\text{AUC} = \int_{0}^{1} \text{ROC}(t) \, dt$$

Application in Finance:

AUC-ROC is instrumental in assessing models like customer churn prediction, where it's essential to understand the trade-offs between sensitivity and specificity across different thresholds.

Confusion Matrix

The confusion matrix is a tabular representation of actual versus predicted classifications, enabling a detailed analysis of model performance:

| | Predicted Positive | Predicted Negative |
|---|---|---|

| | | |
|---|---|---|
| Actual Positive | TP | FN |
| Actual Negative | FP | TN |

Application in Finance:

The confusion matrix is beneficial for visualizing the performance of models like anti-money laundering systems, helping analysts identify areas of improvement.

Specificity

Specificity (True Negative Rate) measures the proportion of true negative predictions among all actual negatives:

$$ \text{Specificity} = \frac{TN}{TN + FP} $$

Application in Finance:

Specificity is crucial in financial applications where minimizing false positives is essential, such as in the detection of non-fraudulent transactions.

Matthews Correlation Coefficient (MCC)

The MCC is a balanced measure that accounts for all four quadrants of the confusion matrix, providing a correlation coefficient between the observed and predicted classifications:

$$ \text{MCC} = \frac{TP \cdot TN - FP \cdot FN}{\sqrt{(TP + FP)(TP + FN)(TN + FP)(TN + FN)}} $$

Application in Finance:

MCC is useful in scenarios like credit risk assessment, where a balanced evaluation of all prediction outcomes is necessary.

Implementing Performance Metrics with Python

Let's implement these performance metrics using Python and Scikit-Learn, focusing on a dataset predicting loan defaults.

```python
from sklearn.metrics import confusion_matrix, accuracy_score, precision_score, recall_score, f1_score, roc_auc_score, matthews_corrcoef

import numpy as np

Sample true and predicted labels

y_true = [1, 0, 1, 1, 0, 1, 0, 0, 1, 0]

y_pred = [1, 0, 1, 0, 0, 1, 0, 0, 1, 1]

Confusion Matrix

cm = confusion_matrix(y_true, y_pred)

print(f"Confusion Matrix:\n{cm}")

 Accuracy

accuracy = accuracy_score(y_true, y_pred)

print(f"Accuracy: {accuracy}")

Precision

precision = precision_score(y_true, y_pred)

print(f"Precision: {precision}")
```

```
Recall
recall = recall_score(y_true, y_pred)
print(f"Recall: {recall}")

F1 Score
f1 = f1_score(y_true, y_pred)
print(f"F1 Score: {f1}")

Area Under ROC Curve (AUC-ROC)
auc = roc_auc_score(y_true, y_pred)
print(f"AUC-ROC: {auc}")

Specificity
tn, fp, fn, tp = cm.ravel()
specificity = tn / (tn + fp)
print(f"Specificity: {specificity}")

Matthews Correlation Coefficient (MCC)
mcc = matthews_corrcoef(y_true, y_pred)
print(f"Matthews Correlation Coefficient (MCC): {mcc}")
```

Choosing the Right Metric

Selecting the appropriate performance metric depends on the specific financial task at hand:

- Accuracy is ideal for balanced datasets where all classes are equally important.

- Precision is critical when the cost of false positives is high, such as in fraud detection.

- Recall is pivotal in applications where missing positive instances has significant consequences, like in identifying credit defaults.

- F1 Score is beneficial when a balance between precision and recall is necessary.

- AUC-ROC provides a comprehensive evaluation across various threshold levels.

- Specificity is crucial in scenarios where minimizing false positives is essential.

- MCC offers a balanced measure accounting for all classification outcomes.

Evaluating the performance of classification models is a nuanced process, essential for ensuring their reliability and effectiveness in financial applications. Metrics such as accuracy, precision, recall, F1 score, AUC-ROC, confusion matrix, specificity, and MCC provide a robust toolkit for financial analysts. By meticulously analyzing these metrics, professionals can craft models that not only perform well but also offer dependable and actionable insights. This thorough evaluation process is vital for making informed financial decisions and maintaining a competitive advantage.

Case Study: Predicting Stock Prices Using Regression Models

In this case study, we dive into the practical application of regression models in predicting stock prices—a quintessential task in the financial domain. Stock price prediction is a complex and dynamic problem, influenced by myriad factors ranging from macroeconomic indicators to company-specific news. By leveraging regression models, we aim to capture these relationships and forecast future stock prices with enhanced accuracy.

Stock price prediction holds significant importance for traders, investors, and financial analysts. Accurate forecasts can lead to profitable trading strategies, better risk management, and informed investment decisions. However, the inherent volatility and stochastic nature of financial markets make this task particularly challenging. This case study demonstrates how supervised learning techniques, specifically regression models, can be effectively utilized to predict stock prices.

Data Collection and Preprocessing

The first step in any predictive modeling task involves gathering and preparing the data. For this case study, we will use historical stock price data from Yahoo Finance. This dataset includes daily open, high, low, close prices, and trading volume.

Python Implementation for Data Collection:

```python
import pandas as pd
import yfinance as yf

Define the stock ticker and the time period
ticker = 'AAPL'
start_date = '2010-01-01'
end_date = '2020-01-01'
```

```
Fetch the historical data
stock_data = yf.download(ticker, start=start_date, end=end_date)

Display the first few rows of the dataset
print(stock_data.head())
```

After obtaining the dataset, the next step is to preprocess it. This involves handling missing values, feature engineering, and data normalization.

Data Preprocessing:

```python
Handle missing values by forward filling
stock_data.fillna(method='ffill', inplace=True)

Feature engineering: Create additional features such as moving averages
stock_data['MA_10'] = stock_data['Close'].rolling(window=10).mean()
stock_data['MA_50'] = stock_data['Close'].rolling(window=50).mean()

Drop rows with NaN values created by moving averages
stock_data.dropna(inplace=True)

Display the first few rows after preprocessing
```

```
print(stock_data.head())
```

Exploratory Data Analysis (EDA)

EDA is crucial to understand the underlying patterns and relationships in the data. We will plot the stock prices and moving averages to visualize trends and patterns.

Plotting Stock Prices and Moving Averages:

```python
import matplotlib.pyplot as plt

plt.figure(figsize=(14, 7))
plt.plot(stock_data['Close'], label='Close Price')
plt.plot(stock_data['MA_10'], label='10-Day MA')
plt.plot(stock_data['MA_50'], label='50-Day MA')
plt.title('Stock Prices and Moving Averages')
plt.xlabel('Date')
plt.ylabel('Price')
plt.legend()
plt.show()
```

Building the Regression Model

With the data prepared, we can now build a regression model to predict future stock prices. We will use Linear Regression as our primary model due to its simplicity and interpretability.

Creating the Training and Test Sets:

```python
from sklearn.model_selection import train_test_split

Define the features and target variable
X = stock_data[['MA_10', 'MA_50']]
y = stock_data['Close']

Split the data into training and test sets
X_train, X_test, y_train, y_test = train_test_split(X, y, test_size=0.2, random_state=42)
```

Training the Linear Regression Model:

```python
from sklearn.linear_model import LinearRegression

Initialize and train the model
lr_model = LinearRegression()
lr_model.fit(X_train, y_train)

 Predict on the test set
y_pred = lr_model.predict(X_test)
```

Evaluating Model Performance

To evaluate the performance of our regression model, we will use performance metrics such as Mean Absolute Error (MAE), Mean Squared Error (MSE), and R-squared ($R^2$).

Calculating Performance Metrics:

```python
from sklearn.metrics import mean_absolute_error, mean_squared_error, r2_score

mae = mean_absolute_error(y_test, y_pred)
mse = mean_squared_error(y_test, y_pred)
r2 = r2_score(y_test, y_pred)

print(f'Mean Absolute Error (MAE): {mae}')
print(f'Mean Squared Error (MSE): {mse}')
print(f'R-squared (R²): {r2}')
```

Improving the Model

While Linear Regression offers a good starting point, more sophisticated models like Polynomial Regression, Decision Trees, and Random Forests can improve predictive accuracy. Here's a brief overview of implementing Polynomial Regression.

Implementing Polynomial Regression:

```python
```

```
from sklearn.preprocessing import PolynomialFeatures
from sklearn.pipeline import make_pipeline

Create a pipeline that includes polynomial features and linear regression
poly_model = make_pipeline(PolynomialFeatures(degree=3), LinearRegression())

Train the model
poly_model.fit(X_train, y_train)

Predict on the test set
y_poly_pred = poly_model.predict(X_test)

Evaluate the polynomial model
mae_poly = mean_absolute_error(y_test, y_poly_pred)
mse_poly = mean_squared_error(y_test, y_poly_pred)
r2_poly = r2_score(y_test, y_poly_pred)

print(f'Polynomial Regression - Mean Absolute Error (MAE): {mae_poly}')
print(f'Polynomial Regression - Mean Squared Error (MSE): {mse_poly}')
print(f'Polynomial Regression - R-squared (R²): {r2_poly}')
```

Practical Considerations

In real-world applications, predicting stock prices involves numerous additional considerations:

- Feature Selection: Incorporating technical indicators, macroeconomic variables, and sentiment analysis from financial news can enhance model performance.

- Model Validation: Implementing cross-validation techniques ensures the model's robustness and generalizability.

- Risk Management: Integrating predicted stock prices into trading strategies must account for risk management techniques to mitigate potential losses.

This case study highlights the practical steps involved in predicting stock prices using regression models. By methodically collecting and preprocessing data, performing exploratory analysis, building and evaluating models, and considering practical factors, financial professionals can develop robust predictive models that aid in making informed investment decisions. While the models presented here offer a foundational approach, continuous iteration, and incorporation of advanced techniques are essential for achieving superior performance in the ever-evolving financial markets.

# CHAPTER 4: UNSUPERVISED LEARNING TECHNIQUES

K-Means Clustering stands as one of the simplest yet robust unsupervised learning algorithms. It partitions the dataset into K distinct, non-overlapping subsets or clusters. The aim is to minimize the variance within each cluster, often referred to as the "within-cluster sum of squares."

Python Implementation of K-Means Clustering:

```python
import pandas as pd
from sklearn.cluster import KMeans
import matplotlib.pyplot as plt

Sample financial dataset (e.g., stock returns and volatilities)
data = {'Return': [0.1, 0.15, 0.2, -0.05, -0.1, 0.02, 0.07, 0.05,
```

```
-0.03, 0.18],
    'Volatility': [0.05, 0.1, 0.2, 0.15, 0.1, 0.05, 0.08, 0.07, 0.06, 0.12]}
df = pd.DataFrame(data)

Initialize K-Means with 3 clusters
kmeans = KMeans(n_clusters=3, random_state=42)
df['Cluster'] = kmeans.fit_predict(df)

Visualizing the clusters
plt.scatter(df['Return'], df['Volatility'], c=df['Cluster'], cmap='viridis')
plt.xlabel('Return')
plt.ylabel('Volatility')
plt.title('K-Means Clustering of Financial Data')
plt.show()
```

In this example, stock returns and volatilities are clustered into three groups, revealing distinct patterns that could inform asset allocation and risk assessment strategies.

Challenges and Considerations:

- Choosing K: Determining the optimal number of clusters (K) is crucial. Techniques like the Elbow Method and Silhouette Analysis can help.
- Scalability: K-Means is efficient for large datasets but may struggle with non-spherical clusters or varying cluster sizes.

Hierarchical Clustering

Hierarchical Clustering builds a tree-like structure of clusters, often visualized through a dendrogram. It comes in two flavors: Agglomerative (bottom-up approach) and Divisive (top-down approach). Agglomerative clustering starts with individual data points and merges them into clusters, while divisive clustering starts with one cluster and splits it into smaller ones.

Python Implementation of Hierarchical Clustering:

```python
from scipy.cluster.hierarchy import dendrogram, linkage
import seaborn as sns

Using the same financial dataset
linked = linkage(df[['Return', 'Volatility']], method='ward')

Plotting the dendrogram
plt.figure(figsize=(10, 7))
dendrogram(linked,
           orientation='top',
           labels=df.index,
           distance_sort='descending',
           show_leaf_counts=True)
plt.title('Dendrogram for Hierarchical Clustering')
plt.xlabel('Sample Index')
plt.ylabel('Distance')
plt.show()
```

The dendrogram provides a visual summary of the hierarchical clustering process, illustrating how clusters are formed based on the distance metric used (e.g., Ward's method).

Advantages and Limitations:

- Interpretability: The dendrogram offers intuitive insights into the relationships between data points.

- Computational Complexity: Hierarchical clustering can be computationally intensive for large datasets, making it less scalable than K-Means.

DBSCAN (Density-Based Spatial Clustering of Applications with Noise)

DBSCAN is a density-based clustering algorithm capable of identifying clusters of varying shapes and sizes. It defines clusters based on the density of data points and can effectively handle noise and outliers. DBSCAN requires two parameters: epsilon (ε) defining the neighborhood radius and the minimum number of points (minPts) to form a dense region.

Python Implementation of DBSCAN:

```python
from sklearn.cluster import DBSCAN

Initialize DBSCAN with epsilon and minPts
dbscan = DBSCAN(eps=0.05, min_samples=2)
df['Cluster'] = dbscan.fit_predict(df[['Return', 'Volatility']])
```

```
Visualizing the clusters
plt.scatter(df['Return'], df['Volatility'], c=df['Cluster'], cmap='viridis')
plt.xlabel('Return')
plt.ylabel('Volatility')
plt.title('DBSCAN Clustering of Financial Data')
plt.show()
```

DBSCAN's ability to classify noise points (indicated by -1 in the cluster labels) makes it particularly useful in financial datasets where outliers are prevalent.

Strengths and Challenges:

- Flexibility: DBSCAN can discover clusters of arbitrary shape and is robust to outliers.
- Parameter Sensitivity: The choice of ε and minPts can significantly impact the results, necessitating careful tuning.

Practical Applications in Finance

Clustering methods hold vast potential for various financial applications:

- Market Segmentation: Identifying groups of stocks or assets with similar performance attributes.
- Anomaly Detection: Detecting unusual trading patterns or fraudulent activities.
- Portfolio Diversification: Grouping assets to achieve optimal risk-return profiles.

For example, clustering can assist in segmenting the market into different regimes (bullish, bearish, and neutral), enabling traders to tailor strategies to prevailing market conditions. Additionally, clustering credit card transactions can highlight fraudulent activities by distinguishing anomalous patterns from regular transactions.

K-Means, Hierarchical Clustering, and DBSCAN each offer distinct methodologies for uncovering patterns in financial data, catering to different needs and dataset characteristics. Mastery of these clustering techniques equips financial analysts with the tools to translate complex datasets into actionable insights, driving informed decision-making in the dynamic world of finance.

## Dimensionality Reduction: PCA and LDA

Dimensionality reduction is a crucial step in financial data analysis, enabling analysts to simplify complex datasets while preserving significant information. This process not only enhances computational efficiency but also helps in visualizing high-dimensional data. Two primary techniques for dimensionality reduction are Principal Component Analysis (PCA) and Linear Discriminant Analysis (LDA). These methods, while different in their approaches, both aim to reduce the number of variables under consideration and highlight the underlying structures of the data.

### Principal Component Analysis (PCA)

Principal Component Analysis (PCA) is an unsupervised learning algorithm used to reduce the dimensionality of large datasets by transforming the data into a set of orthogonal components. The primary objective of PCA is to capture as much variance as possible with fewer components.

Mathematical Intuition:
PCA transforms the original features into a new set of features called principal components. These components are ordered in such a way that the first few retain most of the variation present in all of the original variables.

Python Implementation of PCA:

To illustrate PCA, consider a financial dataset containing various economic indicators:

```python
import pandas as pd
from sklearn.decomposition import PCA
import matplotlib.pyplot as plt

Sample financial dataset (e.g., different financial indicators)
data = {'Indicator1': [2.5, 0.5, 2.2, 1.9, 3.1, 2.3, 2.0, 1.0, 1.5, 1.1],
        'Indicator2': [2.4, 0.7, 2.9, 2.2, 3.0, 2.7, 1.6, 1.1, 1.6, 0.9]}
df = pd.DataFrame(data)

Standardize the data
from sklearn.preprocessing import StandardScaler
scaler = StandardScaler()
scaled_data = scaler.fit_transform(df)

Apply PCA
```

```
pca = PCA(n_components=2)
principal_components = pca.fit_transform(scaled_data)
df_pca = pd.DataFrame(data=principal_components, columns=['PC1', 'PC2'])

Visualizing the principal components
plt.scatter(df_pca['PC1'], df_pca['PC2'])
plt.xlabel('Principal Component 1')
plt.ylabel('Principal Component 2')
plt.title('PCA of Financial Indicators')
plt.show()
```

In this example, PCA reduces the original dataset into two principal components, revealing the primary directions in which the data varies. This reduction allows for improved visualization and understanding of the dataset's structure.

Applications in Finance:

- Portfolio Optimization: PCA can identify the major sources of risk and return, helping in the construction of diversified portfolios.
- Market Analysis: PCA can be used to extract the main factors driving market movements, aiding in the development of trading strategies.
- Risk Management: By reducing the number of variables, PCA helps in creating more manageable and interpretable risk models.

Strengths and Limitations:

- Strengths: PCA is effective in reducing dimensionality while retaining significant variance, enhancing interpretability and computational efficiency.
- Limitations: PCA assumes linear relationships between variables and may not capture complex, nonlinear structures in the data.

Linear Discriminant Analysis (LDA)

Linear Discriminant Analysis (LDA) is a supervised learning algorithm used for both classification and dimensionality reduction. Unlike PCA, which focuses on maximizing variance, LDA aims to maximize the separability between different classes.

Mathematical Intuition:

LDA seeks to find the linear combination of features that best separates two or more classes of objects. It projects the data in such a way that the distance between the means of different classes is maximized, while the spread within each class is minimized.

Python Implementation of LDA:

Consider a financial dataset with labeled classes, such as credit ratings (good, bad):

```python
from sklearn.discriminant_analysis import LinearDiscriminantAnalysis as LDA

Sample financial dataset with labels
data = {'Indicator1': [2.5, 0.5, 2.2, 1.9, 3.1, 2.3, 2.0, 1.0, 1.5, 1.1],
```

```
'Indicator2': [2.4, 0.7, 2.9, 2.2, 3.0, 2.7, 1.6, 1.1, 1.6, 0.9],
'CreditRating': ['good', 'bad', 'good', 'good', 'good', 'bad', 'bad', 'bad', 'good', 'bad']}
df = pd.DataFrame(data)

Extract features and labels
X = df[['Indicator1', 'Indicator2']]
y = df['CreditRating']

Apply LDA
lda = LDA(n_components=1)
X_r2 = lda.fit_transform(X, y)

Visualizing the linear discriminant
plt.scatter(X_r2, [0]*len(X_r2), c=(y == 'good'), cmap='viridis')
plt.xlabel('Linear Discriminant')
plt.title('LDA of Financial Indicators')
plt.show()
```

In this example, LDA transforms the financial indicators into a single linear discriminant that best separates the credit ratings. This reduction is particularly useful for visualizing class separability and improving classification performance.

Applications in Finance:

- Credit Scoring: LDA can enhance the accuracy of credit scoring models by emphasizing the differences between good and bad credit risks.
- Fraud Detection: By maximizing class separability, LDA helps

in identifying fraudulent transactions.

- Market Segmentation: LDA can be used to classify customers into different segments based on their financial behavior.

Strengths and Limitations:

- Strengths: LDA is effective in improving class separability and enhancing the performance of classification models.

- Limitations: LDA assumes normally distributed, homoscedastic classes, which may not always be the case in financial data.

Practical Considerations and Integration

Combining PCA and LDA in financial analysis can yield powerful insights. For instance, PCA can first be used to reduce dimensionality and remove noise, followed by LDA to maximize class separability for classification tasks. This combination leverages the strengths of both techniques, providing a comprehensive approach to dimensionality reduction.

Example Workflow: PCA followed by LDA:

```python
Apply PCA first
pca = PCA(n_components=2)
pca_result = pca.fit_transform(scaled_data)

Apply LDA on PCA-transformed data
lda = LDA(n_components=1)
lda_result = lda.fit_transform(pca_result, y)
```

```
Visualizing the combined PCA and LDA results
plt.scatter(lda_result, [0]*len(lda_result), c=(y == 'good'), cmap='viridis')
plt.xlabel('Linear Discriminant after PCA')
plt.title('Combined PCA and LDA of Financial Indicators')
plt.show()
```

PCA and LDA, while addressing different aspects of dimensionality reduction, both play pivotal roles in the financial sector. Their combined use can lead to robust, accurate, and insightful models, enabling analysts to stay ahead in the fast-paced world of finance.

Anomaly Detection

Anomaly detection is a critical aspect of financial analytics, essential for identifying irregular patterns that may indicate fraud, market manipulation, or systemic risks. For instance, an unexpected spike in trading volume or an unusual transaction pattern can signal fraudulent activities. Moreover, anomalies in financial data can also pinpoint new market trends, offering early investment opportunities.

Methods of Anomaly Detection

Various methods can be employed to detect anomalies, each with its own strengths and applicable scenarios. We'll explore both traditional statistical techniques and advanced machine learning models, focusing on how they can be implemented using Scikit-Learn.

1. Statistical Methods

Statistical methods are some of the earliest approaches used for anomaly detection. They include techniques like:

- Z-Score Method: This approach identifies anomalies by calculating the Z-score, which measures how many standard deviations an element is from the mean. A high absolute Z-score indicates a potential anomaly.
- IQR (Interquartile Range): Utilizes the range between the first and third quartiles to detect outliers. Values outside 1.5 times the IQR from the quartiles are considered anomalies.

2. Machine Learning Methods

Machine learning offers more sophisticated techniques for anomaly detection, which can handle high-dimensional data and complex patterns more effectively than traditional methods.

- Isolation Forest: This ensemble method isolates observations by randomly selecting a feature and then randomly selecting a split value. Anomalies require fewer splits to isolate, making them distinct from normal points.
- One-Class SVM (Support Vector Machine): One-Class SVM is designed for anomaly detection by learning a decision function for outlier detection. It classifies new data points as similar or different from the training set.
- DBSCAN (Density-Based Spatial Clustering of Applications with Noise): While primarily a clustering algorithm, DBSCAN can identify outliers as points that do not fit well into any cluster.

Practical Implementation with Scikit-Learn

Let's walk through practical examples using Scikit-Learn to implement some of these anomaly detection methods.

1. Isolation Forest Example

```python
import numpy as np
import pandas as pd
from sklearn.ensemble import IsolationForest

Generating synthetic data
data = np.random.randn(100, 2)
data[95:] = np.random.uniform(low=-4, high=4, size=(5, 2))
Adding anomalies

Converting to DataFrame
df = pd.DataFrame(data, columns=['Feature1', 'Feature2'])

Initializing and fitting the model
clf = IsolationForest(contamination=0.05)
clf.fit(df)

Predicting anomalies
df['anomaly'] = clf.predict(df)

Filtering out anomalies
anomalies = df[df['anomaly'] == -1]
```

```
print(anomalies)
```

In this example, an Isolation Forest is used to detect anomalies in a synthetic dataset. The `contamination` parameter defines the proportion of outliers in the data, and the `predict` method labels normal points as 1 and anomalies as -1.

2. One-Class SVM Example

```python
from sklearn.svm import OneClassSVM

Initializing the model
clf = OneClassSVM(nu=0.05, kernel="rbf", gamma=0.1)
clf.fit(df[['Feature1', 'Feature2']])

Predicting anomalies
df['anomaly'] = clf.predict(df[['Feature1', 'Feature2']])

Filtering out anomalies
anomalies = df[df['anomaly'] == -1]
print(anomalies)
```

The One-Class SVM model is initialized with `nu`, representing the proportion of anomalies, and `gamma`, the kernel coefficient. Similar to Isolation Forest, it predicts anomalies which are then filtered out.

3. DBSCAN Example

```python
from sklearn.cluster import DBSCAN

Initializing the model
db = DBSCAN(eps=0.5, min_samples=5)
db.fit(df[['Feature1', 'Feature2']])

Adding cluster labels to the DataFrame
df['label'] = db.labels_

Identifying anomalies (label = -1)
anomalies = df[df['label'] == -1]
print(anomalies)
```

DBSCAN identifies anomalies as points with the label -1, which do not belong to any cluster. The `eps` parameter defines the maximum distance between two samples for one to be considered as in the neighborhood of the other, while `min_samples` is the number of samples in a neighborhood for a point to be considered a core point.

Applications in the Financial Sector

Anomaly detection has a wide array of applications in finance, including but not limited to:

- Fraud Detection: Identifying irregular transactions to

prevent financial fraud.

- Risk Management: Monitoring and mitigating risks by detecting unusual patterns in market data.

- Market Surveillance: Detecting market manipulation by identifying abnormal trading behaviors.

- Portfolio Management: Spotting outliers in asset performance to adjust investment strategies.

In the bustling financial districts of global cities like New York or London, the ability to swiftly detect anomalies can mean the difference between a significant loss and a strategic advantage. For instance, during the 2008 financial crisis, better anomaly detection mechanisms could have flagged the impending systemic risks earlier, potentially mitigating some of the fallout.

Anomaly detection is indispensable in the financial sector, offering a shield against fraud and a lens into emerging trends. By leveraging Scikit-Learn's robust library, financial analysts can implement effective anomaly detection models, ensuring data integrity and uncovering valuable insights. The next step in our journey will take us deeper into unsupervised learning, where we will explore how clustering and other advanced techniques can further enhance our financial models.

Principal Component Analysis (PCA) in Portfolio Management

PCA is instrumental in reducing the dimensionality of financial data while preserving its essential characteristics. By transforming correlated variables into a set of uncorrelated principal components, PCA helps in extracting the most significant features of the data. This is particularly beneficial in portfolio management, where it can uncover the underlying drivers of asset returns and assist in constructing more efficient portfolios.

## Understanding Principal Components

To grasp the essence of PCA, let's break down its fundamental concepts:

1. Dimensionality Reduction: Financial data often involves numerous variables, such as different asset returns. High-dimensional data can be challenging to analyze and visualize. PCA reduces this complexity by transforming the data into a lower-dimensional form without significant loss of information.
2. Principal Components: These are the new variables created by PCA. Each principal component is a linear combination of the original variables, ordered by the amount of variance they explain. The first principal component captures the most variance, followed by the second, and so on.
3. Eigenvalues and Eigenvectors: Eigenvalues represent the variance explained by each principal component, while eigenvectors determine the direction of these components in the original variable space.

## Mathematical Foundation of PCA

PCA involves several mathematical steps:

1. Standardization: The first step is standardizing the data to have a mean of zero and a standard deviation of one. This ensures that PCA is not biased by variables with larger scales.
2. Covariance Matrix Computation: The covariance matrix of the standardized data is computed to understand how the

variables are correlated.

3. Eigen Decomposition: The covariance matrix is decomposed into eigenvalues and eigenvectors, which form the basis for the principal components.

4. Principal Component Formation: The principal components are formed by projecting the original data onto the eigenvectors.

Practical Implementation with Scikit-Learn

Let's implement PCA in a portfolio management context using Scikit-Learn. We'll use a dataset comprising daily returns of several stocks.

1. Importing Libraries and Data

```python
import numpy as np
import pandas as pd
from sklearn.decomposition import PCA
import matplotlib.pyplot as plt

Generating synthetic stock return data
np.random.seed(42)
data = np.random.randn(1000, 5)  1000 days of returns for 5 stocks
df = pd.DataFrame(data, columns=['Stock_A', 'Stock_B', 'Stock_C', 'Stock_D', 'Stock_E'])
```

2. Standardizing the Data

```python
from sklearn.preprocessing import StandardScaler

Standardizing the returns
scaler = StandardScaler()
std_data = scaler.fit_transform(df)
```

3. Applying PCA

```python
Initializing PCA and fitting the standardized data
pca = PCA(n_components=5)
principal_components = pca.fit_transform(std_data)

Creating a DataFrame for the principal components
pc_df = pd.DataFrame(data=principal_components, columns=[f'PC{i+1}' for i in range(5)])
```

4. Explained Variance

Understanding the proportion of variance explained by each principal component is crucial for deciding how many components to retain.

```python
```

```
Explained variance
explained_variance = pca.explained_variance_ratio_
print("Explained variance by each component:", explained_variance)

Plotting the explained variance
plt.figure(figsize=(10, 6))
plt.bar(range(1, 6), explained_variance, alpha=0.5, align='center', label='Individual explained variance')
plt.step(range(1, 6), np.cumsum(explained_variance), where='mid', label='Cumulative explained variance')
plt.xlabel('Principal components')
plt.ylabel('Explained variance ratio')
plt.legend(loc='best')
plt.tight_layout()
plt.show()
```

Applications of PCA in Portfolio Management

1. Risk Management

PCA helps in identifying the main sources of risk in a portfolio. By analyzing the principal components, portfolio managers can understand which assets contribute most to the portfolio's risk.

2. Asset Allocation

PCA can be used to cluster assets based on their principal

components, facilitating better diversification. For example, if two assets have similar principal components, they might be redundant in a portfolio.

3. Noise Reduction

Market data often includes noise that can obscure true signals. PCA reduces noise by focusing on the components that explain the most variance, thus enhancing the reliability of financial models.

4. Factor Analysis

PCA allows for the identification of latent factors that drive asset returns. These factors can be used to construct factor-based investment strategies, leading to more robust portfolio performance.

Real-World Example: Portfolio Decomposition

To illustrate PCA's practical application, let's decompose a portfolio of stocks into its principal components and analyze the results.

```python
Example: Decomposing a portfolio
portfolio_weights = np.array([0.2, 0.3, 0.2, 0.2, 0.1])
portfolio_returns = np.dot(std_data, portfolio_weights)

Applying PCA on portfolio returns
portfolio_pca = PCA(n_components=5)
```

```
portfolio_principal_components = portfolio_pca.fit_transform(portfolio_returns.reshape(-1, 1))

Explained variance of portfolio components

portfolio_explained_variance = portfolio_pca.explained_variance_ratio_

print("Portfolio explained variance by each component:", portfolio_explained_variance)
```

In this example, we construct a synthetic portfolio with specific weights assigned to each stock. Applying PCA to the portfolio returns helps in understanding how much of the portfolio's variance is explained by each principal component.

Principal Component Analysis is a powerful technique for simplifying and understanding complex financial data. Its applications in portfolio management are vast, ranging from risk management to asset allocation and noise reduction. By leveraging PCA, financial analysts can gain deeper insights into the underlying structure of their portfolios, enabling more informed investment decisions. As we progress, we'll explore other advanced techniques in unsupervised learning, further enhancing our ability to navigate the world of finance.

Clustering Financial Time Series Data

In the financial world, time series data is ubiquitous. Stock prices, interest rates, exchange rates, and economic indicators are all examples of time series that analysts monitor closely. Clustering these time series can reveal:

1. Market Segmentation: By grouping similar assets, analysts

can identify different market segments, which aids in targeted investment strategies.

2. Anomaly Detection: Clustering can help detect outliers or unusual patterns, which might indicate potential risks or opportunities.

3. Portfolio Diversification: Understanding the relationships between different assets can help in constructing diversified portfolios with reduced risk.

Clustering Techniques for Financial Time Series

Several clustering techniques can be applied to financial time series data. The choice of method depends on the specific characteristics of the data and the goals of the analysis. Here, we will focus on three popular methods: K-Means, Hierarchical Clustering, and DBSCAN.

1. K-Means Clustering

K-Means is a centroid-based clustering method that partitions data into K clusters, where each data point belongs to the cluster with the nearest centroid.

Steps Involved:

1. Initialize K centroids randomly.

2. Assign each time series to the nearest centroid.

3. Update the centroids based on the mean of the assigned time series.

4. Repeat steps 2 and 3 until convergence.

Implementation in Scikit-Learn:

```python
from sklearn.cluster import KMeans

Assuming `time_series_data` is a DataFrame where each row represents a time series
kmeans = KMeans(n_clusters=3, random_state=42)
clusters = kmeans.fit_predict(time_series_data)

Adding cluster labels to the DataFrame
time_series_data['Cluster'] = clusters
```

2. Hierarchical Clustering

Hierarchical Clustering builds a hierarchy of clusters either by continuously merging (agglomerative) or splitting (divisive) clusters.

Steps Involved (Agglomerative):

1. Start with each time series as its own cluster.
2. Merge the two nearest clusters.
3. Repeat step 2 until all time series are in a single cluster.

Implementation in Scikit-Learn:

```python
from sklearn.cluster import AgglomerativeClustering

agg_cluster = AgglomerativeClustering(n_clusters=3)
```

clusters = agg_cluster.fit_predict(time_series_data)

Adding cluster labels to the DataFrame

time_series_data['Cluster'] = clusters

```

3. Density-Based Spatial Clustering of Applications with Noise (DBSCAN)

DBSCAN is a density-based clustering method that can identify clusters of varying shapes and handle noise effectively.

Steps Involved:

1. Identify core points that have a minimum number of neighbors within a specified radius.

2. Merge core points and their neighbors to form clusters.

3. Mark remaining points as noise.

Implementation in Scikit-Learn:

```python
from sklearn.cluster import DBSCAN

dbscan = DBSCAN(eps=0.5, min_samples=5)
clusters = dbscan.fit_predict(time_series_data)

Adding cluster labels to the DataFrame
time_series_data['Cluster'] = clusters
```
```

## Feature Extraction for Time Series Clustering

Clustering time series data often requires extracting meaningful features that capture the essential characteristics of the time series. Common feature extraction techniques include:

1. Statistical Features: Mean, variance, skewness, and kurtosis of the time series.
2. Fourier Transform: Extracting frequency components.
3. Wavelet Transform: Capturing both time and frequency information.
4. Autocorrelation: Measuring the correlation of the time series with its lagged values.

Example of Feature Extraction:

```python
import numpy as np

Example function to extract basic statistical features
def extract_features(time_series):
    return {
        'mean': np.mean(time_series),
        'std': np.std(time_series),
        'skewness': skew(time_series),
        'kurtosis': kurtosis(time_series)
    }
```

```
Applying feature extraction to each time series in the DataFrame
features = time_series_data.apply(extract_features, axis=1)
feature_df = pd.DataFrame(features.tolist())
```

Practical Example: Clustering Stock Returns

To illustrate the application of clustering methods on financial time series data, let us consider the daily returns of multiple stocks. The goal is to group these stocks into clusters based on their return patterns.

1. Importing Libraries and Data

```python
import pandas as pd
import numpy as np
from sklearn.preprocessing import StandardScaler
from sklearn.cluster import KMeans, AgglomerativeClustering, DBSCAN
import matplotlib.pyplot as plt

Assuming `stock_returns` is a DataFrame with daily returns of multiple stocks
stock_returns = pd.read_csv('stock_returns.csv')
```

2. Standardizing the Data

```python
scaler = StandardScaler()
scaled_returns = scaler.fit_transform(stock_returns)
```

3. Applying K-Means Clustering

```python
kmeans = KMeans(n_clusters=3, random_state=42)
clusters = kmeans.fit_predict(scaled_returns)

Adding cluster labels to the DataFrame
stock_returns['Cluster'] = clusters

Plotting the clusters
plt.scatter(stock_returns.index, stock_returns['Stock_A'], c=clusters, cmap='viridis')
plt.xlabel('Index')
plt.ylabel('Stock A Returns')
plt.title('K-Means Clustering of Stock Returns')
plt.show()
```

4. Applying Hierarchical Clustering

```python
agg_cluster = AgglomerativeClustering(n_clusters=3)
clusters = agg_cluster.fit_predict(scaled_returns)
```

```
Adding cluster labels to the DataFrame
stock_returns['Cluster'] = clusters

Plotting the dendrogram
from scipy.cluster.hierarchy import dendrogram, linkage

linked = linkage(scaled_returns, 'ward')
plt.figure(figsize=(10, 7))
dendrogram(linked, labels=stock_returns.index.to_list(), distance_sort='ascending')
plt.title('Hierarchical Clustering Dendrogram')
plt.show()
```

5. Applying DBSCAN

```python
dbscan = DBSCAN(eps=0.5, min_samples=5)
clusters = dbscan.fit_predict(scaled_returns)

Adding cluster labels to the DataFrame
stock_returns['Cluster'] = clusters

Visualizing the clusters
plt.scatter(stock_returns.index, stock_returns['Stock_A'], c=clusters, cmap='plasma')
plt.xlabel('Index')
plt.ylabel('Stock A Returns')
```

```
plt.title('DBSCAN Clustering of Stock Returns')
plt.show()
```

Clustering financial time series data offers a robust approach to understanding complex financial markets. By grouping similar time series, financial analysts can uncover hidden patterns, detect anomalies, and make more informed investment decisions. Techniques such as K-Means, Hierarchical Clustering, and DBSCAN, when combined with effective feature extraction, provide powerful tools for analyzing financial datasets. Practical implementation in Scikit-Learn, as demonstrated, equips analysts with the necessary skills to apply these clustering methods in real-world financial scenarios.

## Feature Extraction with Scikit-Learn

Feature extraction serves several critical purposes in the context of financial data analysis:

1. Dimensionality Reduction: Financial datasets often contain a vast number of variables. Feature extraction helps reduce this complexity while retaining essential information.
2. Improved Model Performance: Quality features can significantly enhance the predictive power and accuracy of machine learning models.
3. Interpretability: Extracted features can provide clearer insights into the underlying patterns and trends within the data.
4. Noise Reduction: By focusing on the most relevant aspects of

the data, feature extraction helps in minimizing the impact of noise and irrelevant information.

Common Feature Extraction Techniques

Feature extraction methods vary depending on the nature of the data and the specific requirements of the analysis. Below, we will explore several commonly used techniques in financial data analysis:

1. Statistical Features
2. Time-Based Features
3. Frequency Domain Features
4. Principal Component Analysis (PCA)
5. Domain-Specific Features

1. Statistical Features

Statistical features capture the essential characteristics of financial time series data. These features include measures of central tendency, dispersion, and shape.

Implementation in Scikit-Learn:

```python
import numpy as np
from scipy.stats import skew, kurtosis

def extract_statistical_features(time_series):
    return {
```

```
        'mean': np.mean(time_series),
        'std': np.std(time_series),
        'skewness': skew(time_series),
        'kurtosis': kurtosis(time_series)
    }

Applying feature extraction to each time series in the DataFrame
stat_features = time_series_data.apply(extract_statistical_features, axis=1)
stat_feature_df = pd.DataFrame(stat_features.tolist())
```

2. Time-Based Features

Time-based features are derived from the temporal aspects of the data. They include lag values, rolling statistics, and seasonal components.

Implementation in Scikit-Learn:

```python
def extract_time_based_features(time_series):
    return {
        'lag_1': time_series.shift(1),
        'rolling_mean_5': time_series.rolling(window=5).mean(),
        'rolling_std_5': time_series.rolling(window=5).std()
    }
```

```
Applying feature extraction to each time series in the DataFrame

time_features =
time_series_data.apply(extract_time_based_features, axis=1)

time_feature_df = pd.DataFrame(time_features.tolist())
```

3. Frequency Domain Features

Frequency domain features are derived from transforming the time series data into the frequency domain using techniques like Fourier Transform. These features capture periodicities and cycles in the data.

Implementation in Scikit-Learn:

```python
from scipy.fft import fft

def extract_frequency_features(time_series):
    fft_values = fft(time_series)
    return {
        'fft_real': np.real(fft_values),
        'fft_imag': np.imag(fft_values)
    }

Applying feature extraction to each time series in the DataFrame

freq_features =
```

time_series_data.apply(extract_frequency_features, axis=1)
freq_feature_df = pd.DataFrame(freq_features.tolist())
```

4. Principal Component Analysis (PCA)

PCA is a dimensionality reduction technique that transforms the data into a set of orthogonal components, capturing the most variance in the data.

Implementation in Scikit-Learn:

```python
from sklearn.decomposition import PCA

pca = PCA(n_components=5)
principal_components = pca.fit_transform(time_series_data)

Converting principal components to DataFrame
pca_df = pd.DataFrame(principal_components, columns=[f'PC_{i+1}' for i in range(principal_components.shape[1])])
```

5. Domain-Specific Features

Domain-specific features are tailored to the unique characteristics of the financial data being analyzed. These could include indicators like Moving Average Convergence Divergence (MACD), Relative Strength Index (RSI), and Bollinger Bands.
```

Example: Extracting MACD

```python
def extract_macd(time_series, short_window=12, long_window=26, signal_window=9):
    short_ema = time_series.ewm(span=short_window, adjust=False).mean()
    long_ema = time_series.ewm(span=long_window, adjust=False).mean()
    macd = short_ema - long_ema
    signal = macd.ewm(span=signal_window, adjust=False).mean()
    return {
        'macd': macd,
        'signal': signal
    }

Applying feature extraction to each time series in the DataFrame
macd_features = time_series_data.apply(extract_macd, axis=1)
macd_feature_df = pd.DataFrame(macd_features.tolist())
```

Practical Example: Feature Extraction from Financial Time Series

To illustrate the application of feature extraction techniques, let us consider the daily closing prices of multiple stocks. The goal is to extract meaningful features that can be used for further analysis, such as clustering or predictive modeling.

1. Importing Libraries and Data

```python
import pandas as pd
import numpy as np
from scipy.stats import skew, kurtosis
from scipy.fft import fft
from sklearn.decomposition import PCA

Assuming `stock_prices` is a DataFrame with daily closing prices of multiple stocks
stock_prices = pd.read_csv('stock_prices.csv')
```

2. Extracting Statistical Features

```python
def extract_stat_features(time_series):
    return {
        'mean': np.mean(time_series),
        'std': np.std(time_series),
        'skewness': skew(time_series),
        'kurtosis': kurtosis(time_series)
    }

Applying feature extraction to each time series in the
```

```
DataFrame
stat_features = stock_prices.apply(extract_stat_features, axis=1)
stat_feature_df = pd.DataFrame(stat_features.tolist())
```

3. Extracting Time-Based Features

```python
def extract_time_features(time_series):
    return {
        'lag_1': time_series.shift(1).fillna(0),
        'rolling_mean_5': time_series.rolling(window=5).mean().fillna(0),
        'rolling_std_5': time_series.rolling(window=5).std().fillna(0)
    }

Applying feature extraction to each time series in the DataFrame
time_features = stock_prices.apply(extract_time_features, axis=1)
time_feature_df = pd.DataFrame(time_features.tolist())
```

4. Extracting Frequency Domain Features

```python
def extract_freq_features(time_series):
```

```
    fft_values = fft(time_series)
    return {
        'fft_real': np.real(fft_values)[1],
        'fft_imag': np.imag(fft_values)[1],
        'fft_magnitude': np.abs(fft_values)[1]
    }

Applying feature extraction to each time series in the DataFrame
freq_features = stock_prices.apply(extract_freq_features, axis=1)
freq_feature_df = pd.DataFrame(freq_features.tolist())
```

5. Extracting Principal Components

```python
pca = PCA(n_components=5)
principal_components = pca.fit_transform(stock_prices)

Converting principal components to DataFrame
pca_df = pd.DataFrame(principal_components, columns=[f'PC_{i+1}' for i in range(principal_components.shape[1])])
```

6. Extracting Domain-Specific Features (MACD)

```python
```

```
def extract_macd_features(time_series, short_window=12, long_window=26, signal_window=9):
    short_ema = time_series.ewm(span=short_window, adjust=False).mean()
    long_ema = time_series.ewm(span=long_window, adjust=False).mean()
    macd = short_ema - long_ema
    signal = macd.ewm(span=signal_window, adjust=False).mean()
    return {
        'macd': macd.iloc[-1],
        'signal': signal.iloc[-1]
    }

Applying feature extraction to each time series in the DataFrame
macd_features = stock_prices.apply(extract_macd_features, axis=1)
macd_feature_df = pd.DataFrame(macd_features.tolist())
```

Integrating Extracted Features

After extracting the features, they can be combined into a single DataFrame for further analysis:

```python
combined_features_df = pd.concat([stat_feature_df, time_feature_df, freq_feature_df, pca_df, macd_feature_df], axis=1)
```

```
```

Feature extraction is a vital step in the machine learning pipeline, especially when dealing with financial time series data. By transforming raw data into meaningful features, we enhance the interpretability, performance, and robustness of our models. The techniques and implementations explored here using Scikit-Learn provide a solid foundation for extracting insightful features from financial datasets. As we move forward, these extracted features will serve as the building blocks for more sophisticated analyses and predictive modeling.

Why Evaluating Clustering Quality is Essential in Finance

1. Model Validation: Ensuring that the clustering model accurately segments financial data into meaningful groups.

2. Investment Decisions: Reliable clusters can inform decisions on portfolio diversification and risk management.

3. Fraud Detection: High-quality clusters help differentiate between normal and anomalous transactions.

4. Market Segmentation: Identifying distinct market segments aids in targeted strategies and better customer insights.

Common Metrics for Evaluating Clustering Quality

1. Inertia (Within-cluster Sum of Squares)

2. Silhouette Score

3. Davies-Bouldin Index

4. Adjusted Rand Index (ARI)

5. Mutual Information-based Metrics

1. Inertia (Within-cluster Sum of Squares)

Inertia measures how tightly the data points within a cluster are grouped around the centroid. Lower inertia indicates more compact clusters.

Implementation in Scikit-Learn:

```python
from sklearn.cluster import KMeans

Applying KMeans clustering
kmeans = KMeans(n_clusters=5, random_state=42)
kmeans.fit(financial_data)

Evaluating inertia
inertia = kmeans.inertia_
print(f'Inertia: {inertia}')
```

2. Silhouette Score

The silhouette score assesses how similar a data point is to its own cluster compared to other clusters. The score ranges from -1 to 1, where higher values indicate better-defined clusters.

Implementation in Scikit-Learn:

```python
```

from sklearn.metrics import silhouette_score

Calculating silhouette score

sil_score = silhouette_score(financial_data, kmeans.labels_)

print(f'Silhouette Score: {sil_score}')

```
```

3. Davies-Bouldin Index

The Davies-Bouldin Index evaluates cluster quality by examining the ratio of within-cluster scatter to between-cluster separation. Lower values signify better clustering.

Implementation in Scikit-Learn:

```python
from sklearn.metrics import davies_bouldin_score

Calculating Davies-Bouldin Index
db_index = davies_bouldin_score(financial_data, kmeans.labels_)
print(f'Davies-Bouldin Index: {db_index}')
```

4. Adjusted Rand Index (ARI)

The Adjusted Rand Index compares the similarity between the clustering results and a ground truth classification. ARI values range from -1 to 1, with higher values indicating better clustering.

Implementation in Scikit-Learn:

```python
from sklearn.metrics import adjusted_rand_score

Assuming `true_labels` is the ground truth classification
ari = adjusted_rand_score(true_labels, kmeans.labels_)
print(f'Adjusted Rand Index: {ari}')
```

5. Mutual Information-based Metrics

Mutual Information-based metrics, such as the Adjusted Mutual Information (AMI) score, measure the agreement between the clustering and ground truth labels, adjusted for chance.

Implementation in Scikit-Learn:

```python
from sklearn.metrics import adjusted_mutual_info_score

Calculating Adjusted Mutual Information score
ami = adjusted_mutual_info_score(true_labels, kmeans.labels_)
print(f'Adjusted Mutual Information Score: {ami}')
```

Practical Example: Evaluating Clustering Quality in Financial

Data

To illustrate these concepts, consider a dataset containing transaction records from various financial accounts. Our objective is to cluster these transactions and evaluate the quality of the resulting clusters.

1. Importing Libraries and Data

```python
import pandas as pd
from sklearn.preprocessing import StandardScaler
from sklearn.cluster import KMeans
from sklearn.metrics import silhouette_score, davies_bouldin_score, adjusted_rand_score, adjusted_mutual_info_score

Assuming `transactions` is a DataFrame with transaction data
transactions = pd.read_csv('transactions.csv')

Standardizing the data
scaler = StandardScaler()
scaled_transactions = scaler.fit_transform(transactions)
```

2. Applying KMeans Clustering

```python
Applying KMeans clustering
```

kmeans = KMeans(n_clusters=5, random_state=42)

kmeans.fit(scaled_transactions)

Assigning cluster labels

transactions['cluster'] = kmeans.labels_

```

3. Evaluating Inertia

```python
Evaluating inertia
inertia = kmeans.inertia_
print(f'Inertia: {inertia}')
```

4. Calculating Silhouette Score

```python
Calculating silhouette score
sil_score = silhouette_score(scaled_transactions, kmeans.labels_)
print(f'Silhouette Score: {sil_score}')
```

5. Calculating Davies-Bouldin Index

```python
Calculating Davies-Bouldin Index
db_index = davies_bouldin_score(scaled_transactions,

kmeans.labels_)
print(f'Davies-Bouldin Index: {db_index}')
```

6. Computing Adjusted Rand Index

```python
Assuming `true_labels` is the ground truth classification
ari = adjusted_rand_score(true_labels, kmeans.labels_)
print(f'Adjusted Rand Index: {ari}')
```

7. Computing Adjusted Mutual Information Score

```python
Calculating Adjusted Mutual Information score
ami = adjusted_mutual_info_score(true_labels, kmeans.labels_)
print(f'Adjusted Mutual Information Score: {ami}')
```

Interpreting the Metrics

1. Inertia: Lower inertia suggests more compact clusters.
2. Silhouette Score: Values close to 1 indicate well-separated clusters.
3. Davies-Bouldin Index: Lower values denote better clustering quality.
4. ARI and AMI: Higher scores reflect greater alignment with
```

the ground truth.

Evaluating clustering quality is an indispensable step in the unsupervised learning pipeline, especially when dealing with financial data. The metrics and techniques discussed provide a robust framework for assessing the effectiveness of clustering algorithms. By implementing these evaluations using Scikit-Learn, we ensure that our models are not only theoretically sound but also practically effective in real-world financial applications. This thorough approach to evaluation helps in making informed decisions, whether it be for investment strategies, fraud detection, or market segmentation.

## Applications in Market Segmentation

Market segmentation involves dividing a broader market into smaller, more manageable segments based on shared characteristics. These segments can be defined by demographic factors, behavioural patterns, geographic locations, or psychographic profiles. The goal is to tailor marketing efforts and financial products to meet the specific needs and preferences of each segment, thereby maximizing customer satisfaction and business profitability.

### Why Clustering in Market Segmentation is Crucial

1. Personalized Marketing: By identifying distinct customer groups, financial institutions can create customized marketing campaigns that resonate with specific segments.

2. Product Innovation: Segmentation helps in understanding the unique needs of different customer groups, leading to the development of tailored financial products and services.

3. Resource Optimization: Efficiently allocate marketing budgets and resources to the most profitable segments.

4. Customer Retention: Enhance customer loyalty by providing targeted offers and personalized experiences.

Key Clustering Techniques in Market Segmentation

1. K-Means Clustering
2. Hierarchical Clustering
3. DBSCAN (Density-Based Spatial Clustering of Applications with Noise)

1. K-Means Clustering

K-Means clustering is one of the most widely used algorithms for market segmentation. It partitions the data into a predetermined number of clusters, minimizing the variance within each cluster.

Implementation in Scikit-Learn:

```python
from sklearn.cluster import KMeans
from sklearn.preprocessing import StandardScaler

Assuming `customer_data` is a DataFrame containing customer features
scaler = StandardScaler()
scaled_data = scaler.fit_transform(customer_data)

Applying KMeans clustering
kmeans = KMeans(n_clusters=4, random_state=42)
```

```
kmeans.fit(scaled_data)

Assigning cluster labels to the original data
customer_data['segment'] = kmeans.labels_
```

2. Hierarchical Clustering

Hierarchical clustering builds a tree (or dendrogram) of clusters. This method is particularly useful for identifying nested and hierarchical relationships within the data.

Implementation in Scikit-Learn:

```python
from sklearn.cluster import AgglomerativeClustering

Applying Hierarchical clustering
hierarchical = AgglomerativeClustering(n_clusters=4)
customer_data['segment'] = hierarchical.fit_predict(scaled_data)
```

3. DBSCAN

DBSCAN is a density-based clustering algorithm that can identify clusters of varying shapes and sizes, and it is robust to noise.

Implementation in Scikit-Learn:

```python
from sklearn.cluster import DBSCAN

Applying DBSCAN clustering
dbscan = DBSCAN(eps=0.5, min_samples=5)
customer_data['segment'] = dbscan.fit_predict(scaled_data)
```

Practical Example: Segmenting Bank Customers

To illustrate the application of clustering in market segmentation, let's consider a dataset containing various attributes of bank customers, such as age, income, account balance, and transaction frequency. Our objective is to segment these customers into distinct groups for targeted financial products.

1. Importing Libraries and Data

```python
import pandas as pd

Load customer data
customer_data = pd.read_csv('bank_customers.csv')

Standardizing the data
scaler = StandardScaler()
scaled_data = scaler.fit_transform(customer_data)
```

2. Applying KMeans Clustering

```python
Applying KMeans clustering
kmeans = KMeans(n_clusters=4, random_state=42)
customer_data['segment'] = kmeans.fit_predict(scaled_data)
```

3. Visualizing the Segments

Visualizing the results helps in understanding the characteristics of each segment.

```python
import matplotlib.pyplot as plt

Plotting the clusters
plt.scatter(customer_data['age'], customer_data['income'], c=customer_data['segment'])
plt.xlabel('Age')
plt.ylabel('Income')
plt.title('Customer Segments')
plt.show()
```

4. Profiling Segments

Once segments are identified, profile each segment to understand their unique characteristics.

```python
segment_profiles = customer_data.groupby('segment').mean()
print(segment_profiles)
```

Interpreting the Results

- Segment 0: Young professionals with high income but moderate account balances.
- Segment 1: Middle-aged customers with moderate income and high transaction frequency.
- Segment 2: Retirees with lower income but high account balances.
- Segment 3: Young students with low income and infrequent transactions.

Applications in Financial Services

1. Targeted Marketing Campaigns: Tailor marketing messages to each segment's unique needs and preferences, increasing engagement and conversion rates.
2. Product Development: Design financial products that cater to the specific requirements of different segments, such as high-interest savings accounts for retirees or student loans for young students.
3. Customer Service Enhancement: Provide personalized customer support based on segment profiles, thereby improving customer satisfaction and loyalty.
4. Risk Management: Identify segments that are more prone to financial risks and develop strategies to mitigate these risks.

Market segmentation through clustering provides a powerful tool for financial institutions to understand and serve their customers better. By applying clustering algorithms like K-Means, hierarchical clustering, and DBSCAN, businesses can uncover valuable insights into customer behaviour and preferences. These insights enable the development of personalized marketing strategies, innovative financial products, and improved customer service. The practical example provided demonstrates how to implement these techniques using Scikit-Learn, transforming raw data into actionable business intelligence that drives growth and profitability.

## Pipeline Creation for Unsupervised Learning

A pipeline in machine learning is akin to an assembly line in manufacturing. It consists of a sequence of steps where each step transforms the data in a specific manner. Pipelines in Scikit-Learn are particularly advantageous because they simplify the workflow by chaining together various preprocessing methods and learning algorithms into a single cohesive unit.

### Why Use Pipelines?

1. Efficiency: Pipelines streamline the workflow, reducing the need for repetitive coding tasks.
2. Reproducibility: Ensure consistent data processing and model training steps, making it easier to reproduce results.
3. Maintainability: Encapsulate the entire processing and learning sequence within a single object, simplifying maintenance and updates.

4. Cross-Validation: Facilitate the application of cross-validation techniques by ensuring that all steps are applied consistently during each fold of the validation process.

Key Components of a Pipeline

1. Preprocessing: Standardizing, normalizing, or transforming data.
2. Feature Extraction: Extracting meaningful features from raw data.
3. Modeling: Applying clustering algorithms to uncover patterns in the data.
4. Evaluation: Assessing the performance and quality of the clustering results.

Constructing a Pipeline for Unsupervised Learning

We will illustrate the construction of a pipeline using a practical example involving clustering of financial transaction data. The goal is to segment transactions into meaningful clusters based on their attributes.

Step 1: Import Libraries and Load Data

```python
import pandas as pd
from sklearn.preprocessing import StandardScaler
from sklearn.pipeline import Pipeline
from sklearn.cluster import KMeans

Load transaction data
```

```
data = pd.read_csv('financial_transactions.csv')
features = data[['amount', 'transaction_type', 'account_balance']]
```

Step 2: Define the Pipeline Components

```python
Standardize the data
scaler = StandardScaler()

Define the clustering algorithm
kmeans = KMeans(n_clusters=5, random_state=42)

Create the pipeline
pipeline = Pipeline([
    ('scaler', scaler),
    ('kmeans', kmeans)
])
```

Step 3: Fit the Pipeline to the Data

```python
Fit the pipeline
pipeline.fit(features)

Assign cluster labels to the original data
data['cluster'] = pipeline.predict(features)
```

Step 4: Evaluate the Clustering Results

Evaluation of clustering models typically involves examining the characteristics of each cluster. However, since unsupervised learning lacks predefined labels, alternative evaluation metrics such as silhouette scores or visual inspection must be used.

```python
from sklearn.metrics import silhouette_score

Calculate silhouette score
score = silhouette_score(features, data['cluster'])
print(f'Silhouette Score: {score}')
```

Step 5: Visualize the Clusters

Visualizing the clustering results provides insights into the data and helps identify meaningful patterns and anomalies.

```python
import matplotlib.pyplot as plt

Plotting the clusters based on selected features
plt.scatter(data['amount'], data['account_balance'], c=data['cluster'])
plt.xlabel('Transaction Amount')
```

```
plt.ylabel('Account Balance')
plt.title('Transaction Clusters')
plt.show()
```

Enhancing Pipelines with Additional Steps

Pipelines can be further enhanced by incorporating additional preprocessing steps, such as feature selection or dimensionality reduction. For instance, Principal Component Analysis (PCA) can be added to reduce the dimensionality of the data before applying clustering.

Adding PCA to the Pipeline

```python
from sklearn.decomposition import PCA

Define the PCA component
pca = PCA(n_components=2)

Create an enhanced pipeline with PCA
enhanced_pipeline = Pipeline([
    ('scaler', scaler),
    ('pca', pca),
    ('kmeans', kmeans)
])

Fit the enhanced pipeline
enhanced_pipeline.fit(features)
```

```
Assign cluster labels to the original data
data['enhanced_cluster'] =
enhanced_pipeline.predict(features)

Visualize the enhanced clusters
plt.scatter(data['amount'], data['account_balance'],
c=data['enhanced_cluster'])
plt.xlabel('Transaction Amount')
plt.ylabel('Account Balance')
plt.title('Enhanced Transaction Clusters with PCA')
plt.show()
```

Practical Considerations in Pipeline Creation

1. Parameter Tuning: Optimize hyperparameters using techniques like GridSearchCV within pipelines.
2. Pipeline Persistence: Save and load pipelines for future use with joblib or pickle, ensuring consistency across sessions.
3. Handling Imbalanced Data: Integrate oversampling or undersampling methods to address imbalanced datasets within the pipeline.

Saving and Loading Pipelines

```python
import joblib

Save pipeline
```

```
joblib.dump(enhanced_pipeline, 'enhanced_pipeline.pkl')

Load pipeline
loaded_pipeline = joblib.load('enhanced_pipeline.pkl')

Predict with loaded pipeline
data['loaded_cluster'] = loaded_pipeline.predict(features)
```

Case Study: Detecting Fraudulent Transactions Using Clustering

Detecting fraudulent transactions is paramount. The vast volume of daily transactions necessitates sophisticated methods to identify anomalies. Clustering, a powerful unsupervised learning technique, offers a solution by grouping transactions based on similarity, thereby highlighting outliers indicative of fraud. This case study illustrates the practical application of clustering techniques to detect fraudulent transactions, providing a detailed walkthrough of the process, from data preprocessing to evaluation.

Understanding the Problem

Financial institutions constantly battle fraud, seeking methods to identify suspicious activities among millions of legitimate transactions. Traditional rule-based systems often fall short due to their rigidity and inability to adapt to new fraud patterns. Clustering algorithms, however, can automatically detect anomalies by learning from the data itself, making them highly effective for this task.

Dataset Overview

For this case study, we'll use a dataset comprising various features that describe transactions, such as transaction amount, transaction type, account balance, and timestamp. The goal is to cluster transactions and identify those that deviate significantly from the norm, flagging them as potential fraud.

Step-by-Step Implementation

Step 1: Import Libraries and Load Data

```python
import pandas as pd
from sklearn.preprocessing import StandardScaler
from sklearn.pipeline import Pipeline
from sklearn.cluster import DBSCAN

Load the transaction dataset
data = pd.read_csv('financial_transactions.csv')
features = data[['amount', 'transaction_type', 'account_balance', 'timestamp']]
```

Step 2: Data Preprocessing

Data preprocessing is crucial for the accuracy of clustering algorithms. Standardization ensures that all features contribute equally to the clustering process.

```python
Convert the timestamp to a numerical value
data['timestamp'] = pd.to_datetime(data['timestamp'])
data['timestamp'] = data['timestamp'].astype(int) / 109 Convert to seconds

Standardize the features
scaler = StandardScaler()
features_scaled = scaler.fit_transform(features)
```

Step 3: Choose the Clustering Algorithm

For fraud detection, DBSCAN (Density-Based Spatial Clustering of Applications with Noise) is particularly effective as it can identify clusters of varying shapes and sizes and detect noise, which in this context can be potential fraudulent transactions.

```python
Define the DBSCAN clustering algorithm
dbscan = DBSCAN(eps=0.5, min_samples=5)

Fit the model to the scaled features
dbscan.fit(features_scaled)

Assign cluster labels to the data
data['cluster'] = dbscan.labels_
```

Step 4: Identify Anomalies

In DBSCAN, points labeled as `-1` are considered noise and are potential anomalies.

```python
Identify potential fraudulent transactions
fraudulent_transactions = data[data['cluster'] == -1]
print(f'Number of potential fraudulent transactions: {len(fraudulent_transactions)}')
```

Step 5: Evaluate the Results

Evaluating the effectiveness of anomaly detection in clustering involves analyzing the identified anomalies and their characteristics.

```python
Summary statistics of the potential fraudulent transactions
print(fraudulent_transactions.describe())

Visual inspection of clusters
import matplotlib.pyplot as plt

plt.scatter(data['amount'], data['account_balance'], c=data['cluster'])
plt.xlabel('Transaction Amount')
plt.ylabel('Account Balance')
```

```
plt.title('Transaction Clusters with DBSCAN')
plt.show()
```

Step 6: Refining the Model

Refinement involves tuning parameters like `eps` (the maximum distance between two samples for one to be considered as in the neighborhood of the other) and `min_samples` (the number of samples in a neighborhood for a point to be considered as a core point). GridSearchCV can aid in this process, even for unsupervised learning where evaluation metrics might differ.

```python
from sklearn.model_selection import GridSearchCV
from sklearn.metrics import make_scorer, silhouette_score

Define a scoring function for GridSearchCV
def dbscan_scorer(estimator, X):
    cluster_labels = estimator.fit_predict(X)
    if len(set(cluster_labels)) > 1:
        return silhouette_score(X, cluster_labels)
    else:
        return -1

Define parameter grid
param_grid = {'eps': [0.3, 0.5, 0.7], 'min_samples': [3, 5, 10]}

Perform Grid Search for the best parameters
```

grid_search = GridSearchCV(DBSCAN(), param_grid, scoring=dbscan_scorer, cv=[(slice(None), slice(None))])

grid_search.fit(features_scaled)

Best parameters

best_params = grid_search.best_params_

print(f'Best parameters: {best_params}')

```

Step 7: Implement the Tuned Model

```python

Apply the best parameters to DBSCAN

dbscan_tuned = DBSCAN(eps=best_params['eps'], min_samples=best_params['min_samples'])

data['tuned_cluster'] = dbscan_tuned.fit_predict(features_scaled)

Identify anomalies with tuned model

tuned_fraudulent_transactions = data[data['tuned_cluster'] == -1]

print(f'Number of potential fraudulent transactions with tuned model: {len(tuned_fraudulent_transactions)}')

Visualize the clusters from the tuned model

plt.scatter(data['amount'], data['account_balance'], c=data['tuned_cluster'])

plt.xlabel('Transaction Amount')

plt.ylabel('Account Balance')

plt.title('Tuned Transaction Clusters with DBSCAN')

```
plt.show()
```

Detecting fraudulent transactions using clustering techniques like DBSCAN demonstrates the power of unsupervised learning in financial analytics. By effectively preprocessing data, selecting appropriate algorithms, and tuning parameters, you can uncover hidden patterns and anomalies that signify potential fraud. This case study has walked through practical steps, from data preprocessing to model evaluation and refinement, illustrating how clustering can be a robust tool in the arsenal of financial fraud detection.

# CHAPTER 5: MODEL SELECTION AND HYPERPARAMETER TUNING

In the arena of quantitative finance, the importance of model selection cannot be overstated. Picking the right model is akin to selecting the correct tool for a job - it can mean the difference between insightful predictions and costly errors. Unlike other fields where the implications of a poor model might be limited to academic interest, in finance, the stakes are real and high. Financial decisions driven by machine learning models impact everything from investment strategies to risk management, making the expertise in model selection a critical skill.

The financial markets are dynamic and often unpredictable, characterized by complex relationships among numerous variables. This complexity necessitates sophisticated analytical techniques. The selection of a model has to account for various factors including the type of data, the specific financial problem, and the desired outcome. For instance, predicting stock prices, assessing credit risk, and optimizing portfolios each demands a tailored approach.

Predictive accuracy is paramount in finance because even minor inaccuracies can lead to significant financial losses. For example, an over-optimistic credit scoring model might underestimate the likelihood of defaults, leading to substantial financial setbacks for lending institutions. Conversely, an overly conservative model might reject potentially profitable opportunities. Thus, the choice of model directly influences the financial health and profitability of an organization.

Consider the scenario of predicting stock prices. A linear regression model might offer simplicity and interpretability, but it may not capture the  patterns in highly volatile market data. On the other hand, more sophisticated models like Support Vector Machines (SVM) or Gradient Boosting Machines (GBM) can provide better predictive power, albeit at the cost of increased complexity and computational resources.

Handling High-Dimensional Financial Data

Financial datasets often encompass a high dimensionality with numerous features, such as historical prices, trading volumes, economic indicators, and even textual data from news articles and social media. In such cases, dimensionality reduction techniques like Principal Component Analysis (PCA) or more complex deep learning models might be necessary to handle the data effectively.

For example, in portfolio management, the goal is to maximize returns while minimizing risks. This involves constructing a model that can analyze the historical performance of various assets and predict future price movements. Models like

PCA can reduce the dimensionality of the data, simplifying the problem and enhancing the performance of subsequent predictive models.

Adaptability to Changing Market Conditions

The financial markets are not static; they evolve over time due to various factors such as economic cycles, regulatory changes, and technological advancements. Therefore, the selected model must be adaptable to changing market conditions. Machine learning models that can update themselves with new data, such as online learning algorithms, are particularly valuable in this context.

Moreover, ensemble methods, combining the strengths of multiple models, often provide a robust solution. Techniques like Random Forests and Gradient Boosting aggregate the predictions of several models to improve accuracy and generalizability. This approach is particularly useful in finance, where the ability to generalize across different market conditions can significantly enhance the reliability of predictions.

Risk Management and Regulatory Compliance

Risk management is a cornerstone of any financial strategy. The chosen model must not only predict outcomes accurately but also quantify uncertainties and risks associated with those predictions. Financial regulators require institutions to demonstrate that their predictive models are not only effective but also transparent and unbiased.

For instance, logistic regression models are often preferred for credit scoring due to their simplicity and interpretability, which facilitate regulatory compliance. However, more complex models like Neural Networks, despite their superior predictive power, may face scrutiny due to their 'black-box' nature. Therefore, model selection in finance often involves a trade-off between accuracy and interpretability, especially in regulated environments.

Case Study: Credit Scoring Models

To illustrate the importance of model selection, consider a case study on credit scoring. Credit scoring models assess the risk of lending to individuals by predicting the likelihood of default. Traditional models like logistic regression have been widely used due to their simplicity and ease of interpretation. However, with the advent of machine learning, more sophisticated models such as Gradient Boosting and Neural Networks have shown superior predictive performance.

A logistic regression model might use features such as credit history, current debt, and income levels to predict default risk. While this model is straightforward and easy to explain to stakeholders and regulators, it may not capture complex nonlinear relationships in the data. In contrast, a Gradient Boosting model can handle these complexities better, leading to more accurate predictions. However, it requires careful tuning of hyperparameters and more computational resources.

This trade-off between accuracy and complexity exemplifies the critical nature of model selection in finance. The chosen model must align with the specific requirements of the financial application, balancing predictive performance with practical considerations like interpretability, ease of implementation, and regulatory compliance.

The importance of model selection in finance cannot be understated. It encompasses understanding the unique characteristics of financial data, balancing accuracy with complexity, adapting to changing market conditions, and meeting regulatory requirements. By selecting the appropriate model, financial analysts and data scientists can derive meaningful insights, make informed decisions, and ultimately drive better financial outcomes. In the world of finance, mastering the art of model selection is not just a technical necessity but a strategic imperative.

## Grid Search vs. Random Search

As financial professionals delve deeper into machine learning, optimizing model performance becomes paramount. Two prevalent hyperparameter tuning techniques, Grid Search and Random Search, offer distinct strategies for achieving this goal. Each method has its strengths and limitations, and understanding their differences is crucial for effectively leveraging them in the financial landscape.

### Hyperparameter Tuning: The Backbone of Model Optimization

Before we dissect the methodologies, it's essential to grasp the concept of hyperparameter tuning. Unlike model parameters, which are learned from the training data, hyperparameters are set prior to training and govern the model's learning process. Examples include the learning rate in gradient boosting, the number of trees in a random forest, or the regularization strength in a support vector machine.

Proper tuning of these hyperparameters is vital as it can significantly impact the model's performance. In financial contexts, where predictive accuracy can directly influence investment decisions and risk management, fine-tuning these parameters ensures that the model generalizes well to unseen data, mitigating overfitting or underfitting.

Grid Search: Exhaustive and Structured

Grid Search is a methodical and exhaustive approach to hyperparameter tuning. It involves defining a grid of possible hyperparameter values and testing all possible combinations. For instance, if you are tuning a random forest model, you might create a grid with different numbers of trees (e.g., 50, 100, 150) and various maximum depths (e.g., 10, 20, 30). Grid Search evaluates each combination to identify the optimal set of hyperparameters.

Advantages of Grid Search

1. Comprehensive Exploration: Grid Search explores all possible combinations within the defined grid, ensuring that no potential hyperparameter setting is overlooked. This thoroughness can be particularly beneficial in financial models where specific hyperparameter configurations might yield significant improvements.

2. Deterministic Nature: The exhaustive nature of Grid Search ensures reproducibility. Given the same grid and data, it will consistently produce the same results, providing a stable foundation for model selection.

Limitations of Grid Search

1. Computationally Intensive: The main drawback of Grid

Search lies in its computational cost. As the number of hyperparameters and their potential values increase, the number of combinations grows exponentially. This can lead to prohibitively long training times, especially with complex financial datasets and models.

2. Rigid Search Space: Grid Search's predefined grid can be overly restrictive. If the optimal hyperparameter values fall outside the defined grid, Grid Search won't find them, potentially missing better-performing configurations.

Random Search: Efficient and Flexible

In contrast to Grid Search, Random Search approaches hyperparameter tuning with a stochastic mindset. Instead of evaluating all possible combinations, Random Search selects a random subset of combinations to evaluate. This method is particularly effective when the hyperparameter space is vast.

Advantages of Random Search

1. Efficiency: Random Search is computationally more efficient. By evaluating random samples, it can uncover good hyperparameter settings without the need to exhaustively explore the entire grid. This efficiency is invaluable in financial applications where timely model updates are crucial.

2. Flexibility: Random Search's flexibility allows it to explore a broader range of hyperparameter values, increasing the likelihood of discovering optimal or near-optimal settings. This adaptability can be especially advantageous in complex financial models with high-dimensional hyperparameter spaces.

3. Scalability: Random Search scales better with the number of hyperparameters. Since it does not need to evaluate every possible combination, it can handle more extensive hyperparameter spaces, making it suitable for models with numerous tuning parameters.

### Limitations of Random Search

1. Non-Deterministic Nature: Due to its stochastic nature, Random Search may yield different results on different runs. This variability can be a disadvantage when consistent reproducibility is required in a financial setting.

2. Potentially Missed Combinations: While Random Search is efficient, it may miss optimal hyperparameter combinations simply because they were not sampled. This randomness can lead to suboptimal performance in some cases.

### Practical Implementation with Scikit-Learn

In practice, Scikit-Learn provides robust implementations for both Grid Search and Random Search. Let's delve into their usage with an example of tuning a Random Forest model for credit scoring.

### Grid Search Implementation

```python
from sklearn.ensemble import RandomForestClassifier
from sklearn.model_selection import GridSearchCV
```

```
Define the model and the parameter grid
model = RandomForestClassifier(random_state=42)
param_grid = {
    'n_estimators': [50, 100, 150],
    'max_depth': [10, 20, 30]
}

Initialize Grid Search
grid_search = GridSearchCV(estimator=model, param_grid=param_grid, cv=5, scoring='accuracy', n_jobs=-1)
grid_search.fit(X_train, y_train)

 Best parameters and score
print(f"Best Parameters: {grid_search.best_params_}")
print(f"Best Score: {grid_search.best_score_}")
```

Random Search Implementation

```python
from sklearn.ensemble import RandomForestClassifier
from sklearn.model_selection import RandomizedSearchCV
from scipy.stats import randint

Define the model and the parameter distribution
model = RandomForestClassifier(random_state=42)
param_dist = {
    'n_estimators': randint(50, 200),
```

```
    'max_depth': randint(10, 40)
}

Initialize Random Search
random_search = RandomizedSearchCV(estimator=model, param_distributions=param_dist, n_iter=100, cv=5, scoring='accuracy', n_jobs=-1, random_state=42)
random_search.fit(X_train, y_train)

 Best parameters and score
print(f"Best Parameters: {random_search.best_params_}")
print(f"Best Score: {random_search.best_score_}")
```

Choosing the Right Method

Selecting between Grid Search and Random Search hinges on the specific requirements and constraints of your financial application. Grid Search offers a comprehensive and deterministic approach, making it suitable for situations where computational resources are ample and reproducibility is critical. Conversely, Random Search provides efficiency and flexibility, ideal for high-dimensional hyperparameter spaces and scenarios demanding quick model iterations.

Ultimately, mastering both techniques equips financial analysts with the tools to fine-tune their models effectively, ensuring robust and accurate predictions in the ever-evolving financial landscape. By judiciously applying these hyperparameter tuning methods, you can enhance your machine learning models, driving better financial decisions and outcomes.

## Using Scikit-Learn's GridSearchCV

In the world of finance, where the accuracy of predictive models can have profound implications, fine-tuning hyperparameters is not just an enhancement—it's a necessity. The GridSearchCV utility in Scikit-Learn provides a powerful and systematic approach to this fine-tuning, ensuring that your models operate at peak performance.

### The Essence of GridSearchCV

GridSearchCV stands as a cornerstone in the toolbox of any quantitative analyst. It automates the process of searching for the best hyperparameter configuration by performing an exhaustive search over a specified parameter grid. This methodically ensures that every possible combination within the grid is evaluated, leaving no stone unturned in the quest for optimal model performance.

Hyperparameters, unlike model parameters, are not learned from the data. They are defined a priori and govern various aspects of the model learning process. Examples include the number of estimators in a Random Forest, the learning rate in a Gradient Boosting Machine, or the penalty parameter in a Support Vector Machine. Properly tuning these hyperparameters can significantly influence the model's predictive power, particularly in financial applications where precision is paramount.

### Setting Up GridSearchCV

To leverage GridSearchCV, one must define a model and the hyperparameter grid. Let's consider a practical example using a Random Forest classifier for a credit scoring problem, a common application in finance where distinguishing between good and bad credit risks is crucial.

```python
from sklearn.ensemble import RandomForestClassifier
from sklearn.model_selection import GridSearchCV

Define the model
model = RandomForestClassifier(random_state=42)

Define the parameter grid
param_grid = {
    'n_estimators': [50, 100, 150],
    'max_depth': [10, 20, 30],
    'min_samples_split': [2, 5, 10]
}

Initialize Grid Search
grid_search = GridSearchCV(estimator=model, param_grid=param_grid, cv=5, scoring='accuracy', n_jobs=-1)
grid_search.fit(X_train, y_train)

 Best parameters and score
print(f"Best Parameters: {grid_search.best_params_}")
print(f"Best Score: {grid_search.best_score_}")
```

## Detailed Breakdown of GridSearchCV

### Initialization and Parameter Grid

The first step involves importing the required libraries and defining the model. The parameter grid (`param_grid`) encompasses various hyperparameters and their respective values. For our Random Forest example, these include the number of trees (`n_estimators`), the maximum depth of each tree (`max_depth`), and the minimum number of samples required to split an internal node (`min_samples_split`). These values are chosen based on domain knowledge, empirical evidence, or exploratory data analysis.

### Execution Workflow

1. Model Definition: The `RandomForestClassifier` is initialized with a fixed random state for reproducibility.

2. Parameter Grid Definition: The `param_grid` dictionary specifies the hyperparameter values to be explored.

3. GridSearchCV Initialization: The `GridSearchCV` object is created with the model, parameter grid, and additional settings such as the cross-validation strategy (`cv=5`), scoring metric (`accuracy`), and number of parallel jobs (`n_jobs=-1`).

4. Fitting the Model: The `fit` method is called with the training data (`X_train` and `y_train`), initiating the grid search process.

5. Result Extraction: After fitting, the best hyperparameters and the corresponding accuracy score are printed.

## Practical Considerations in Financial Applications

GridSearchCV's exhaustive nature ensures thorough exploration, which is vital in financial contexts where even slight improvements in model accuracy can translate to significant economic gains. However, this thoroughness comes at a computational cost. Here are some practical tips:

### Balancing Computational Cost

Given the complexity of financial datasets, running an exhaustive search can be computationally intensive. Utilize parallel processing (`n_jobs=-1` in GridSearchCV) to distribute the workload across multiple CPU cores, significantly reducing the execution time.

### Handling Large Datasets

When dealing with large financial datasets, consider sampling techniques to create a representative subset for the grid search. This approach reduces computational load while maintaining the integrity of the parameter search.

### Cross-Validation Strategy

The choice of cross-validation strategy (`cv`) is crucial. For financial time series data, use techniques like TimeSeriesSplit to preserve the temporal ordering and prevent data leakage.

## Advanced Usage and Customization

### Custom Scoring Metrics

In finance, accuracy may not always be the preferred metric. Custom scoring functions can be implemented to optimize for metrics like AUC-ROC, precision, recall, or F1-score, aligning the model evaluation with specific business objectives.

```python
from sklearn.metrics import make_scorer, f1_score

Define a custom scorer
f1_scorer = make_scorer(f1_score, average='weighted')

Initialize Grid Search with custom scorer
grid_search = GridSearchCV(estimator=model, param_grid=param_grid, cv=5, scoring=f1_scorer, n_jobs=-1)
grid_search.fit(X_train, y_train)

 Best parameters and score
print(f"Best Parameters: {grid_search.best_params_}")
print(f"Best Score: {grid_search.best_score_}")
```

Pipeline Integration

Integrate GridSearchCV with Scikit-Learn Pipelines to streamline preprocessing and model tuning. This integration ensures that all steps, including data scaling, feature selection, and model fitting, are properly validated within the cross-validation process.

```python
```

```
from sklearn.pipeline import Pipeline
from sklearn.preprocessing import StandardScaler

Define a pipeline
pipeline = Pipeline([
    ('scaler', StandardScaler()),
    ('classifier', RandomForestClassifier(random_state=42))
])

Define the parameter grid
param_grid = {
    'classifier__n_estimators': [50, 100, 150],
    'classifier__max_depth': [10, 20, 30],
    'classifier__min_samples_split': [2, 5, 10]
}

Initialize Grid Search with pipeline
grid_search = GridSearchCV(estimator=pipeline, param_grid=param_grid, cv=5, scoring='accuracy', n_jobs=-1)
grid_search.fit(X_train, y_train)

Best parameters and score
print(f"Best Parameters: {grid_search.best_params_}")
print(f"Best Score: {grid_search.best_score_}")
```

Leveraging GridSearchCV for Financial Mastery

GridSearchCV's systematic and exhaustive approach to

hyperparameter tuning makes it an invaluable tool for financial analysts. By methodically exploring the hyperparameter space, it ensures that models are fine-tuned to their optimal performance, crucial for making accurate and reliable financial predictions.

Whether you are developing models for credit scoring, stock price prediction, or risk management, mastering GridSearchCV will enhance your ability to build robust and precise machine learning models, driving better financial outcomes and decision-making.

## Cross-Validation Techniques

In the high-stakes arena of financial modeling, the importance of cross-validation cannot be overstated. It is the bedrock upon which the credibility and robustness of a machine learning model rest. Cross-validation techniques provide a systematic way to assess the performance of a model, ensuring that it generalizes well to unseen data, a critical requirement given the volatile nature of financial markets.

### Understanding Cross-Validation

Cross-validation is a statistical method used to estimate the skill of machine learning models. It primarily helps in mitigating the risk of overfitting, which occurs when a model performs well on training data but poorly on new, unseen data. By partitioning the dataset into multiple subsets, cross-validation allows for more rigorous testing and validation, leading to more reliable models.

## Types of Cross-Validation Techniques

Several cross-validation techniques are available, each with its advantages and specific use cases. Let's delve into some of the most commonly employed methods:

### 1. K-Fold Cross-Validation

K-Fold Cross-Validation is one of the most widely used and straightforward cross-validation techniques. The entire dataset is divided into 'k' equally sized folds. The model is trained on 'k-1' folds and tested on the remaining fold. This process is repeated 'k' times, with each fold serving as the test set exactly once. The final performance metric is the average of the 'k' test results.

For instance, in a 5-Fold Cross-Validation, the dataset is split into five parts. The model is trained on four parts and tested on the fifth part, repeated five times.

```python
from sklearn.model_selection import KFold
from sklearn.ensemble import RandomForestClassifier
from sklearn.metrics import accuracy_score

Initialize the model
model = RandomForestClassifier(random_state=42)

Define the K-Fold Cross-Validator
kf = KFold(n_splits=5)
```

```
Perform Cross-Validation
accuracies = []
for train_index, test_index in kf.split(X):
    X_train, X_test = X[train_index], X[test_index]
    y_train, y_test = y[train_index], y[test_index]
    model.fit(X_train, y_train)
    predictions = model.predict(X_test)
    accuracy = accuracy_score(y_test, predictions)
    accuracies.append(accuracy)

Average accuracy
print(f"Average Accuracy: {sum(accuracies) / len(accuracies)}")
```

2. Stratified K-Fold Cross-Validation

In financial datasets, class imbalance is a common issue, particularly in scenarios like credit scoring, where the number of defaulters might be significantly lower than non-defaulters. Stratified K-Fold Cross-Validation ensures that each fold has the same proportion of each class as the whole dataset, providing a more accurate and reliable measure of model performance.

```python
from sklearn.model_selection import StratifiedKFold

Define the Stratified K-Fold Cross-Validator
```

```
skf = StratifiedKFold(n_splits=5)

Perform Stratified Cross-Validation
accuracies = []
for train_index, test_index in skf.split(X, y):
    X_train, X_test = X[train_index], X[test_index]
    y_train, y_test = y[train_index], y[test_index]
    model.fit(X_train, y_train)
    predictions = model.predict(X_test)
    accuracy = accuracy_score(y_test, predictions)
    accuracies.append(accuracy)

Average accuracy
print(f"Average Accuracy: {sum(accuracies) / len(accuracies)}")
```

3. Leave-One-Out Cross-Validation (LOOCV)

Leave-One-Out Cross-Validation is an extreme case of K-Fold Cross-Validation where 'k' equals the number of data points in the dataset. Each observation is used once as a test set while the remaining observations form the training set. Although this method provides an unbiased estimate of model performance, it can be computationally expensive, especially for large datasets.

```python
from sklearn.model_selection import LeaveOneOut
```

```
Define the Leave-One-Out Cross-Validator
loo = LeaveOneOut()

Perform Leave-One-Out Cross-Validation
accuracies = []
for train_index, test_index in loo.split(X):
    X_train, X_test = X[train_index], X[test_index]
    y_train, y_test = y[train_index], y[test_index]
    model.fit(X_train, y_train)
    predictions = model.predict(X_test)
    accuracy = accuracy_score(y_test, predictions)
    accuracies.append(accuracy)

Average accuracy
print(f"Average Accuracy: {sum(accuracies) / len(accuracies)}")
```

Time Series Cross-Validation

In finance, data often comes in the form of time series, where the temporal ordering of observations is crucial. Traditional cross-validation methods might not be suitable as they can lead to data leakage by mixing training and testing data across time periods. Time Series Cross-Validation techniques, such as TimeSeriesSplit, maintain the temporal order, ensuring that the model is trained on past data and tested on future data.

4. TimeSeriesSplit

TimeSeriesSplit is designed for time series data, where the training set is always before the test set in chronological order. This method is particularly useful for financial applications like stock price prediction or risk management, where the model's ability to predict future values is assessed.

```python
from sklearn.model_selection import TimeSeriesSplit

Define the Time Series Split Cross-Validator
tscv = TimeSeriesSplit(n_splits=5)

Perform Time Series Cross-Validation
accuracies = []
for train_index, test_index in tscv.split(X):
    X_train, X_test = X[train_index], X[test_index]
    y_train, y_test = y[train_index], y[test_index]
    model.fit(X_train, y_train)
    predictions = model.predict(X_test)
    accuracy = accuracy_score(y_test, predictions)
    accuracies.append(accuracy)

Average accuracy
print(f"Average Accuracy: {sum(accuracies) / len(accuracies)}")
```

Practical Considerations in Financial Applications

## Choosing the Right Cross-Validation Technique

Selecting the appropriate cross-validation technique depends on the nature of the financial dataset and the specific modeling objectives. For balanced datasets, K-Fold Cross-Validation is often sufficient. For imbalanced classes, Stratified K-Fold Cross-Validation is preferred. Time series data necessitates TimeSeriesSplit to preserve temporal integrity.

### Balancing Bias and Variance

Cross-validation helps in balancing the bias-variance tradeoff. High bias models (underfitting) and high variance models (overfitting) are both detrimental in financial contexts. Cross-validation provides a robust framework to tune models, ensuring they generalize well to new data.

### Computational Efficiency

While techniques like LOOCV offer unbiased performance estimates, they can be computationally prohibitive for large datasets. K-Fold and Stratified K-Fold Cross-Validation strike a balance between computational efficiency and reliability, making them suitable for most financial applications.

## The Power of Cross-Validation in Financial Modeling

Cross-validation is an indispensable tool for financial quantitative analysts, providing a rigorous framework for model validation and selection. By employing appropriate cross-validation techniques, you ensure that your models are robust, reliable, and capable of delivering accurate predictions in the volatile and complex world of finance. Mastering cross-validation is a crucial step towards building high-performance financial models that drive better decision-making and foster innovation.

## Balancing Bias-Variance Tradeoff

### Understanding Bias and Variance

Before diving into the tradeoff, let's clarify what bias and variance entail:

- Bias refers to the error introduced by approximating a real-world problem, which may be complex, by a simplified model. High bias can cause underfitting, where the model is too simplistic to capture the underlying trends in the data. This results in poor performance on both training and test datasets.

- Variance refers to the model's sensitivity to small fluctuations in the training data. High variance can cause overfitting, where the model learns the noise and details of the training data to such an extent that it performs well on training data but poorly on new, unseen data.

The goal is to find a model with low bias and low variance. However, reducing one often increases the other, hence the tradeoff.

### The Bias-Variance Tradeoff in Financial Models

In the context of financial modeling, the bias-variance tradeoff is particularly pertinent due to the inherent volatility and complexity of financial data. Models with high bias may miss out on important market signals, leading to suboptimal investment strategies or risk assessments. On the other hand, models with high variance may react too sensitively to market noise, resulting in unreliable predictions and poor generalization to future data.

Strategies to Balance Bias and Variance

Several techniques can help manage the bias-variance tradeoff. Below, we discuss some of the most effective strategies, illustrated with Scikit-Learn implementations.

1. Model Complexity

Choosing the right level of model complexity is pivotal. Simple models like linear regression have high bias but low variance, while complex models like decision trees may have low bias but high variance. To illustrate, let's compare linear regression and decision trees for a financial dataset predicting stock prices.

Example: Linear Regression vs Decision Tree

```python
from sklearn.linear_model import LinearRegression
from sklearn.tree import DecisionTreeRegressor
from sklearn.model_selection import cross_val_score
```

```
Initialize models
linear_model = LinearRegression()
tree_model = DecisionTreeRegressor(max_depth=5)

Evaluate models using cross-validation
linear_scores = cross_val_score(linear_model, X, y, cv=5, scoring='neg_mean_squared_error')
tree_scores = cross_val_score(tree_model, X, y, cv=5, scoring='neg_mean_squared_error')

print(f"Linear Regression MSE: {-linear_scores.mean()}")
print(f"Decision Tree MSE: {-tree_scores.mean()}")
```

This example highlights the tradeoff: Linear Regression may exhibit higher bias, while Decision Tree Regressor may exhibit higher variance depending on the complexity of the data.

2. Regularization

Regularization techniques, such as Ridge and Lasso regression, add a penalty for larger coefficients, effectively balancing bias and variance by shrinking coefficients. These methods are particularly useful for financial datasets with many predictors, where multicollinearity is a concern.

Example: Ridge and Lasso Regression

```python
from sklearn.linear_model import Ridge, Lasso
```

```
Initialize models with regularization
ridge_model = Ridge(alpha=1.0)
lasso_model = Lasso(alpha=0.1)

Evaluate models using cross-validation
ridge_scores = cross_val_score(ridge_model, X, y, cv=5, scoring='neg_mean_squared_error')
lasso_scores = cross_val_score(lasso_model, X, y, cv=5, scoring='neg_mean_squared_error')

print(f"Ridge Regression MSE: {-ridge_scores.mean()}")
print(f"Lasso Regression MSE: {-lasso_scores.mean()}")
```

Regularization helps in managing overfitting by penalizing large coefficients, thus balancing variance.

3. Ensemble Methods

Ensemble methods, such as Random Forests and Gradient Boosting, combine multiple models to mitigate the bias-variance tradeoff. These methods often result in models that generalize better than individual models.

Example: Random Forest Regression

```python
from sklearn.ensemble import RandomForestRegressor

Initialize the Random Forest model
```

rf_model = RandomForestRegressor(n_estimators=100, max_depth=10, random_state=42)

Evaluate the model using cross-validation

rf_scores = cross_val_score(rf_model, X, y, cv=5, scoring='neg_mean_squared_error')

print(f"Random Forest Regression MSE: {-rf_scores.mean()}")

```

Random Forests reduce variance by averaging multiple decision trees, thus offering a balance between bias and variance.

4. Cross-Validation

Cross-validation itself is a powerful technique to assess model performance and ensure that it generalizes well to unseen data. Employing techniques like K-Fold or TimeSeriesSplit ensures that the model is neither too biased nor too variant.

Example: Cross-Validation with Ridge Regression

```python
from sklearn.model_selection import KFold

Define the K-Fold Cross-Validator
kf = KFold(n_splits=5)

Initialize the Ridge Regression model
ridge_model = Ridge(alpha=1.0)
```
```

```
Perform Cross-Validation
mse_scores = []
for train_index, test_index in kf.split(X):
    X_train, X_test = X[train_index], X[test_index]
    y_train, y_test = y[train_index], y[test_index]
    ridge_model.fit(X_train, y_train)
    predictions = ridge_model.predict(X_test)
    mse = mean_squared_error(y_test, predictions)
    mse_scores.append(mse)

Average MSE
print(f"Average MSE: {sum(mse_scores) / len(mse_scores)}")
```

Cross-validation provides a robust estimate of model performance, helping to balance bias and variance effectively.

Practical Considerations in Financial Applications

Data Quality and Preprocessing

High-quality data and rigorous preprocessing can significantly impact the bias-variance tradeoff. Ensuring that the dataset is free from noise and accurately represents the underlying financial phenomena is crucial. Techniques like feature scaling, normalization, and handling missing values can improve model performance.

Feature Engineering

Creating meaningful features from raw financial data can help in reducing both bias and variance. Feature engineering involves domain knowledge to create predictors that capture the underlying financial trends, leading to better model performance.

Hyperparameter Tuning

Careful tuning of hyperparameters, such as the depth of a decision tree or the regularization strength in ridge regression, can help achieve an optimal balance between bias and variance. Using techniques like GridSearchCV or RandomizedSearchCV in Scikit-Learn can aid in finding the best hyperparameters.

Example: Hyperparameter Tuning with GridSearchCV

```python
from sklearn.model_selection import GridSearchCV

Define the parameter grid for Ridge Regression
param_grid = {'alpha': [0.1, 1.0, 10.0]}

Initialize the Ridge Regression model
ridge_model = Ridge()

Perform Grid Search with Cross-Validation
grid_search = GridSearchCV(ridge_model, param_grid, cv=5, scoring='neg_mean_squared_error')
grid_search.fit(X, y)
```

```
Best parameter and score
print(f"Best alpha: {grid_search.best_params_['alpha']}")
print(f"Best MSE: {-grid_search.best_score_}")
```

Hyperparameter tuning ensures that the model is neither too simple nor too complex, balancing bias and variance.

## Mastering the Bias-Variance Tradeoff

Balancing the bias-variance tradeoff is a critical aspect of building robust and reliable financial models. By understanding the underlying principles and employing strategies like model complexity adjustment, regularization, ensemble methods, and careful cross-validation, you can develop models that generalize well to new data. Mastering this balance will empower you to create predictive models that are not only accurate but also resilient in the fast-paced and often unpredictable world of finance.

## Regularization Techniques in Finance Models

### Understanding Regularization

Regularization introduces a penalty for larger coefficients in a model to prevent overfitting. By constraining the magnitude of these coefficients, regularization forces the model to prioritize features that contribute most significantly to the prediction, leading to simpler and more interpretable models.

The two primary forms of regularization are Ridge Regression (L2 regularization) and Lasso Regression (L1 regularization).

Ridge Regression (L2 Regularization)

Ridge Regression adds a penalty equivalent to the sum of the squared magnitude of coefficients. This form of regularization shrinks the coefficients evenly, mitigating the impact of multicollinearity.

Example: Implementing Ridge Regression

```python
from sklearn.linear_model import Ridge
from sklearn.model_selection import train_test_split
from sklearn.metrics import mean_squared_error

Splitting the dataset
X_train, X_test, y_train, y_test = train_test_split(X, y, test_size=0.2, random_state=42)

Ridge Regression model
ridge_model = Ridge(alpha=1.0)

Fitting the model
ridge_model.fit(X_train, y_train)

Making predictions
y_pred = ridge_model.predict(X_test)
```

Evaluating the model

mse = mean_squared_error(y_test, y_pred)

print(f"Ridge Regression Mean Squared Error: {mse}")

```

In financial datasets, where predictors might be highly correlated (e.g., stock prices of companies within the same sector), Ridge Regression can help drive more stable and reliable predictions.

Lasso Regression (L1 Regularization)

Lasso Regression introduces a penalty equal to the absolute value of the coefficients. This has the effect of shrinking some coefficients to zero, effectively performing feature selection.

Example: Implementing Lasso Regression

```python
from sklearn.linear_model import Lasso

Lasso Regression model
lasso_model = Lasso(alpha=0.1)

Fitting the model
lasso_model.fit(X_train, y_train)

Making predictions
y_pred = lasso_model.predict(X_test)

```
Evaluating the model
mse = mean_squared_error(y_test, y_pred)
print(f"Lasso Regression Mean Squared Error: {mse}")
```

In practice, Lasso Regression can be highly advantageous for financial models where interpretability and feature selection are critical. By shrinking some coefficients to zero, Lasso helps in identifying the most influential predictors, thus simplifying the model without substantial loss of predictive power.

Elastic Net: A Hybrid Approach

Elastic Net combines the penalties of Ridge and Lasso, offering a balanced approach that leverages the strengths of both methods. This flexibility makes it particularly useful for financial data, where the number of predictors can be very high, and multicollinearity is common.

Example: Implementing Elastic Net

```python
from sklearn.linear_model import ElasticNet

Elastic Net model
elastic_net_model = ElasticNet(alpha=0.1, l1_ratio=0.7)

Fitting the model
elastic_net_model.fit(X_train, y_train)
```

```
Making predictions
y_pred = elastic_net_model.predict(X_test)

Evaluating the model
mse = mean_squared_error(y_test, y_pred)
print(f"Elastic Net Mean Squared Error: {mse}")
```

Elastic Net is particularly effective in scenarios where the dataset contains multiple correlated features. By combining L1 and L2 regularization, it ensures robust feature selection while maintaining model stability.

Practical Considerations in Finance

Dealing with Multicollinearity

Financial datasets often suffer from multicollinearity, where predictors are highly correlated. Regularization techniques like Ridge and Elastic Net are particularly effective in such scenarios. By penalizing large coefficients, these methods reduce the impact of multicollinearity, leading to more stable and interpretable models.

Feature Selection and Interpretability

In financial modeling, interpretability is often as important as accuracy. Lasso and Elastic Net aid in feature selection, simplifying models and making them more interpretable. This can be invaluable for financial analysts who need to explain and justify their models to stakeholders.

## Hyperparameter Tuning

The effectiveness of regularization is highly dependent on the choice of hyperparameters, such as the regularization strength (alpha) and the mixing ratio (l1_ratio for Elastic Net). Techniques like GridSearchCV can be employed to find the optimal hyperparameters, ensuring the best balance between bias, variance, and interpretability.

Example: Hyperparameter Tuning with GridSearchCV for Elastic Net

```python
from sklearn.model_selection import GridSearchCV

Define the parameter grid
param_grid = {
    'alpha': [0.1, 1.0, 10.0],
    'l1_ratio': [0.1, 0.5, 0.7, 1.0]
}

Initialize the Elastic Net model
elastic_net_model = ElasticNet()

Perform Grid Search with Cross-Validation
grid_search = GridSearchCV(elastic_net_model, param_grid, cv=5, scoring='neg_mean_squared_error')
grid_search.fit(X, y)

Best parameters and score
```

```
print(f"Best parameters: {grid_search.best_params_}")
print(f"Best Mean Squared Error: {-grid_search.best_score_}")
```

Case Study: Credit Scoring with Regularization

To illustrate the practical application of regularization techniques in finance, let's consider a case study on credit scoring. Credit scoring models aim to predict the likelihood of a borrower defaulting on a loan. Given the high stakes, it's crucial to use models that are both accurate and interpretable.

Dataset Preparation

```python
import pandas as pd
from sklearn.preprocessing import StandardScaler

Load the dataset
data = pd.read_csv('credit_data.csv')

Feature selection and preprocessing
X = data.drop(columns=['default'])
y = data['default']

scaler = StandardScaler()
X_scaled = scaler.fit_transform(X)
```

Model Building

```python
Splitting the dataset
X_train, X_test, y_train, y_test = train_test_split(X_scaled, y, test_size=0.2, random_state=42)

Initialize and fit the Ridge Regression model
ridge_model = Ridge(alpha=1.0)
ridge_model.fit(X_train, y_train)

Predictions and evaluation
y_pred = ridge_model.predict(X_test)
mse = mean_squared_error(y_test, y_pred)
print(f"Ridge Regression Mean Squared Error: {mse}")

Initialize and fit the Lasso Regression model
lasso_model = Lasso(alpha=0.1)
lasso_model.fit(X_train, y_train)

Predictions and evaluation
y_pred = lasso_model.predict(X_test)
mse = mean_squared_error(y_test, y_pred)
print(f"Lasso Regression Mean Squared Error: {mse}")

Initialize and fit the Elastic Net model
elastic_net_model = ElasticNet(alpha=0.1, l1_ratio=0.7)
elastic_net_model.fit(X_train, y_train)

Predictions and evaluation
```

```
y_pred = elastic_net_model.predict(X_test)
mse = mean_squared_error(y_test, y_pred)
print(f"Elastic Net Mean Squared Error: {mse}")
```

In this case study, we see how regularization techniques can be applied to a critical financial task like credit scoring. By penalizing large coefficients, these methods help in building robust models that generalize well to new data, ensuring accurate and reliable credit risk assessments.

## Harnessing Regularization for Financial Models

Regularization techniques are indispensable tools for financial modeling, offering a robust solution to the challenges of high-dimensional data and multicollinearity. By understanding and effectively implementing methods like Ridge, Lasso, and Elastic Net, you can develop models that are both accurate and interpretable. These techniques enable you to harness the full potential of your financial data, leading to more reliable predictions and informed decision-making.

As you continue to explore and apply regularization methods in your financial models, remember that the right balance of bias and variance, combined with thoughtful feature selection and hyperparameter tuning, will empower you to create predictive models that stand strong against the volatile and complex nature of financial markets.

## Handling Imbalanced Datasets in Financial Models

## Understanding Imbalanced Datasets

Imbalanced datasets occur when the distribution of classes is skewed. This imbalance can drastically affect the performance of machine learning algorithms, which often assume an even distribution of classes. As a result, models may become biased towards the majority class, leading to poor performance on the minority class. Key metrics such as accuracy can be misleading in these situations, making it essential to adopt evaluation metrics like precision, recall, and the F1-score.

## Techniques to Handle Imbalanced Datasets

1. Resampling Methods
2. Algorithmic Approaches
3. Evaluation Metrics

## Resampling Methods

Resampling involves modifying the dataset to balance the class distribution. There are two primary resampling techniques:

### Oversampling the Minority Class

Oversampling involves increasing the number of instances in the minority class by duplicating or creating synthetic samples.

Example: Implementing Synthetic Minority Over-sampling

Technique (SMOTE)

```python
from imblearn.over_sampling import SMOTE
from sklearn.model_selection import train_test_split
from sklearn.ensemble import RandomForestClassifier
from sklearn.metrics import classification_report

Splitting the dataset
X_train, X_test, y_train, y_test = train_test_split(X, y, test_size=0.2, random_state=42)

Applying SMOTE
smote = SMOTE(random_state=42)
X_train_resampled, y_train_resampled = smote.fit_resample(X_train, y_train)

 Training a model
rf_model = RandomForestClassifier(random_state=42)
rf_model.fit(X_train_resampled, y_train_resampled)

Making predictions
y_pred = rf_model.predict(X_test)

Evaluation
print(classification_report(y_test, y_pred))
```

SMOTE generates synthetic samples for the minority class

by interpolating between existing samples. This technique is particularly effective in maintaining the variability of minority class instances, leading to better generalization.

Undersampling the Majority Class

Undersampling balances the dataset by reducing the number of instances in the majority class.

Example: Implementing Random Under-Sampling

```python
from imblearn.under_sampling import RandomUnderSampler

Applying Random Under-Sampling
rus = RandomUnderSampler(random_state=42)
X_train_resampled, y_train_resampled = rus.fit_resample(X_train, y_train)

 Training a model
rf_model.fit(X_train_resampled, y_train_resampled)

Making predictions
y_pred = rf_model.predict(X_test)

Evaluation
print(classification_report(y_test, y_pred))
```

While undersampling can help balance the classes, it might lead to a loss of important information from the majority class. Careful consideration and possibly combining it with oversampling can provide a balanced approach.

Algorithmic Approaches

Some algorithms are inherently better at handling imbalanced datasets. Adjustments can also be made to existing algorithms to improve their performance on imbalanced data.

Cost-Sensitive Learning

Cost-sensitive learning assigns different misclassification costs to classes. This approach penalizes misclassifications of the minority class more heavily, encouraging the model to perform better on the minority class.

Example: Implementing Cost-Sensitive Random Forest

```python
Defining class weights
class_weights = {0: 1, 1: 10}   Assuming 0 is majority class and 1 is minority class

Training a cost-sensitive Random Forest
rf_model = RandomForestClassifier(class_weight=class_weights, random_state=42)
rf_model.fit(X_train, y_train)
```

```
Making predictions
y_pred = rf_model.predict(X_test)

Evaluation
print(classification_report(y_test, y_pred))
```

By assigning higher weights to the minority class, cost-sensitive learning ensures the model pays more attention to correctly predicting minority class instances.

Ensemble Methods

Ensemble methods, such as Balanced Random Forests and EasyEnsemble, combine multiple models to improve performance on imbalanced datasets.

Example: Implementing EasyEnsemble

```python
from imblearn.ensemble import EasyEnsembleClassifier

Initializing EasyEnsembleClassifier
eec = EasyEnsembleClassifier(random_state=42)
eec.fit(X_train, y_train)

Making predictions
y_pred = eec.predict(X_test)
```

```
Evaluation
print(classification_report(y_test, y_pred))
```

EasyEnsemble iteratively samples subsets of the majority class and combines them with the minority class to create balanced training sets for multiple weak classifiers. The predictions from these classifiers are then aggregated, improving overall performance on the minority class.

Evaluation Metrics

When dealing with imbalanced datasets, traditional accuracy metrics can be misleading as they don't account for the model's performance on the minority class. Alternative metrics provide a more accurate picture of the model's effectiveness.

Precision, Recall, and F1-Score

- Precision: The ratio of true positive predictions to the total predicted positives.
- Recall: The ratio of true positive predictions to the total actual positives.
- F1-Score: The harmonic mean of precision and recall, balancing the trade-off between the two.

Confusion Matrix

A confusion matrix provides a detailed breakdown of the model's performance by displaying True Positives (TP), True

Negatives (TN), False Positives (FP), and False Negatives (FN).

Example: Evaluating with a Confusion Matrix

```python
from sklearn.metrics import confusion_matrix

Generating the confusion matrix
cm = confusion_matrix(y_test, y_pred)
print(cm)
```

The confusion matrix helps visualize the model's performance across both classes, making it easier to identify areas for improvement.

Practical Considerations in Finance

Fraud Detection

Fraudulent transactions are rare but costly. Efficiently handling the imbalance between fraudulent and legitimate transactions is crucial for accurate fraud detection models.

Credit Scoring

Defaulting on loans is far less common than successful repayments. Balancing the dataset ensures the credit risk models can accurately predict defaults without being biased towards the majority class.

Portfolio Management

In portfolio management, certain market events or asset behaviors might be rare but significant. Handling imbalanced datasets can help in predicting these rare events more accurately, leading to better risk management and decision-making.

Case Study: Fraud Detection with Imbalanced Data

To illustrate the practical application of these techniques, let's consider a case study on fraud detection in credit card transactions.

Dataset Preparation

```python
import pandas as pd
from sklearn.preprocessing import StandardScaler

Load the dataset
data = pd.read_csv('credit_card_fraud.csv')

Feature selection and preprocessing
X = data.drop(columns=['fraud'])
y = data['fraud']

scaler = StandardScaler()
X_scaled = scaler.fit_transform(X)
```

Model Building with SMOTE and Random Forest

```python
Splitting the dataset
X_train, X_test, y_train, y_test = train_test_split(X_scaled, y, test_size=0.2, random_state=42)

Applying SMOTE
smote = SMOTE(random_state=42)
X_train_resampled, y_train_resampled = smote.fit_resample(X_train, y_train)

Training a Random Forest model
rf_model = RandomForestClassifier(random_state=42)
rf_model.fit(X_train_resampled, y_train_resampled)

Making predictions
y_pred = rf_model.predict(X_test)

Evaluation
print(classification_report(y_test, y_pred))
print(confusion_matrix(y_test, y_pred))
```

In this case study, the combination of SMOTE and Random Forest demonstrates how oversampling the minority class can lead to better fraud detection, resulting in a more balanced and accurate model.

## Mastering Imbalanced Datasets for Financial Modeling

Handling imbalanced datasets is pivotal in financial modeling. By employing techniques like resampling, cost-sensitive learning, and ensemble methods, and adopting appropriate evaluation metrics, you can build models that perform well even in the presence of imbalance. These methods not only improve the accuracy and reliability of your predictions but also ensure that the models are robust and interpretable, leading to better financial decision-making.

As you continue your journey in financial modeling, remember that addressing class imbalance is not merely a technical challenge but a step towards achieving more equitable and effective models. By mastering these techniques, you can unlock the true potential of your financial data, leading to more accurate predictions and informed decisions.

## Ensemble Methods for Robust Forecasts

### Understanding Ensemble Methods

Ensemble methods are predicated on the concept that a group of weak learners can come together to form a strong learner. The collective wisdom of multiple models tends to outperform individual models, especially in complex and dynamic environments such as finance. There are several key ensemble methodologies, including bagging, boosting, and stacking, each with its unique approach to model aggregation and error reduction.

Types of Ensemble Methods

1. Bagging (Bootstrap Aggregating)
2. Boosting
3. Stacking

Bagging (Bootstrap Aggregating)

Bagging involves generating multiple subsets of the original dataset through random sampling with replacement. Each subset is used to train a separate model, typically of the same type, and the final output is obtained by averaging (for regression) or majority voting (for classification) the predictions of all models. Bagging helps reduce variance, thus preventing overfitting.

Example: Implementing Random Forests

Random Forests, an extension of bagging, creates multiple decision trees using different subsets of data and features.

```python
from sklearn.ensemble import RandomForestClassifier

from sklearn.model_selection import train_test_split

from sklearn.metrics import classification_report

Splitting the dataset

X_train, X_test, y_train, y_test = train_test_split(X, y, test_size=0.2, random_state=42)
```

```
Training a Random Forest model
rf_model = RandomForestClassifier(n_estimators=100, random_state=42)
rf_model.fit(X_train, y_train)

 Making predictions
y_pred = rf_model.predict(X_test)

Evaluation
print(classification_report(y_test, y_pred))
```

Random Forests decorrelate the individual trees by selecting random subsets of features, leading to diverse and robust predictions.

Boosting

Boosting sequentially trains models, each focusing on the errors of its predecessor. This method aims to convert weak learners into strong learners by incrementally reducing errors. Boosting methods like AdaBoost, Gradient Boosting, and XGBoost are highly effective in improving model accuracy.

Example: Implementing Gradient Boosting

Gradient Boosting builds models sequentially, each new model correcting the errors of the previous ones.

```python
```

```
from sklearn.ensemble import GradientBoostingClassifier

Training a Gradient Boosting model
gb_model = GradientBoostingClassifier(n_estimators=100, learning_rate=0.1, random_state=42)
gb_model.fit(X_train, y_train)

 Making predictions
y_pred = gb_model.predict(X_test)

Evaluation
print(classification_report(y_test, y_pred))
```

Gradient Boosting adjusts model weights to minimize the loss function, resulting in highly accurate predictions, albeit at the cost of increased computational complexity.

Stacking

Stacking involves training multiple models (base learners) and using their predictions as inputs to a higher-level meta-model. The meta-model synthesizes the predictions of the base learners to produce the final output, leveraging the strengths of each base learner.

Example: Implementing Stacking

```python
from sklearn.ensemble import StackingClassifier
from sklearn.linear_model import LogisticRegression
```

```
from sklearn.svm import SVC

Defining base learners
base_learners = [
    ('rf', RandomForestClassifier(n_estimators=100, random_state=42)),
    ('gb', GradientBoostingClassifier(n_estimators=100, learning_rate=0.1, random_state=42))
]

Defining meta-model
meta_model = LogisticRegression()

Training a Stacking model
stack_model = StackingClassifier(estimators=base_learners, final_estimator=meta_model)
stack_model.fit(X_train, y_train)

 Making predictions
y_pred = stack_model.predict(X_test)

Evaluation
print(classification_report(y_test, y_pred))
```

Stacking leverages diverse model architectures and learning paradigms, leading to robust and generalized predictions.

Practical Applications in Finance

Stock Price Prediction

Ensemble methods have proven highly effective in predicting stock prices, where the complexity and noise of financial markets demand robust and accurate models. By combining models like decision trees, support vector machines, and neural networks, ensemble methods capture diverse aspects of market behavior.

Credit Scoring

In credit scoring, ensemble methods help improve the accuracy of predicting loan defaults. By aggregating multiple models, these methods enhance the model's ability to identify high-risk borrowers while minimizing false positives and negatives.

Portfolio Optimization

Portfolio optimization often requires balancing multiple conflicting objectives. Ensemble methods integrate predictions from various models to provide a balanced and optimized portfolio, considering risk-return trade-offs and market conditions.

Fraud Detection

Fraud detection benefits significantly from ensemble methods' ability to handle class imbalance and rare events. Techniques like Random Forests and Gradient Boosting help identify fraudulent transactions with high precision and recall.

Case Study: Predicting Stock Prices Using Ensemble Methods

To illustrate the power of ensemble methods in finance, let's consider a case study on predicting stock prices.

Dataset Preparation

```python
import pandas as pd
from sklearn.preprocessing import StandardScaler

Load the dataset
data = pd.read_csv('stock_prices.csv')

Feature selection and preprocessing
X = data.drop(columns=['price'])
y = data['price']

scaler = StandardScaler()
X_scaled = scaler.fit_transform(X)
```

Model Building with Stacking

```python
Splitting the dataset
X_train, X_test, y_train, y_test = train_test_split(X_scaled, y, test_size=0.2, random_state=42)
```

```
Defining base learners
base_learners = [
    ('rf', RandomForestRegressor(n_estimators=100, random_state=42)),
    ('gb', GradientBoostingRegressor(n_estimators=100, learning_rate=0.1, random_state=42))
]

Defining meta-model
meta_model = LinearRegression()

Training a Stacking model
stack_model = StackingRegressor(estimators=base_learners, final_estimator=meta_model)
stack_model.fit(X_train, y_train)

 Making predictions
y_pred = stack_model.predict(X_test)

Evaluation
from sklearn.metrics import mean_squared_error

mse = mean_squared_error(y_test, y_pred)
print(f'Mean Squared Error: {mse}')
```

In this case study, stacking demonstrates how integrating predictions from various models, including Random Forest and Gradient Boosting, leads to more accurate stock price forecasts.

Ensemble Methods as a Game-Changer in Financial Forecasting

Ensemble methods offer a powerful toolkit for financial forecasting, combining the strengths of different models to produce robust and reliable predictions. By employing techniques such as bagging, boosting, and stacking, financial analysts can enhance their predictive capabilities, reduce errors, and make more informed decisions. As financial markets continue to evolve in complexity, the adaptability and effectiveness of ensemble methods will remain indispensable, guiding practitioners towards greater accuracy and success.

These methods not only improve model performance but also provide a safeguard against the inherent uncertainties and volatilities of financial markets. Mastering ensemble techniques equips you with the tools to navigate these challenges, ensuring your financial models are not just accurate but resilient and insightful.

## 0.53sub 9. Practical Considerations in Hyperparameter Tuning

Understanding Hyperparameters

Hyperparameters are the settings that govern the training process of a machine learning model. Unlike model parameters, which are learned during training, hyperparameters are set prior to the learning process. Examples include the learning rate in gradient descent, the number of trees in a random forest, and the penalty term in regularized regression. Choosing the right hyperparameters can drastically affect a model's performance, making it imperative to approach tuning methodically.

Strategies for Hyperparameter Tuning

1. Grid Search: This brute-force method involves specifying a set of hyperparameter values and exhaustively searching through all possible combinations. While thorough, grid search can be computationally expensive, especially with a large number of hyperparameters or values.

```python
from sklearn.model_selection import GridSearchCV
from sklearn.ensemble import RandomForestClassifier

 Define the model
rf = RandomForestClassifier()

 Define the hyperparameters grid
param_grid = {
    'n_estimators': [100, 200, 300],
    'max_depth': [None, 10, 20, 30],
    'min_samples_split': [2, 5, 10]
}

 Set up the grid search
```

```
grid_search = GridSearchCV(estimator=rf, param_grid=param_grid, cv=5, scoring='accuracy', n_jobs=-1)

Fit the grid search
grid_search.fit(X_train, y_train)

Best hyperparameters
print("Best Hyperparameters:", grid_search.best_params_)
```

2. Random Search: Instead of exhaustively searching all combinations, random search samples a fixed number of hyperparameter settings from the specified distributions. This method is often more efficient and can find good solutions with fewer iterations.

```python
from sklearn.model_selection import RandomizedSearchCV

Define the random search
random_search = RandomizedSearchCV(estimator=rf, param_distributions=param_grid, n_iter=100, cv=5, scoring='accuracy', n_jobs=-1, random_state=42)

Fit the random search
random_search.fit(X_train, y_train)

Best hyperparameters
print("Best Hyperparameters:", random_search.best_params_)
```

```

3. Bayesian Optimization: This advanced method uses probabilistic models to predict the performance of hyperparameter configurations. It iteratively updates its beliefs based on observed performance, efficiently navigating the hyperparameter space.

```python
from skopt import BayesSearchCV

Define the Bayesian search
bayes_search = BayesSearchCV(estimator=rf, search_spaces=param_grid, n_iter=32, cv=5, scoring='accuracy', n_jobs=-1)

Fit the Bayesian search
bayes_search.fit(X_train, y_train)

Best hyperparameters
print("Best Hyperparameters:", bayes_search.best_params_)
```

Best Practices for Hyperparameter Tuning

1. Start Simple: Begin with a simple model and a small hyperparameter grid. Gradually increase complexity as you gain more insights into the model's behavior.

2. Use Cross-Validation: Employ cross-validation to assess
```

the model's performance across different datasets. This helps ensure that the hyperparameters generalize well to unseen data.

3. Monitor Overfitting: Regularly check for overfitting by comparing training and validation performance. Overfitting can often be mitigated by adjusting hyperparameters related to regularization or model complexity.

4. Leverage Computational Resources: Utilize parallel processing and distributed computing to expedite the tuning process. Tools like Dask and joblib can help distribute the workload across multiple cores or machines.

5. Iterative Tuning: Hyperparameter tuning is often an iterative process. Start with a coarse search to identify promising regions in the hyperparameter space, followed by a finer search within those regions.

6. Domain Expertise: Incorporate domain knowledge when setting up hyperparameter ranges. For instance, in finance, certain hyperparameters may have known effective ranges based on historical data and established practices.

7. Consider Model Stability: Financial data can be volatile. Ensure that your hyperparameters lead to stable and consistent model performance across different time periods and market conditions.

Practical Example: Tuning a Gradient Boosting Model for Credit Scoring

Credit scoring models are critical in finance for assessing the creditworthiness of individuals or entities. Let's walk through a practical example of tuning a gradient boosting model for this application.

```python
from sklearn.ensemble import GradientBoostingClassifier
from sklearn.model_selection import GridSearchCV

Define the model
gb = GradientBoostingClassifier()

Define the hyperparameters grid
param_grid = {
    'n_estimators': [50, 100, 150],
    'learning_rate': [0.01, 0.1, 0.2],
    'max_depth': [3, 5, 7],
    'subsample': [0.8, 1.0]
}

Set up the grid search
grid_search = GridSearchCV(estimator=gb, param_grid=param_grid, cv=5, scoring='roc_auc', n_jobs=-1)

Fit the grid search
grid_search.fit(X_train, y_train)

Best hyperparameters
print("Best Hyperparameters:", grid_search.best_params_)
```

```
Evaluate the best model
best_model = grid_search.best_estimator_
y_pred = best_model.predict(X_test)
roc_auc_score = roc_auc_score(y_test, y_pred)
print("Test ROC AUC Score:", roc_auc_score)
```

In this example, we use the ROC AUC score as the evaluation metric, which is particularly useful for imbalanced datasets common in credit scoring.

By following these practical considerations and employing the right strategies, you can effectively tune hyperparameters to enhance the performance and reliability of your financial models. This meticulous approach to hyperparameter tuning will ensure that your models are not only accurate but also robust and dependable in the dynamic world of finance.

## 0.54sub 10. Case Study: Hyperparameter Tuning for Credit Scoring Models

In the world of finance, credit scoring models hold a pivotal role in assessing the creditworthiness of individuals and entities. These models inform decisions that can range from loan approvals to interest rate settings. The efficacy of such models heavily relies on precise hyperparameter tuning, ensuring that predictions are both accurate and reliable. In this detailed case study, we will explore the nuances of hyperparameter tuning for a credit scoring model using the Gradient Boosting Classifier (GBC) from Scikit-Learn.

## The Credit Scoring Scenario

Imagine a financial institution aiming to refine its credit scoring system to minimize defaults and maximize repayment rates. The dataset comprises various features, including credit history, loan amount, income level, and demographic details. The target variable indicates whether a borrower defaults on a loan.

Dataset Overview:

- Features: Credit history, income level, loan amount, age, employment status, etc.
- Target: Loan default (1 for default, 0 for no default)

## Step-by-Step Guide to Hyperparameter Tuning

### Step 1: Data Preparation

Before diving into hyperparameter tuning, the data must be preprocessed and split into training and testing sets.

```python
import pandas as pd
from sklearn.model_selection import train_test_split

Load the dataset
data = pd.read_csv('credit_data.csv')

Feature and target separation
X = data.drop('default', axis=1)
```

```
y = data['default']

Train-test split
X_train, X_test, y_train, y_test = train_test_split(X, y, test_size=0.2, random_state=42)
```

Step 2: Initializing the Gradient Boosting Classifier

We begin by setting up the Gradient Boosting Classifier, a powerful ensemble method ideal for this scenario.

```python
from sklearn.ensemble import GradientBoostingClassifier

Initialize the model
gb = GradientBoostingClassifier(random_state=42)
```

Step 3: Defining the Hyperparameter Grid

A comprehensive hyperparameter grid is crucial for effective tuning. The grid encompasses key parameters such as the number of estimators, learning rate, maximum depth, and subsample size.

```python
param_grid = {
    'n_estimators': [50, 100, 150],
    'learning_rate': [0.01, 0.1, 0.2],
```

```
    'max_depth': [3, 5, 7],
    'subsample': [0.8, 1.0]
}
```

Step 4: Setting Up Grid Search

Grid Search is employed to systematically explore the hyperparameter combinations. We use 5-fold cross-validation to ensure robust evaluation.

```python
from sklearn.model_selection import GridSearchCV
from sklearn.metrics import roc_auc_score

Set up the grid search
grid_search = GridSearchCV(estimator=gb, param_grid=param_grid, cv=5, scoring='roc_auc', n_jobs=-1)

Fit the grid search
grid_search.fit(X_train, y_train)

Retrieve the best hyperparameters
best_params = grid_search.best_params_
print("Best Hyperparameters:", best_params)
```

Step 5: Evaluating the Best Model

Once the best hyperparameters are identified, we evaluate the model on the test set to gauge its performance.

```python
Best model
best_model = grid_search.best_estimator_

Predict on the test set
y_pred = best_model.predict(X_test)

Calculate ROC AUC score
roc_auc = roc_auc_score(y_test, y_pred)
print("Test ROC AUC Score:", roc_auc)
```

Step 6: Detailed Interpretation and Analysis

Understanding the impact of each hyperparameter is crucial. Here we delve into the significance of the selected hyperparameters:

- n_estimators: Represents the number of boosting stages. More estimators can improve performance but also increase the risk of overfitting.
- learning_rate: Controls the contribution of each tree. Lower values necessitate more trees but can enhance generalization.
- max_depth: Limits the depth of the individual trees. Deeper trees can capture more complex patterns but may overfit.
- subsample: Fraction of samples used for fitting individual base learners. Introducing subsampling can reduce variance and prevent overfitting.

Practical Insights and Best Practices

1. Iterative Refinement: Begin with a broad grid and iteratively narrow down the hyperparameter space based on initial results.

2. Regular Monitoring: Continuously monitor overfitting by comparing performance on the training and validation sets.

3. Computational Efficiency: Utilize parallel processing to speed up the grid search, especially when dealing with large datasets.

4. Domain Knowledge: Leverage domain expertise to set realistic hyperparameter ranges, reducing the search space and improving efficiency.

5. Robust Evaluation: Employ multiple evaluation metrics, such as ROC AUC, precision, recall, and F1-score, to gain a comprehensive understanding of model performance.

Hyperparameter tuning is not just a technical exercise—it is a blend of art and science, requiring meticulous attention to detail and a deep understanding of both machine learning techniques and domain-specific knowledge. By following the outlined steps and best practices, you can optimize your credit scoring models, ensuring they are not only accurate but also robust and reliable in the dynamic financial landscape. This meticulous approach to hyperparameter tuning will significantly enhance your ability to make informed, data-driven decisions, ultimately translating to improved financial outcomes.

# CHAPTER 6: TIME SERIES FORECASTING

Time series data is ubiquitous and critical. It encompasses a sequence of data points indexed in temporal order, reflecting how financial variables evolve over time. From stock prices and interest rates to economic indicators and trading volumes, time series data forms the backbone of financial analysis and forecasting. Understanding its nuances is paramount for any financial professional seeking to leverage machine learning for predictive insights.

Defining Time Series Data

Time series data consists of observations recorded at successive points in time, typically at uniform intervals. Unlike cross-sectional data, which provides a snapshot at a single point in time, time series data captures the dynamic behavior of financial variables, enabling the analysis of trends, cycles, and seasonal patterns.

Examples of Time Series Data in Finance:

- Stock Prices: Daily closing prices of a particular stock.

- Interest Rates: Monthly interest rates on government bonds.
- GDP Growth Rates: Quarterly GDP growth figures.

Characteristics of Time Series Data

1. Trend: The long-term movement in the data. It represents the underlying direction in which the data is moving over an extended period.
2. Seasonality: Regular, repeating patterns or cycles in the data, often tied to calendar events such as quarters, months, or days of the week.
3. Cyclic Patterns: Fluctuations in the data that occur at irregular intervals, typically influenced by economic cycles.
4. Noise: Random variations or irregularities in the data that cannot be attributed to trend, seasonality, or cycles.

Understanding these characteristics is crucial for building effective time series models. Each component must be analyzed and accounted for to create accurate and reliable forecasts.

Time Series Data in Financial Models

Financial time series data is integral to various models and analyses, including:

- Forecasting Stock Prices: Predicting future stock prices based on historical data.
- Volatility Modeling: Estimating and forecasting the volatility of financial instruments.
- Risk Management: Assessing and managing financial risks by analyzing historical returns.

- Economic Forecasting: Projecting future economic indicators like GDP growth and inflation rates.

Data Preparation for Time Series Analysis

Effective time series analysis begins with meticulous data preparation. This involves several steps:

1. Data Collection: Gathering historical data from reliable sources. Financial data can be sourced from stock exchanges, financial institutions, and government agencies.
2. Data Cleaning: Handling missing values, outliers, and inconsistencies in the data.
3. Data Transformation: Applying transformations like differencing and logarithms to stabilize variance and make the data stationary, a crucial requirement for many time series models.
4. Feature Engineering: Creating additional features that capture important aspects of the data, such as lagged variables and moving averages.

Example: Preparing Stock Price Data

Consider the example of preparing stock price data for time series analysis:

```python
import pandas as pd

Load the stock price data
data = pd.read_csv('stock_prices.csv', parse_dates=['Date'], index_col='Date')
```

```
Handle missing values by forward filling
data.fillna(method='ffill', inplace=True)

Log transformation to stabilize variance
data['Log_Close'] = np.log(data['Close'])

Differencing to make the series stationary
data['Diff_Log_Close'] = data['Log_Close'].diff().dropna()

Create lagged features
data['Lag_1'] = data['Diff_Log_Close'].shift(1)
data['Lag_2'] = data['Diff_Log_Close'].shift(2)

Drop missing values after differencing and lagging
data.dropna(inplace=True)

print(data.head())
```

Exploratory Data Analysis (EDA)

Before diving into modeling, conducting exploratory data analysis (EDA) on time series data is essential. EDA involves visualizing the data, identifying patterns, and gaining insights into its structure.

Visualization Techniques:

- Line Plots: Display the data over time to observe trends, seasonality, and anomalies.

- Autocorrelation Plots: Show the correlation of the time series with its own lagged values, helping identify seasonality and cycles.
- Decomposition Plots: Decompose the time series into trend, seasonal, and residual components for a clearer understanding.

Example: Visualizing Stock Price Data

```python
import matplotlib.pyplot as plt

import statsmodels.api as sm

Line plot

plt.figure(figsize=(10, 6))

plt.plot(data['Close'])

plt.title('Stock Prices Over Time')

plt.xlabel('Date')

plt.ylabel('Price')

plt.show()

Autocorrelation plot

sm.graphics.tsa.plot_acf(data['Diff_Log_Close'].dropna(), lags=30)

plt.show()

Seasonal decomposition

decomposition = sm.tsa.seasonal_decompose(data['Close'], model='multiplicative', period=252)  Assuming daily data with yearly seasonality
```

```
decomposition.plot()
plt.show()
```

Time Series Models

Time series data requires specialized models that account for its temporal structure. Some of the widely used time series models in finance include:

1. Autoregressive (AR) Models: Models that use past values of the variable to predict future values.
2. Moving Average (MA) Models: Models that use past forecast errors to predict future values.
3. Autoregressive Integrated Moving Average (ARIMA) Models: Combining AR and MA models with differencing to handle non-stationary data.
4. Exponential Smoothing Models: Models that apply exponentially decreasing weights to past observations.

Practical Applications in Finance

Time series models are applied across various financial domains:

- High-Frequency Trading: Predicting short-term price movements based on historical tick data.
- Portfolio Management: Forecasting asset returns and volatilities to optimize portfolio allocation.
- Economic Policy Analysis: Projecting economic indicators to inform policy decisions.

Embracing the complexity and potential of time series data, you position yourself at the forefront of financial innovation. This understanding lays the foundation for more advanced topics, such as time series forecasting, explored in subsequent sections.

Seasonal and Trend Decomposition

Seasonal and trend decomposition breaks down a time series into three fundamental components:

1. Trend Component (T): Represents the long-term progression of the series. It captures the underlying movement, whether upward or downward, over an extended period.
2. Seasonal Component (S): Reflects regular, repeating patterns within fixed periods, such as quarters, months, or days. This component is crucial in finance, where seasonal effects can be driven by fiscal quarters, holidays, or market cycles.
3. Residual (or Irregular) Component (R): Accounts for the random, irregular fluctuations that cannot be explained by the trend or seasonal components. This noise represents the unpredictable variations in the data.

The decomposition of a time series can follow either an additive or multiplicative model:

- Additive Model: Assumes that the components add together linearly.

$$ Y(t) = T(t) + S(t) + R(t) $$

- Multiplicative Model: Assumes that the components multiply together, often used when the seasonal variations change proportionally with the trend.

$$Y(t) = T(t) \times S(t) \times R(t)$$

Methods of Decomposition

Several methods exist for decomposing time series data, with two of the most prominent being Classical Decomposition and Seasonal-Trend Decomposition using Loess (STL).

Classical Decomposition:

Classical decomposition involves the following steps:

1. Estimate the Trend Component: Apply a moving average to smooth the series, isolating the long-term trend.
2. Isolate the Seasonal Component: Subtract the trend component from the original series and average the resulting detrended series over the period of seasonality.
3. Calculate the Residual Component: Subtract both the trend and seasonal components from the original series to obtain the residual component.

Example using Python:

```python
import pandas as pd

import numpy as np

import matplotlib.pyplot as plt

Load the financial time series data

data = pd.read_csv('financial_data.csv', parse_dates=['Date'], index_col='Date')
```

Apply a moving average to estimate the trend component

```
data['Trend'] = data['Value'].rolling(window=12, center=True).mean()
```

Detrend the series

```
data['Detrended'] = data['Value'] - data['Trend']
```

Estimate the seasonal component by averaging the detrended series

```
data['Seasonal'] = data['Detrended'].groupby(data.index.month).transform('mean')
```

Calculate the residual component

```
data['Residual'] = data['Value'] - data['Trend'] - data['Seasonal']
```

Plot the decomposed components

```
plt.figure(figsize=(12, 8))
plt.subplot(411)
plt.plot(data['Value'], label='Original')
plt.legend(loc='upper left')
plt.subplot(412)
plt.plot(data['Trend'], label='Trend')
plt.legend(loc='upper left')
plt.subplot(413)
plt.plot(data['Seasonal'], label='Seasonal')
plt.legend(loc='upper left')
plt.subplot(414)
```

```
plt.plot(data['Residual'], label='Residual')
plt.legend(loc='upper left')
plt.tight_layout()
plt.show()
```

Seasonal-Trend Decomposition using Loess (STL):

STL is a more flexible and robust method compared to classical decomposition. It uses locally weighted regression (Loess) to iteratively estimate and remove the trend and seasonal components, accommodating non-linear trends and complex seasonal patterns.

Example using Python:

```python
from statsmodels.tsa.seasonal import STL

Apply STL decomposition
stl = STL(data['Value'], seasonal=13)
result = stl.fit()

Extract the components
trend = result.trend
seasonal = result.seasonal
residual = result.resid

Plot the decomposed components
plt.figure(figsize=(12, 8))
```

```
plt.subplot(411)
plt.plot(data['Value'], label='Original')
plt.legend(loc='upper left')
plt.subplot(412)
plt.plot(trend, label='Trend')
plt.legend(loc='upper left')
plt.subplot(413)
plt.plot(seasonal, label='Seasonal')
plt.legend(loc='upper left')
plt.subplot(414)
plt.plot(residual, label='Residual')
plt.legend(loc='upper left')
plt.tight_layout()
plt.show()
```

Practical Applications of Seasonal and Trend Decomposition in Finance

1. Stock Price Analysis:

Decomposing stock prices helps in understanding the underlying trends and seasonal patterns that influence price movements. For instance, retail stocks often show seasonality driven by holiday shopping periods, while technology stocks may exhibit trends related to product release cycles.

2. Economic Indicators:

Economic time series, such as GDP growth rates or unemployment rates, often exhibit seasonal patterns linked to fiscal quarters and other periodic factors. Decomposing these series can provide clearer insights for economic policy analysis and forecasting.

3. Volatility Modeling:

Understanding the trend and seasonal components of volatility can enhance risk management practices. For example, volatility often increases during specific periods, such as earnings announcements or economic downturns. Decomposing volatility time series helps in isolating these effects and improving forecasts.

4. Sales Forecasting:

Financial institutions and businesses use seasonal decomposition to forecast sales and revenue, accounting for regular patterns like end-of-quarter surges or holiday spikes. This enables more accurate budgeting, inventory management, and strategic planning.

Autoregressive Models (AR)

An autoregressive model predicts the value of a variable based on its own previous values. The fundamental idea is that past values have a linear relationship with the current value. The AR model can be formally defined as follows:

$$ Y_t = c + \sum_{i=1}^{p} \phi_i Y_{t-i} + \epsilon_t $$

where:

- $Y_t$ is the value of the time series at time $t$.
- $c$ is a constant term.
- $\phi_i$ are the coefficients of the model.

- $p$ is the order of the autoregressive model, indicating how many previous time steps are considered.
- $\epsilon_t$ is the error term, assumed to be white noise.

The primary task in developing an AR model is to determine the appropriate order $p$ and estimate the coefficients $\phi_i$.

Estimating the Order of the AR Model

The order $p$ of an AR model can be selected using criteria such as the Akaike Information Criterion (AIC), the Bayesian Information Criterion (BIC), or the Partial Autocorrelation Function (PACF). The PACF helps in identifying the number of significant lags to include in the model.

Example: Determining the Order Using PACF

```python
import pandas as pd

import numpy as np

import matplotlib.pyplot as plt

from statsmodels.graphics.tsaplots import plot_pacf

Load the financial time series data

data = pd.read_csv('financial_data.csv', parse_dates=['Date'], index_col='Date')

Plot the PACF

plot_pacf(data['Value'], lags=20)

plt.show()
```

## Building and Fitting an AR Model

Once the order $p$ is determined, the next step is to fit the AR model to the data. This involves estimating the coefficients $\phi_i$ and the constant term $c$. The method of least squares is commonly used for this purpose.

### Example: Fitting an AR Model

```python
from statsmodels.tsa.ar_model import AutoReg

Determine the order of the model
p = 3  Example order, determined from PACF

Fit the AR model
model = AutoReg(data['Value'], lags=p)
model_fit = model.fit()

Print the model summary
print(model_fit.summary())
```

## Evaluating the Model

After fitting the AR model, it is essential to evaluate its performance using various metrics and diagnostic plots. Commonly used metrics include Mean Absolute Error (MAE), Mean Squared Error (MSE), and Root Mean Squared Error

(RMSE). Diagnostic plots such as residual plots and the Q-Q plot are also useful for assessing model assumptions.

Example: Evaluating the AR Model

```python
from sklearn.metrics import mean_squared_error
import statsmodels.api as sm

Make predictions
data['Predicted'] = model_fit.predict(start=p, end=len(data)-1)

Calculate the RMSE
rmse = np.sqrt(mean_squared_error(data['Value'][p:], data['Predicted'][p:]))
print(f'RMSE: {rmse}')

Plot the original and predicted values
plt.figure(figsize=(12, 6))
plt.plot(data['Value'], label='Original')
plt.plot(data['Predicted'], label='Predicted', linestyle='--')
plt.legend()
plt.show()

Diagnostic plots
sm.graphics.qqplot(model_fit.resid, line='s')
plt.show()
sm.graphics.tsa.plot_acf(model_fit.resid)
plt.show()
```

` ` `

Practical Applications of Autoregressive Models in Finance

1. Stock Price Prediction:

AR models are widely used to forecast stock prices based on historical data. By capturing the temporal dependencies in price movements, AR models can provide valuable insights for trading strategies and risk management.

2. Interest Rate Forecasting:

Interest rates often exhibit autoregressive behavior, making AR models suitable for predicting future rates. Accurate forecasts of interest rates are crucial for portfolio management, bond pricing, and financial planning.

3. Volatility Modeling:

In financial markets, volatility tends to cluster, meaning periods of high volatility are followed by more high volatility, and the same for low volatility. AR models can capture this behavior, aiding in the prediction of future volatility and the assessment of risk.

4. Economic Indicators:

Economic time series, such as GDP growth rates, inflation rates, and unemployment rates, often follow autoregressive patterns. AR models help in forecasting these indicators, providing valuable inputs for economic policy and business planning.

With a solid grasp of autoregressive models, you are now well-equipped to explore more advanced time series forecasting techniques. This knowledge will be invaluable as you delve into financial data analysis and prediction in the subsequent sections.

## Moving Average Models (MA)

A Moving Average (MA) model predicts the value of a variable by averaging past error terms. The rationale behind MA models is that the current value of a time series can be expressed as a linear combination of past white noise error terms. An MA model of order $q$ can be formally defined as follows:

$$Y_t = \mu + \epsilon_t + \theta_1 \epsilon_{t-1} + \theta_2 \epsilon_{t-2} + \ldots + \theta_q \epsilon_{t-q}$$

where:

- $Y_t$ is the value of the time series at time $t$.
- $\mu$ is the mean of the series.
- $\epsilon_t$ is the white noise error term at time $t$.
- $\theta_i$ are the coefficients of the model.
- $q$ is the order of the Moving Average model, indicating how many past error terms are considered.

The key task in developing an MA model is to determine the appropriate order $q$ and estimate the coefficients $\theta_i$.

### Estimating the Order of the MA Model

The order $q$ of an MA model can be selected using criteria such as the Akaike Information Criterion (AIC), the Bayesian Information Criterion (BIC), or the Autocorrelation Function (ACF). The ACF helps in identifying the number of significant past error terms to include in the model.

Example: Determining the Order Using ACF

```python
import pandas as pd
import numpy as np
import matplotlib.pyplot as plt
from statsmodels.graphics.tsaplots import plot_acf

Load the financial time series data
data = pd.read_csv('financial_data.csv', parse_dates=['Date'], index_col='Date')

Plot the ACF
plot_acf(data['Value'], lags=20)
plt.show()
```

Building and Fitting an MA Model

Once the order $q$ is determined, the next step is to fit the MA model to the data. This involves estimating the coefficients $\theta_i$ and the mean term $\mu$. The method of maximum likelihood is commonly used for this purpose.

Example: Fitting an MA Model

```python
from statsmodels.tsa.arima.model import ARIMA

Determine the order of the model
q = 2  Example order, determined from ACF

Fit the MA model
model = ARIMA(data['Value'], order=(0, 0, q))
model_fit = model.fit()

Print the model summary
print(model_fit.summary())
```

Evaluating the Model

After fitting the MA model, it is essential to evaluate its performance using various metrics and diagnostic plots. Commonly used metrics include Mean Absolute Error (MAE), Mean Squared Error (MSE), and Root Mean Squared Error (RMSE). Diagnostic plots such as residual plots and the Q-Q plot are also useful for assessing model assumptions.

Example: Evaluating the MA Model

```python
from sklearn.metrics import mean_squared_error
```

```
import statsmodels.api as sm

Make predictions
data['Predicted'] = model_fit.predict(start=q, end=len(data)-1)

Calculate the RMSE
rmse = np.sqrt(mean_squared_error(data['Value'][q:], data['Predicted'][q:]))
print(f'RMSE: {rmse}')

Plot the original and predicted values
plt.figure(figsize=(12, 6))
plt.plot(data['Value'], label='Original')
plt.plot(data['Predicted'], label='Predicted', linestyle='--')
plt.legend()
plt.show()

Diagnostic plots
sm.graphics.qqplot(model_fit.resid, line='s')
plt.show()
sm.graphics.tsa.plot_acf(model_fit.resid)
plt.show()
```

Practical Applications of Moving Average Models in Finance

1. Stock Price Smoothing:

MA models are frequently used to smooth stock prices, filtering out short-term noise and highlighting long-term trends. This is particularly useful for identifying support and resistance levels, making informed trading decisions, and developing trend-following strategies.

2. Volatility Modeling:

In financial markets, periods of high volatility are often followed by more high volatility, and the same for low volatility. MA models can capture and forecast this behavior, aiding in risk management and the development of volatility-based trading strategies.

3. Economic Indicator Analysis:

Economic indicators, such as inflation rates and unemployment rates, often show temporal dependencies that can be modeled using MA models. By capturing these dependencies, MA models assist in forecasting future economic conditions and informing policy decisions.

4. Interest Rate Forecasting:

Interest rates exhibit mean-reverting behavior, making them suitable for modeling with MA models. Accurate interest rate forecasts are crucial for bond pricing, portfolio management, and financial planning.

Armed with the knowledge of Moving Average models, you are now prepared to delve into more sophisticated time series forecasting techniques. This expertise will be invaluable as you continue to explore financial data analysis and prediction in the subsequent sections.

Autoregressive Integrated Moving Average (ARIMA)

The ARIMA model is a comprehensive approach that combines

three key components: Autoregression (AR), Integration (I), and Moving Average (MA). Each component plays a critical role in modeling different aspects of the time series data:

1. Autoregression (AR): The AR part of the model involves regressing the variable against its own lagged values. An AR model of order $p$ can be represented as:

$$Y_t = \phi_1 Y_{t-1} + \phi_2 Y_{t-2} + \ldots + \phi_p Y_{t-p} + \epsilon_t$$

where $Y_t$ is the current value, $\phi_i$ are the coefficients, and $\epsilon_t$ is the white noise error term.

2. Integration (I): The I component accounts for differencing the data to achieve stationarity. Differencing helps remove trends and seasonal patterns. If the data needs to be differenced $d$ times to become stationary, the series is said to be integrated of order $d$.

3. Moving Average (MA): The MA part models the dependency between a variable and the residual errors from a moving average model applied to lagged observations. An MA model of order $q$ is given by:

$$Y_t = \mu + \epsilon_t + \theta_1 \epsilon_{t-1} + \theta_2 \epsilon_{t-2} + \ldots + \theta_q \epsilon_{t-q}$$

where $\theta_i$ are the coefficients.

The general form of an ARIMA model is denoted as ARIMA($p, d, q$), where $p$ is the order of the AR part, $d$ is the degree of differencing, and $q$ is the order of the MA part.

Identifying the Order of ARIMA Model

The order of the ARIMA model components (\( p, d, q \)) can be identified using several techniques, including:

1. Autocorrelation Function (ACF): Helps determine the order of \( q \) by examining the correlation between the current value and its lagged values.
2. Partial Autocorrelation Function (PACF): Assists in identifying the order of \( p \) by measuring the correlation between the current value and its lagged values, after removing the effects of intermediate lags.
3. Differencing and Stationarity Tests: The Augmented Dickey-Fuller (ADF) test is commonly used to determine the degree of differencing (\( d \)) required to make the series stationary.

Example: Identifying the Order Using ACF and PACF

```python
import pandas as pd

import numpy as np

import matplotlib.pyplot as plt

from statsmodels.graphics.tsaplots import plot_acf, plot_pacf

from statsmodels.tsa.stattools import adfuller

Load the financial time series data

data = pd.read_csv('financial_data.csv', parse_dates=['Date'], index_col='Date')

Check for stationarity using ADF test

result = adfuller(data['Value'])

print(f'ADF Statistic: {result[0]}')
```

```
print(f'p-value: {result[1]}')

Plot ACF and PACF
fig, axes = plt.subplots(1, 2, figsize=(16, 6))
plot_acf(data['Value'], lags=20, ax=axes[0])
plot_pacf(data['Value'], lags=20, ax=axes[1])
plt.show()
```

Building and Fitting an ARIMA Model

Once the orders \( p, d, q \) are determined, the ARIMA model can be built and fitted to the data. The `statsmodels` library in Python provides robust tools for this purpose.

Example: Fitting an ARIMA Model

```python
from statsmodels.tsa.arima.model import ARIMA

Define the order of the model
p, d, q = 2, 1, 2  Example orders

Fit the ARIMA model
model = ARIMA(data['Value'], order=(p, d, q))
model_fit = model.fit()

Print the model summary
print(model_fit.summary())
```

```
```

## Forecasting with ARIMA

Forecasting future values is one of the primary applications of ARIMA models. After fitting the model, predictions can be made for future time points, providing valuable insights for financial decision-making.

Example: Forecasting with ARIMA

```python
Forecast future values
forecast_steps = 10
forecast = model_fit.forecast(steps=forecast_steps)

Plot the original data and the forecast
plt.figure(figsize=(12, 6))
plt.plot(data['Value'], label='Original')
plt.plot(pd.date_range(data.index[-1], periods=forecast_steps, freq='D'), forecast, label='Forecast', linestyle='--')
plt.legend()
plt.show()
```

## Evaluating the ARIMA Model

Evaluation of the ARIMA model's performance is crucial to ensure its reliability. Commonly used metrics include Mean Absolute Error (MAE), Mean Squared Error (MSE), and Root

Mean Squared Error (RMSE). Residual diagnostics are also performed to check for normality and independence of residuals.

Example: Evaluating the ARIMA Model

```python
from sklearn.metrics import mean_absolute_error, mean_squared_error

Calculate the forecast errors
forecast_errors = data['Value'].iloc[-forecast_steps:] - forecast

Calculate evaluation metrics
mae = mean_absolute_error(data['Value'].iloc[-forecast_steps:], forecast)
mse = mean_squared_error(data['Value'].iloc[-forecast_steps:], forecast)
rmse = np.sqrt(mse)
print(f'MAE: {mae}')
print(f'MSE: {mse}')
print(f'RMSE: {rmse}')

Plot residual diagnostics
sm.graphics.qqplot(model_fit.resid, line='s')
plt.show()
sm.graphics.tsa.plot_acf(model_fit.resid)
plt.show()
```

Practical Applications of ARIMA Models in Finance

1. Stock Price Forecasting:

ARIMA models are widely used to forecast stock prices by analyzing historical price data. Accurate stock price predictions can inform trading strategies and investment decisions.

2. Economic Time Series Analysis:

Economic indicators such as GDP, inflation rates, and unemployment rates often exhibit temporal patterns that can be effectively modeled using ARIMA. This helps in forecasting economic conditions and planning accordingly.

3. Interest Rate Modeling:

Interest rates typically show mean-reverting behavior, making them suitable for ARIMA modeling. Accurate interest rate forecasts are essential for bond pricing and portfolio management.

4. Demand Forecasting:

Financial institutions use ARIMA models to forecast demand for various financial products, aiding in resource allocation and strategic planning.

The Autoregressive Integrated Moving Average (ARIMA) model is a powerful and versatile tool for financial time series forecasting. By understanding its components and mastering its implementation, you can significantly enhance your ability to predict and analyze financial data. The practical examples and methodologies discussed here provide a solid foundation for leveraging ARIMA models in various financial applications.

## Exponential Smoothing Methods

Exponential smoothing methods revolve around the concept of weighted averages, where more recent observations receive higher weights. This approach allows the model to be more responsive to recent changes, making it ideal for forecasting financial data which often exhibits rapid fluctuations.

The general formula for simple exponential smoothing can be expressed as:

$$S_t = \alpha Y_t + (1 - \alpha) S_{t-1}$$

where:

- $S_t$ is the smoothed statistic at time $t$,
- $Y_t$ is the actual value at time $t$,
- $\alpha$ (alpha) is the smoothing factor, ranging between 0 and 1.

## Types of Exponential Smoothing

1. Simple Exponential Smoothing (SES): Suitable for time series data without trends or seasonality. It applies a single smoothing parameter $\alpha$.

2. Holt's Linear Trend Model: An extension of SES that includes a trend component, making it suitable for data with a linear trend. It uses two smoothing parameters: $\alpha$ for the level and $\beta$ for the trend.

$$S_t = \alpha Y_t + (1 - \alpha)(S_{t-1} + T_{t-1})$$

$$T_t = \beta (S_t - S_{t-1}) + (1 - \beta) T_{t-1}$$

where $T_t$ represents the trend estimate at time $t$.

3. Holt-Winters Seasonal Model: This method extends Holt's model by incorporating a seasonal component, making it apt for series with trends and seasonality. There are two variations: additive and multiplicative.

- Additive Model:

$$S_t = \alpha (Y_t - I_{t-L}) + (1 - \alpha) (S_{t-1} + T_{t-1})$$

$$T_t = \beta (S_t - S_{t-1}) + (1 - \beta) T_{t-1}$$

$$I_t = \gamma (Y_t - S_t) + (1 - \gamma) I_{t-L}$$

- Multiplicative Model:

$$S_t = \alpha \left( \frac{Y_t}{I_{t-L}} \right) + (1 - \alpha) (S_{t-1} + T_{t-1})$$

$$T_t = \beta (S_t - S_{t-1}) + (1 - \beta) T_{t-1}$$

$$I_t = \gamma \left( \frac{Y_t}{S_t} \right) + (1 - \gamma) I_{t-L}$$

where $I_t$ represents the seasonal component, and $L$ is the length of the seasonality cycle.

Implementing Exponential Smoothing in Python

The `statsmodels` library in Python provides comprehensive tools for implementing exponential smoothing methods. Below are examples showcasing the implementation of various exponential smoothing techniques.

Example: Simple Exponential Smoothing (SES)

```python
import pandas as pd
import numpy as np
```

```
import matplotlib.pyplot as plt
from statsmodels.tsa.holtwinters import SimpleExpSmoothing

Load the financial time series data
data = pd.read_csv('financial_data.csv', parse_dates=['Date'], index_col='Date')

Fit the SES model
model = SimpleExpSmoothing(data['Value']).fit(smoothing_level=0.2, optimized=False)

Forecast future values
forecast = model.forecast(steps=10)

Plot the original data and the forecast
plt.figure(figsize=(12, 6))
plt.plot(data['Value'], label='Original')
plt.plot(forecast, label='Forecast', linestyle='--')
plt.legend()
plt.show()
```

Example: Holt's Linear Trend Model

```python
from statsmodels.tsa.holtwinters import Holt

Fit Holt's linear trend model
```

```
model = Holt(data['Value']).fit(smoothing_level=0.8, smoothing_slope=0.2)

Forecast future values
forecast = model.forecast(steps=10)

Plot the original data and the forecast
plt.figure(figsize=(12, 6))
plt.plot(data['Value'], label='Original')
plt.plot(forecast, label='Forecast', linestyle='--')
plt.legend()
plt.show()
```

Example: Holt-Winters Seasonal Model

```python
from statsmodels.tsa.holtwinters import ExponentialSmoothing

Fit Holt-Winters seasonal model
model = ExponentialSmoothing(data['Value'], seasonal='add', seasonal_periods=12).fit()

Forecast future values
forecast = model.forecast(steps=12)

Plot the original data and the forecast
plt.figure(figsize=(12, 6))
```

```
plt.plot(data['Value'], label='Original')
plt.plot(forecast, label='Forecast', linestyle='--')
plt.legend()
plt.show()
```

Evaluating Exponential Smoothing Models

The performance of exponential smoothing models can be evaluated using similar metrics as those for ARIMA models, including MAE, MSE, and RMSE. Residual diagnostics are also essential to ensure the model's validity.

Example: Evaluating a Holt-Winters Model

```python
from sklearn.metrics import mean_absolute_error, mean_squared_error

Calculate the forecast errors
forecast_errors = data['Value'].iloc[-12:] - forecast

Calculate evaluation metrics
mae = mean_absolute_error(data['Value'].iloc[-12:], forecast)
mse = mean_squared_error(data['Value'].iloc[-12:], forecast)
rmse = np.sqrt(mse)
print(f'MAE: {mae}')
print(f'MSE: {mse}')
print(f'RMSE: {rmse}')
```

```
Plot residual diagnostics
import statsmodels.api as sm
sm.graphics.qqplot(model.resid, line='s')
plt.show()
sm.graphics.tsa.plot_acf(model.resid)
plt.show()
```

Practical Applications of Exponential Smoothing in Finance

1. Stock Price Forecasting:

Exponential smoothing methods are frequently used for short-term stock price forecasts due to their ability to quickly adapt to recent changes.

2. Revenue and Sales Forecasting:

Financial analysts use these methods to predict future revenues and sales, aiding in budgeting and strategic planning.

3. Inventory Management:

Accurate demand forecasts are crucial for inventory management. Exponential smoothing helps in predicting future demand, optimizing stock levels, and reducing holding costs.

4. Risk Management:

In financial risk management, exponential smoothing can model and forecast volatility and other risk metrics, providing insights for hedging strategies.

Exponential smoothing methods are invaluable tools in the arsenal of financial analysts. Their ability to handle trends and seasonality with simplicity and efficiency makes them particularly suited for the dynamic nature of financial data. By mastering these techniques and their practical applications, you can significantly enhance your forecasting capabilities and make more informed financial decisions.

Equipped with exponential smoothing techniques, you are well-prepared to explore advanced time series forecasting methods. Continue to build on this foundation to navigate the complexities of financial data analysis and prediction with confidence.

## Evaluation Metrics for Time Series Forecasts

One of the most straightforward metrics, Mean Absolute Error (MAE), measures the average magnitude of errors in a set of predictions, without considering their direction. It is calculated as follows:

$$ {MAE} = \frac{1}{n} \sum_{t=1}^n | y_t - \hat{y}_t | $$

Where:

- $y_t$ is the actual value at time $t$
- $\hat{y}_t$ is the forecasted value at time $t$
- $n$ is the number of observations

MAE provides a clear indication of the average error magnitude, making it particularly useful when you need an easily interpretable metric that conveys the typical deviation between your forecasts and actual values.

Mean Squared Error (MSE)

Another fundamental metric is the Mean Squared Error (MSE), which measures the average of the squared differences between predicted and actual values. It is defined as:

$$\text{MSE} = \frac{1}{n} \sum_{t=1}^n (y_t - \hat{y}_t)^2$$

The squaring of errors has the effect of penalizing larger errors more than smaller ones, making MSE particularly sensitive to outliers. This sensitivity can be both an advantage and a disadvantage, depending on the nature of your data and the specific requirements of your forecasting task.

Root Mean Squared Error (RMSE)

Root Mean Squared Error (RMSE) is a derivative of MSE, providing a measure of error in the same units as the original data by taking the square root of MSE. It is calculated as follows:

$$\text{RMSE} = \sqrt{\frac{1}{n} \sum_{t=1}^n (y_t - \hat{y}_t)^2}$$

RMSE is widely used due to its interpretability and the emphasis it places on large errors, similar to MSE. However, unlike MSE, it presents the error in the same scale as the data, making it more intuitive.

### Mean Absolute Percentage Error (MAPE)

Mean Absolute Percentage Error (MAPE) expresses the error as a percentage of the actual values, which can be particularly informative when comparing the accuracy of models across different datasets or scales. It is calculated as:

$$ \text{MAPE} = \frac{100\%}{n} \sum_{t=1}^n \left| \frac{y_t - \hat{y}_t}{y_t} \right| $$

While MAPE provides a normalized measure of error, it can be problematic when actual values are close to zero, leading to inflated error percentages.

### Mean Directional Accuracy (MDA)

Mean Directional Accuracy (MDA) is a less common but insightful metric that measures the percentage of times the predicted direction of change coincides with the actual direction of change. It is calculated as:

$$ \text{MDA} = \frac{1}{n} \sum_{t=1}^n \mathbf{1}[(y_t - y_{t-1})(\hat{y}_t - y_{t-1}) > 0] $$

Where $\mathbf{1}$ is an indicator function that returns 1 if the condition is true and 0 otherwise. MDA is particularly useful in financial contexts where the direction of change is more critical than the magnitude of error.

### Symmetric Mean Absolute Percentage Error (sMAPE)

To address the issues associated with MAPE, the Symmetric Mean Absolute Percentage Error (sMAPE) offers an alternative that avoids the problem of division by zero. It is defined as:

$$\text{sMAPE} = \frac{100\%}{n} \sum_{t=1}^n \frac{| y_t - \hat{y}_t |}{(| y_t | + | \hat{y}_t |) / 2}$$

sMAPE ensures a balanced view of error rates, making it useful for datasets with varying scales.

R-squared (Coefficient of Determination)

R-squared measures the proportion of the variance in the dependent variable that is predictable from the independent variables. For time series forecasting, it is adapted as follows:

$$R^2 = 1 - \frac{\sum_{t=1}^n (y_t - \hat{y}_t)^2}{\sum_{t=1}^n (y_t - \bar{y})^2}$$

Where $\bar{y}$ is the mean of the actual values. An R-squared value of 1 indicates a perfect fit, while a value close to 0 suggests that the model does not explain much of the variance.

Practical Application and Example

Consider the following Python code example to illustrate the evaluation of a time series forecast using Scikit-Learn:

```python
import numpy as np
```

```
from sklearn.metrics import mean_absolute_error, mean_squared_error, r2_score

Example actual and forecasted values
y_actual = np.array([120, 130, 125, 140, 135])
y_forecast = np.array([118, 133, 124, 138, 137])

Calculate metrics
mae = mean_absolute_error(y_actual, y_forecast)
mse = mean_squared_error(y_actual, y_forecast)
rmse = np.sqrt(mse)
r2 = r2_score(y_actual, y_forecast)

print(f"MAE: {mae}")
print(f"MSE: {mse}")
print(f"RMSE: {rmse}")
print(f"R-squared: {r2}")
```

This code snippet demonstrates how to compute MAE, MSE, RMSE, and R-squared values, providing a practical framework for evaluating your time series models.

choosing the right evaluation metric depends on the specific requirements of your financial forecasting task. Each metric has its strengths and weaknesses, and often, multiple metrics are used in tandem to gain a comprehensive understanding of model performance. By mastering these metrics, you can ensure that your time series forecasts are both accurate and reliable, equipping you with the insights needed to make informed financial decisions.

---

By integrating these evaluation techniques into your model development process, you will be better equipped to refine your forecasts and achieve greater precision in your financial analysis. As you continue to explore time series forecasting, remember that the right metrics are vital tools in your arsenal, enabling you to measure, compare, and enhance your predictive models effectively.

## 6.8 Using Scikit-Learn for Time Series Analysis

### Preparing Time Series Data

Before diving into model building, the first step is to prepare the data. Time series data often comes with its own set of challenges, such as missing values, seasonality, and trends. Let's start with a basic time series dataset and walk through the preprocessing steps.

Consider a dataset of daily closing prices for a stock:

```python
import pandas as pd

Load dataset
data = pd.read_csv('stock_prices.csv', parse_dates=['Date'], index_col='Date')
```

```
Display the first few rows
print(data.head())
```

The dataset might look like this:

| Date | Close |
|------------|--------|
| 2022-01-01 | 150.75 |
| 2022-01-02 | 152.80 |
| 2022-01-03 | 153.25 |
| 2022-01-04 | 151.50 |
| 2022-01-05 | 154.00 |

Handling Missing Values

Missing values are common in time series data and can significantly impact model performance. A simple way to handle missing values is to use forward filling or backward filling:

```python
Forward fill missing values
data_ffill = data.ffill()

Backward fill missing values
data_bfill = data.bfill()
```

## Feature Engineering

Feature engineering is crucial in time series analysis. Creating features like moving averages, lagged values, and rolling statistics can help capture the underlying patterns in the data:

```python
Create lagged features
data['Close_lag1'] = data['Close'].shift(1)
data['Close_lag2'] = data['Close'].shift(2)

Create rolling statistics
data['Roll_mean'] = data['Close'].rolling(window=3).mean()
data['Roll_std'] = data['Close'].rolling(window=3).std()
```

## Train-Test Split for Time Series

Unlike typical data, time series data requires a different approach for splitting into training and test sets. The split must respect the temporal order of the data:

```python
Split data
train_size = int(len(data) * 0.8)
train, test = data[:train_size], data[train_size:]

Ensure no look-ahead bias
X_train, y_train = train.drop(columns=['Close']), train['Close']
```

```
X_test, y_test = test.drop(columns=['Close']), test['Close']
```

Building a Time Series Model with Scikit-Learn

Now that the data is prepared, we can build and train a machine learning model. Let's use a Decision Tree Regressor as an example:

```python
from sklearn.tree import DecisionTreeRegressor
from sklearn.metrics import mean_absolute_error

Initialize the model
model = DecisionTreeRegressor()

Fit the model
model.fit(X_train, y_train)

Make predictions
predictions = model.predict(X_test)

Evaluate the model
mae = mean_absolute_error(y_test, predictions)
print(f'Mean Absolute Error: {mae}')
```

Incorporating Time Series Cross-Validation

Cross-validation is essential for robust model evaluation,

especially in time series forecasting. Time series cross-validation can be implemented using the `TimeSeriesSplit` class in Scikit-Learn:

```python
from sklearn.model_selection import TimeSeriesSplit, cross_val_score

Initialize TimeSeriesSplit
tscv = TimeSeriesSplit(n_splits=5)

Perform cross-validation
cv_scores = cross_val_score(model, X_train, y_train, cv=tscv, scoring='neg_mean_absolute_error')
print(f'Cross-Validation MAE: {-cv_scores.mean()}')
```

Hyperparameter Tuning

Hyperparameter tuning can significantly enhance model performance. Using GridSearchCV with `TimeSeriesSplit` ensures that the temporal order of the data is maintained:

```python
from sklearn.model_selection import GridSearchCV

Define parameter grid
param_grid = {'max_depth': [3, 5, 7, 9]}

Initialize GridSearchCV
```

```
grid_search = GridSearchCV(model, param_grid, cv=tscv, scoring='neg_mean_absolute_error')

Fit GridSearchCV
grid_search.fit(X_train, y_train)

Best parameters and score
print(f'Best Parameters: {grid_search.best_params_}')
print(f'Best CV MAE: {-grid_search.best_score_}')
```

Incorporating External Variables

External variables, or exogenous variables, can provide additional information that improves the accuracy of time series forecasts. For example, incorporating economic indicators when forecasting stock prices:

```python
Load external data (e.g., economic indicators)
economic_data = pd.read_csv('economic_indicators.csv', parse_dates=['Date'], index_col='Date')

Merge with the main dataset
data = data.merge(economic_data, on='Date')

Prepare features and target
X = data.drop(columns=['Close'])
y = data['Close']
```

Practical Implementation Example

To illustrate the complete workflow, let's build a time series forecasting model step-by-step using Scikit-Learn:

1. Loading and Preprocessing Data
2. Feature Engineering
3. Splitting Data Respecting Temporal Order
4. Building and Training the Model
5. Evaluating and Tuning the Model

Here is a consolidated code snippet:

```python
import pandas as pd
import numpy as np
from sklearn.tree import DecisionTreeRegressor
from sklearn.model_selection import TimeSeriesSplit, GridSearchCV
from sklearn.metrics import mean_absolute_error

Load dataset
data = pd.read_csv('stock_prices.csv', parse_dates=['Date'], index_col='Date')

Handle missing values
data = data.ffill()

Feature Engineering
```

```
data['Close_lag1'] = data['Close'].shift(1)
data['Close_lag2'] = data['Close'].shift(2)
data['Roll_mean'] = data['Close'].rolling(window=3).mean()
data['Roll_std'] = data['Close'].rolling(window=3).std()
data = data.dropna()

Split data
train_size = int(len(data) * 0.8)
train, test = data[:train_size], data[train_size:]
X_train, y_train = train.drop(columns=['Close']), train['Close']
X_test, y_test = test.drop(columns=['Close']), test['Close']

Initialize and train model
model = DecisionTreeRegressor()
model.fit(X_train, y_train)

 Predictions and evaluation
predictions = model.predict(X_test)
mae = mean_absolute_error(y_test, predictions)
print(f'Mean Absolute Error: {mae}')

Cross-validation
tscv = TimeSeriesSplit(n_splits=5)
cv_scores = cross_val_score(model, X_train, y_train, cv=tscv, scoring='neg_mean_absolute_error')
print(f'Cross-Validation MAE: {-cv_scores.mean()}')

Hyperparameter tuning
```

```
param_grid = {'max_depth': [3, 5, 7, 9]}
grid_search = GridSearchCV(model, param_grid, cv=tscv, scoring='neg_mean_absolute_error')
grid_search.fit(X_train, y_train)
print(f'Best Parameters: {grid_search.best_params_}')
print(f'Best CV MAE: {-grid_search.best_score_}')
```

Incorporating these steps, you can develop, train, and evaluate time series forecasting models using Scikit-Learn. This practical approach ensures that your models are not only accurate but also robust and reliable for making informed financial decisions.

By mastering the use of Scikit-Learn for time series analysis, you enhance your ability to decode complex financial data, paving the way for more precise predictions and better decision-making in the ever-evolving financial landscape.

## 6.9 Incorporating External Variables in Time Series Models

### Understanding External Variables

External variables can range from economic indicators, weather data, social media sentiment, to macroeconomic factors. The key is to identify variables that have a plausible and significant impact on the target variable. For instance, when forecasting stock prices, relevant external variables might include interest rates, inflation rates, GDP growth, or even market sentiment indicators.

Preparing External Data

The first step in incorporating external variables is to gather and preprocess the data. It's crucial to align these variables with your primary time series data in terms of frequency and time frames.

Let's assume we have a dataset of daily stock prices and an additional dataset containing daily economic indicators such as interest rates and GDP growth:

```python
import pandas as pd

Load main dataset
stock_data = pd.read_csv('stock_prices.csv', parse_dates=['Date'], index_col='Date')

Load external dataset
economic_data = pd.read_csv('economic_indicators.csv', parse_dates=['Date'], index_col='Date')

Display the first few rows of both datasets
print(stock_data.head())
print(economic_data.head())
```

The datasets might look like this:

Stock Prices:

| Date | Close |
|---|---|
| 2022-01-01 | 150.75 |
| 2022-01-02 | 152.80 |
| 2022-01-03 | 153.25 |
| 2022-01-04 | 151.50 |
| 2022-01-05 | 154.00 |

Economic Indicators:

| Date | Interest_Rate | GDP_Growth |
|---|---|---|
| 2022-01-01 | 1.5 | 2.3 |
| 2022-01-02 | 1.55 | 2.4 |
| 2022-01-03 | 1.6 | 2.5 |
| 2022-01-04 | 1.58 | 2.4 |
| 2022-01-05 | 1.57 | 2.3 |

Merging Datasets

Once the data is loaded, the next step is to merge the main dataset with the external variables based on the date:

```python
Merge the datasets on the Date column
merged_data = stock_data.merge(economic_data, on='Date')
```

```
Display the merged dataset
print(merged_data.head())
```

Merged Data:

| Date | Close | Interest_Rate | GDP_Growth |
|------------|--------|---------------|------------|
| 2022-01-01 | 150.75 | 1.5 | 2.3 |
| 2022-01-02 | 152.80 | 1.55 | 2.4 |
| 2022-01-03 | 153.25 | 1.6 | 2.5 |
| 2022-01-04 | 151.50 | 1.58 | 2.4 |
| 2022-01-05 | 154.00 | 1.57 | 2.3 |

Feature Engineering

Just like with the primary time series data, feature engineering is essential when incorporating external variables. You can create lagged features, rolling statistics, and other derived features to capture the temporal dynamics:

```python
Create lagged features for the Close price
merged_data['Close_lag1'] = merged_data['Close'].shift(1)
merged_data['Close_lag2'] = merged_data['Close'].shift(2)

Create rolling statistics for the external variables
merged_data['Interest_Rate_Roll_Mean'] =
merged_data['Interest_Rate'].rolling(window=3).mean()
```

```
merged_data['GDP_Growth_Roll_Mean'] = merged_data['GDP_Growth'].rolling(window=3).mean()

Drop rows with NaN values generated by lagging
merged_data = merged_data.dropna()

Display the processed dataset
print(merged_data.head())
```

Processed Data:

| Date | Close | Interest_Rate | GDP_Growth | Close_lag1 | Close_lag2 | Interest_Rate_Roll_Mean | GDP_Growth_Roll_Mean |
|---|---|---|---|---|---|---|---|
| 2022-01-03 | 153.25 | 1.6 | 2.5 | 152.80 | 150.75 | 1.55 | 2.40 |
| 2022-01-04 | 151.50 | 1.58 | 2.4 | 153.25 | 152.80 | 1.58 | 2.43 |
| 2022-01-05 | 154.00 | 1.57 | 2.3 | 151.50 | 153.25 | 1.58 | 2.40 |

Splitting the Dataset

With the merged and processed dataset ready, the next step is to split it into training and testing sets, maintaining the temporal order:

```python
```

Define the target variable and features

X = merged_data.drop(columns=['Close'])

y = merged_data['Close']

Split the data

train_size = int(len(merged_data) * 0.8)

X_train, X_test = X[:train_size], X[train_size:]

y_train, y_test = y[:train_size], y[train_size:]

Display the shapes of the training and testing sets

print(X_train.shape, X_test.shape, y_train.shape, y_test.shape)

```

Building the Time Series Model

With the data prepared, we can build and train a machine learning model. For this example, we'll use a Random Forest Regressor to capture the relationships between the target variable and the external variables:

```python

from sklearn.ensemble import RandomForestRegressor

from sklearn.metrics import mean_absolute_error

Initialize the model

model = RandomForestRegressor(n_estimators=100, random_state=42)

Fit the model

model.fit(X_train, y_train)

Make predictions

predictions = model.predict(X_test)

Evaluate the model

mae = mean_absolute_error(y_test, predictions)

print(f'Mean Absolute Error: {mae}')

```

Cross-Validation and Hyperparameter Tuning

To ensure the robustness of our model, we can perform time series cross-validation and hyperparameter tuning using `TimeSeriesSplit` and `GridSearchCV`:

```python
from sklearn.model_selection import TimeSeriesSplit, GridSearchCV

Initialize TimeSeriesSplit

tscv = TimeSeriesSplit(n_splits=5)

Define parameter grid

param_grid = {'n_estimators': [50, 100, 200], 'max_depth': [5, 10, 20]}

Initialize GridSearchCV

grid_search = GridSearchCV(model, param_grid, cv=tscv, scoring='neg_mean_absolute_error')

Fit GridSearchCV

grid_search.fit(X_train, y_train)

Best parameters and score

print(f'Best Parameters: {grid_search.best_params_}')

print(f'Best CV MAE: {-grid_search.best_score_}')

` ` `

Case Study: Forecasting Stock Prices with Economic Indicators

To illustrate the complete workflow of incorporating external variables into time series models, let's summarize the key steps:

1. Loading and Merging Datasets: Combine your primary time series data with relevant external variables.
2. Preprocessing and Feature Engineering: Handle missing values, create lagged features, and compute rolling statistics.
3. Splitting the Data: Ensure the temporal order is retained when splitting data into training and testing sets.
4. Building and Training the Model: Use machine learning models to capture the relationships between the target variable and external variables.
5. Evaluating and Tuning the Model: Perform cross-validation and hyperparameter tuning to optimize model performance.

By following these steps, you can enhance your time series forecasts with additional information, leading to more accurate and reliable predictions.

Incorporating external variables into your time series models not only improves forecast accuracy but also provides deeper insights into the underlying factors driving financial trends. As you continue to explore and integrate diverse data sources, you'll be better equipped to make informed and strategic financial decisions.

## 6.10 Case Study: Forecasting Market Trends

Forecasting market trends is a quintessential application of machine learning in finance, leveraging historical data, patterns, and various influencing factors to predict future market movements. In this comprehensive case study, we will analyze how to build a robust forecasting model using Scikit-Learn, focusing on practical steps and detailed coding examples to demonstrate the entire workflow.

### Understanding Market Trends

Market trends refer to the general direction in which a financial market or asset moves. Identifying these trends can provide significant insights for investment strategies, risk management, and overall financial planning. Trends can be upward (bullish), downward (bearish), or sideways (neutral), influenced by a multitude of factors including economic indicators, geopolitical events, and investor sentiment.

### Data Collection and Preparation

The first step in forecasting market trends is collecting relevant data. For this case study, we'll use historical stock prices combined with external variables such as economic indicators. Ensuring data quality and preprocessing are crucial for accurate predictions.

Let's start by loading the dataset:

```python
import pandas as pd

Load historical stock prices
stock_data = pd.read_csv('historical_stock_prices.csv', parse_dates=['Date'], index_col='Date')

Load economic indicators
economic_data = pd.read_csv('economic_indicators.csv', parse_dates=['Date'], index_col='Date')

Display the first few rows of both datasets
print(stock_data.head())
print(economic_data.head())
```

Here's what the datasets might look like:

Historical Stock Prices:

| Date | Close |
|------------|--------|
| 2022-01-01 | 150.75 |
| 2022-01-02 | 152.80 |

| 2022-01-03 | 153.25 |

| 2022-01-04 | 151.50 |

| 2022-01-05 | 154.00 |

Economic Indicators:

| Date | Interest_Rate | GDP_Growth |
|---|---|---|
| 2022-01-01 | 1.5 | 2.3 |
| 2022-01-02 | 1.55 | 2.4 |
| 2022-01-03 | 1.6 | 2.5 |
| 2022-01-04 | 1.58 | 2.4 |
| 2022-01-05 | 1.57 | 2.3 |

Merging Datasets

To ensure our model captures the interactions between stock prices and economic indicators, we merge the datasets based on the Date column:

```python
Merge datasets on the Date column
merged_data = stock_data.merge(economic_data, on='Date')

Display the merged dataset
print(merged_data.head())
```

Merged Data:

| Date | Close | Interest_Rate | GDP_Growth |
|---|---|---|---|
| 2022-01-01 | 150.75 | 1.5 | 2.3 |
| 2022-01-02 | 152.80 | 1.55 | 2.4 |
| 2022-01-03 | 153.25 | 1.6 | 2.5 |
| 2022-01-04 | 151.50 | 1.58 | 2.4 |
| 2022-01-05 | 154.00 | 1.57 | 2.3 |

Feature Engineering

Feature engineering is critical in time series forecasting. We create lagged features and rolling statistics to capture temporal dependencies:

```python
Create lagged features for the Close price
merged_data['Close_lag1'] = merged_data['Close'].shift(1)
merged_data['Close_lag2'] = merged_data['Close'].shift(2)

Create rolling statistics for the external variables
merged_data['Interest_Rate_Roll_Mean'] = merged_data['Interest_Rate'].rolling(window=3).mean()
merged_data['GDP_Growth_Roll_Mean'] = merged_data['GDP_Growth'].rolling(window=3).mean()

Drop rows with NaN values generated by lagging
merged_data = merged_data.dropna()

Display the processed dataset
```

print(merged_data.head())
```

Processed Data:

| Date | Close | Interest_Rate | GDP_Growth | Close_lag1 | Close_lag2 | Interest_Rate_Roll_Mean | GDP_Growth_Roll_Mean |
|---|---|---|---|---|---|---|---|
| 2022-01-03 | 153.25 | 1.6 | 2.5 | 152.80 | 150.75 | 1.55 | 2.40 |
| 2022-01-04 | 151.50 | 1.58 | 2.4 | 153.25 | 152.80 | 1.58 | 2.43 |
| 2022-01-05 | 154.00 | 1.57 | 2.3 | 151.50 | 153.25 | 1.58 | 2.40 |

Splitting the Data

We split the data into training and testing sets, keeping the temporal order intact:

```python
Define the target variable and features
X = merged_data.drop(columns=['Close'])
y = merged_data['Close']

Split the data
train_size = int(len(merged_data) * 0.8)
X_train, X_test = X[:train_size], X[train_size:]
```
```

```
y_train, y_test = y[:train_size], y[train_size:]

 Display the shapes of the training and testing sets
print(X_train.shape, X_test.shape, y_train.shape, y_test.shape)
```

Building and Training the Model

We use a Random Forest Regressor to model the relationships between the target and external variables:

```python
from sklearn.ensemble import RandomForestRegressor
from sklearn.metrics import mean_absolute_error

Initialize the model
model = RandomForestRegressor(n_estimators=100, random_state=42)

Fit the model
model.fit(X_train, y_train)

Make predictions
predictions = model.predict(X_test)

Evaluate the model
mae = mean_absolute_error(y_test, predictions)
print(f'Mean Absolute Error: {mae}')
```

Evaluating Model Performance

Assessing the model's performance involves comparing the predictions with actual values. We use the Mean Absolute Error (MAE) as our evaluation metric:

```python
import matplotlib.pyplot as plt

Plot actual vs. predicted values
plt.figure(figsize=(10, 6))
plt.plot(y_test.index, y_test, label='Actual')
plt.plot(y_test.index, predictions, label='Predicted', linestyle='--')
plt.legend()
plt.xlabel('Date')
plt.ylabel('Stock Price')
plt.title('Actual vs Predicted Stock Prices')
plt.show()
```

Cross-Validation and Hyperparameter Tuning

To enhance model robustness, we perform time series cross-validation and hyperparameter tuning:

```python
from sklearn.model_selection import TimeSeriesSplit, GridSearchCV
```

```
Initialize TimeSeriesSplit
tscv = TimeSeriesSplit(n_splits=5)

Define parameter grid
param_grid = {'n_estimators': [50, 100, 200], 'max_depth': [5, 10, 20]}

Initialize GridSearchCV
grid_search = GridSearchCV(model, param_grid, cv=tscv, scoring='neg_mean_absolute_error')

Fit GridSearchCV
grid_search.fit(X_train, y_train)

Best parameters and score
print(f'Best Parameters: {grid_search.best_params_}')
print(f'Best CV MAE: {-grid_search.best_score_}')
```

Case Study Summary

To encapsulate the process of forecasting market trends:

1. Data Collection and Preparation: Integrate historical stock prices with external economic indicators to create a comprehensive dataset.
2. Feature Engineering: Generate lagged features and compute rolling statistics to capture temporal dependencies.
3. Splitting the Data: Maintain the temporal order when

dividing data into training and testing sets.

4. Building and Training the Model: Utilize machine learning models, such as Random Forest Regressors, to learn relationships between variables.

5. Evaluating and Tuning the Model: Assess model performance using metrics and enhance robustness through cross-validation and hyperparameter tuning.

By following these steps, you can create models that not only forecast market trends with greater accuracy but also provide valuable insights into the factors driving these trends. This approach equips you with the tools to make informed and strategic financial decisions, enhancing your ability to navigate the complex landscape of financial markets.

# CHAPTER 7: ADVANCED TOPICS

Deep learning models are inspired by the human brain's structure, composed of layers of interconnected nodes (neurons). These models excel in tasks where traditional machine learning algorithms struggle, such as image and speech recognition, due to their ability to automatically learn feature representations from raw data.

Neural Networks:

A neural network consists of an input layer, hidden layers, and an output layer. Each neuron in a layer computes a weighted sum of its inputs, passes it through an activation function, and forwards the result to the next layer. This process enables the network to learn complex mappings from inputs to outputs.

Backpropagation:

training neural networks is backpropagation, a method for updating the weights of the model to minimize the error between predicted and actual outputs. This is achieved through gradient descent, which iteratively adjusts the weights in the direction that reduces the error.

## Practical Applications of Deep Learning in Finance

Deep learning has found numerous applications in finance, transforming how financial institutions operate and make decisions. Below are some key areas where deep learning has made a significant impact:

1. High-Frequency Trading:

Deep learning models can analyze vast amounts of market data in real-time, identifying patterns and making rapid trading decisions. These models can capture subtle market signals that traditional algorithms may miss, providing a competitive edge in high-frequency trading.

2. Fraud Detection:

Financial institutions use deep learning to detect fraudulent transactions. By training models on historical transaction data, they can learn to identify anomalies that indicate potential fraud, improving the accuracy and efficiency of fraud detection systems.

3. Sentiment Analysis:

Analyzing sentiment from news articles, social media, and other textual data sources helps predict market movements. Deep learning models, particularly those using Natural Language Processing (NLP), can process and interpret large volumes of text, extracting sentiments that influence market trends.

4. Portfolio Management:

Deep learning assists in optimizing portfolios by evaluating a wide range of factors, including historical performance, market conditions, and economic indicators. Models can predict asset prices and determine the optimal asset allocation to maximize returns while minimizing risk.

Integrating Deep Learning with Scikit-Learn

While Scikit-Learn is a powerful tool for traditional machine learning, it integrates seamlessly with deep learning frameworks to extend its capabilities. Libraries such as TensorFlow and Keras can be used alongside Scikit-Learn to build and train deep learning models.

Installation:

Before you can start integrating deep learning models with Scikit-Learn, you need to install the necessary libraries. TensorFlow and Keras are popular choices:

```bash
pip install tensorflow keras
```

Building a Deep Learning Model:

Let's walk through an example of building a deep learning model for stock price prediction using Keras and integrating it with Scikit-Learn.

Step 1: Data Preparation

Prepare the dataset, ensuring it is suitable for training a neural network. For this example, we'll use historical stock prices and create lagged features:

```python
import pandas as pd
from sklearn.preprocessing import MinMaxScaler

Load historical stock prices
data = pd.read_csv('historical_stock_prices.csv', parse_dates=['Date'], index_col='Date')

Feature scaling
scaler = MinMaxScaler()
data_scaled = scaler.fit_transform(data[['Close']])

Create lagged features
def create_lagged_features(data, lag=1):
    df = pd.DataFrame(data)
    for i in range(1, lag + 1):
        df[f'lag_{i}'] = df[0].shift(i)
    df.dropna(inplace=True)
    return df

data_lagged = create_lagged_features(data_scaled, lag=3)

Split the data into features and target
X = data_lagged.drop(columns=[0]).values
y = data_lagged[0].values
```

Step 2: Building the Model

Define and compile the neural network using Keras:

```python
from keras.models import Sequential
from keras.layers import Dense

Initialize the model
model = Sequential()

Add input and first hidden layer
model.add(Dense(units=50, activation='relu',
input_dim=X.shape[1]))

Add second hidden layer
model.add(Dense(units=25, activation='relu'))

Add output layer
model.add(Dense(units=1))

Compile the model
model.compile(optimizer='adam', loss='mean_squared_error')
```

Step 3: Training the Model

Train the model using the prepared dataset:

```python
Train the model
```

```
model.fit(X, y, epochs=50, batch_size=32, validation_split=0.2)
```

Step 4: Integration with Scikit-Learn

To integrate this deep learning model with Scikit-Learn, we can use the `keras.wrappers.scikit_learn` library. This allows us to incorporate the model into Scikit-Learn's pipeline and utilize its tools for cross-validation, hyperparameter tuning, and more.

```python
from keras.wrappers.scikit_learn import KerasRegressor

from sklearn.model_selection import cross_val_score, KFold

Create a function to build the model (required by KerasRegressor)
def build_model():
    model = Sequential()
    model.add(Dense(units=50, activation='relu', input_dim=X.shape[1]))
    model.add(Dense(units=25, activation='relu'))
    model.add(Dense(units=1))
    model.compile(optimizer='adam', loss='mean_squared_error')
    return model

Wrap the model using KerasRegressor
keras_model = KerasRegressor(build_fn=build_model,
```

```
epochs=50, batch_size=32, verbose=0)

Evaluate the model using cross-validation
kfold = KFold(n_splits=5)
results = cross_val_score(keras_model, X, y, cv=kfold)
print(f'Cross-Validation MAE: {results.mean()}')
```

Hyperparameter Tuning

Optimizing the hyperparameters of deep learning models can significantly enhance their performance. Using Scikit-Learn's `GridSearchCV` with `KerasRegressor`, we can perform an exhaustive search over specified hyperparameter values:

```python
from sklearn.model_selection import GridSearchCV

Define the parameter grid
param_grid = {
    'batch_size': [16, 32, 64],
    'epochs': [50, 100],
    'build_fn': [build_model]
}

Initialize GridSearchCV with KerasRegressor
grid_search = GridSearchCV(estimator=keras_model, param_grid=param_grid, cv=kfold, scoring='neg_mean_squared_error')
```

```
Perform grid search
grid_result = grid_search.fit(X, y)

Display the best parameters and score
print(f'Best Parameters: {grid_result.best_params_}')
print(f'Best CV Score: {-grid_result.best_score_}')
```

Deep learning has transformed the landscape of financial modeling, offering powerful tools to uncover hidden patterns and make accurate predictions. By integrating deep learning frameworks like TensorFlow and Keras with Scikit-Learn, financial analysts can leverage the strengths of both traditional and deep learning models. This integration empowers you to build sophisticated models, perform hyperparameter tuning, and ensure robust performance, ultimately leading to more informed and strategic financial decisions.

## Reinforcement Learning Applications

Reinforcement learning (RL) has emerged as a powerful tool in finance, offering a dynamic approach to decision-making under uncertainty. Unlike traditional supervised learning techniques, which rely on labeled datasets, RL involves an agent learning to make decisions by interacting with an environment, receiving rewards or penalties based on the actions it takes. This trial-and-error process enables the agent to develop strategies that maximize cumulative rewards, making RL particularly suited for complex financial problems where optimal decisions are not immediately apparent.

## Theoretical Foundations of Reinforcement Learning

RL is inspired by behavioral psychology, where agents learn from the consequences of their actions. The primary components of an RL framework include the agent, environment, state, action, reward, and policy.

### Agent and Environment:

The agent is the decision-maker, while the environment represents everything outside the agent that it interacts with. For instance, in a stock trading scenario, the agent could be a trading algorithm, and the environment could be the stock market.

### State and Action:

The state is a representation of the environment's current conditions. For example, the state could include the current price of a stock, the agent's holdings, and market indicators. Actions are the decisions the agent can make, such as buying, selling, or holding a stock.

### Reward:

Rewards are signals received by the agent after taking an action. The goal is to maximize the cumulative reward over time. In finance, rewards could be the profit or loss resulting from a trade.

### Policy:

A policy defines the agent's behavior, mapping states to actions. The agent's objective is to learn an optimal policy that maximizes cumulative rewards.

Value Function and Q-Learning:

The value function estimates the expected cumulative reward from a given state, guiding the agent towards more rewarding states. Q-Learning, a popular RL algorithm, extends this concept by estimating the value of taking a specific action in a given state (Q-value). The agent iteratively updates its Q-values based on the rewards received, refining its policy.

Practical Applications of Reinforcement Learning in Finance

Reinforcement learning has found numerous applications in finance, where its ability to learn and adapt makes it an invaluable tool for a variety of tasks.

1. Algorithmic Trading:

One of the most prominent applications of RL in finance is algorithmic trading. RL agents can develop trading strategies by learning from historical market data and real-time trading environments. These agents can adapt to changing market conditions, identifying profitable opportunities and making timely trades. For example, an RL agent might learn to buy stocks when prices are expected to rise and sell them before a downturn, optimizing trade execution to maximize returns.

2. Portfolio Management:

RL is also used in portfolio management to optimize asset allocation. An RL agent can learn to adjust the portfolio's composition based on market conditions, risk tolerance, and investment goals. By continuously interacting with market data, the agent can identify the optimal asset mix that balances risk and return, ensuring the portfolio remains aligned with the investor's objectives.

3. Option Pricing:

In the domain of derivative pricing, RL can be employed to develop pricing models that account for market dynamics and volatility. Traditional models like the Black-Scholes assume constant volatility, which may not accurately reflect market conditions. RL agents can learn to price options by considering factors such as changing volatility, interest rates, and underlying asset prices, leading to more accurate pricing and hedging strategies.

4. Credit Scoring:

Reinforcement learning can enhance credit scoring models by learning from borrowers' behavior and repayment patterns. An RL agent can identify credit risk more effectively by considering a wide range of factors, including historical payment data, economic indicators, and borrower characteristics. This leads to more accurate assessments of creditworthiness and better risk management for financial institutions.

Integrating Reinforcement Learning with Scikit-Learn

While Scikit-Learn is not specifically designed for reinforcement learning, it can be integrated with other libraries such as TensorFlow, Keras, or OpenAI Gym to build and train RL models. These libraries provide the necessary tools for defining environments, agents, and policies, allowing seamless integration with Scikit-Learn's preprocessing and evaluation capabilities.

Installation:

To get started with RL, you need to install the required

libraries:

```bash
pip install tensorflow keras gym
```

Building an RL Environment:

Let's walk through an example of building an RL agent for stock trading using TensorFlow and OpenAI Gym, and integrating it with Scikit-Learn.

Step 1: Define the Environment

First, we define the trading environment using OpenAI Gym:

```python
import gym
import numpy as np

class StockTradingEnv(gym.Env):
    def __init__(self, data):
        super(StockTradingEnv, self).__init__()
        self.data = data
        self.current_step = 0
        self.action_space = gym.spaces.Discrete(3)  Buy, Hold, Sell
        self.observation_space = gym.spaces.Box(low=0, high=1, shape=(len(data.columns),), dtype=np.float32)
```

```
    def reset(self):
        self.current_step = 0
        return self._next_observation()

    def _next_observation(self):
        return self.data.iloc[self.current_step].values

    def step(self, action):
        self.current_step += 1
        done = self.current_step >= len(self.data) - 1
        reward = self._take_action(action)
        obs = self._next_observation()
        return obs, reward, done, {}

    def _take_action(self, action):
         Simplified reward calculation for illustration
        if action == 0:  Buy
            return self.data['Close'].iloc[self.current_step] - self.data['Close'].iloc[self.current_step - 1]
        elif action == 2:  Sell
            return self.data['Close'].iloc[self.current_step - 1] - self.data['Close'].iloc[self.current_step]
        else:  Hold
            return 0
```

Step 2: Building the RL Agent

Next, we build the RL agent using TensorFlow and Keras:

```python
import tensorflow as tf
from tensorflow.keras.models import Sequential
from tensorflow.keras.layers import Dense
from tensorflow.keras.optimizers import Adam

class DQNAgent:
    def __init__(self, state_size, action_size):
        self.state_size = state_size
        self.action_size = action_size
        self.memory = []
        self.gamma = 0.95
        self.epsilon = 1.0
        self.epsilon_decay = 0.995
        self.epsilon_min = 0.01
        self.learning_rate = 0.001
        self.model = self._build_model()

    def _build_model(self):
        model = Sequential()
        model.add(Dense(24,              input_dim=self.state_size,
activation='relu'))
        model.add(Dense(24, activation='relu'))
        model.add(Dense(self.action_size, activation='linear'))
        model.compile(loss='mse',
```

```
optimizer=Adam(lr=self.learning_rate))
        return model

    def remember(self, state, action, reward, next_state, done):
        self.memory.append((state, action, reward, next_state,
done))

    def act(self, state):
        if np.random.rand() <= self.epsilon:
            return np.random.choice(self.action_size)
        act_values = self.model.predict(state)
        return np.argmax(act_values[0])

    def replay(self, batch_size):
        minibatch = np.random.choice(self.memory, batch_size)
        for state, action, reward, next_state, done in minibatch:
            target = reward
            if not done:
                target += self.gamma *
np.amax(self.model.predict(next_state)[0])
            target_f = self.model.predict(state)
            target_f[0][action] = target
            self.model.fit(state, target_f, epochs=1, verbose=0)
        if self.epsilon > self.epsilon_min:
            self.epsilon *= self.epsilon_decay
```

Step 3: Training the Agent

Finally, we train the RL agent in the defined environment:

```python
import pandas as pd

Load historical stock prices
data = pd.read_csv('historical_stock_prices.csv', parse_dates=['Date'], index_col='Date')
env = StockTradingEnv(data)

state_size = env.observation_space.shape[0]
action_size = env.action_space.n
agent = DQNAgent(state_size, action_size)

episodes = 100
batch_size = 32

for e in range(episodes):
    state = env.reset()
    state = np.reshape(state, [1, state_size])
    for time in range(env.data.shape[0]):
        action = agent.act(state)
        next_state, reward, done, _ = env.step(action)
        reward = reward if not done else -10
        next_state = np.reshape(next_state, [1, state_size])
        agent.remember(state, action, reward, next_state, done)
        state = next_state
        if done:
```

```
        print(f"episode: {e+1}/{episodes}, score: {time}, e: {agent.epsilon:.2}")
        break
    if len(agent.memory) > batch_size:
        agent.replay(batch_size)
```

Reinforcement learning offers a transformative approach to financial decision-making, enabling agents to learn and adapt in complex, dynamic environments. By integrating RL with Scikit-Learn and other powerful libraries, financial professionals can develop sophisticated models that enhance trading strategies, portfolio management, option pricing, and credit scoring. As you delve deeper into RL applications in finance, remain observant of evolving methodologies and stay engaged with the continuous advancements in this exciting field. Embrace the potential of RL to revolutionize your financial analyses and decisions.

## Transfer Learning and Its Use Cases

In the ever-evolving landscape of machine learning, Transfer Learning has emerged as a revolutionary technique, enabling models to leverage pre-existing knowledge to solve new, but related, problems more efficiently and effectively. This concept, widely recognized in the domains of image and natural language processing, is increasingly finding its footing in the financial sector, where data sparsity and the high cost of labeled data often pose significant challenges.

### Understanding Transfer Learning

Transfer Learning is predicated on the idea of using a model trained on one task as a starting point for a different, but related, task. Instead of training a new model from scratch, which can be time-consuming and computationally expensive, Transfer Learning allows for the re-utilization of pre-trained models, thereby accelerating the learning process and often improving performance.

Key Components:

Source Domain and Task: This is the original problem domain and the task on which the model is initially trained. For instance, a model trained to predict stock prices in the US market.

Target Domain and Task: This is the new problem domain and the task where the transfer learning will be applied. For example, using the US stock price prediction model to forecast prices in the European market.

Transfer Mechanisms: Techniques such as fine-tuning, where the pre-trained model's parameters are adjusted to better suit the new task, or feature extraction, where the representations learned by the model are used as inputs to a new model.

Theoretical Foundations

Transfer Learning operates on the principle that there exist underlying patterns and features that are common across different, yet related, tasks. By transferring these learned representations, models can quickly adapt to new tasks with fewer data requirements and less computational power.

Types of Transfer Learning:

Inductive Transfer Learning: The source and target tasks are different, but related. For instance, transferring knowledge from predicting stock prices to predicting bond prices.

Transductive Transfer Learning: The tasks remain the same, but the domains differ. An example is using a model trained on US stock market data to predict trends in the European stock market.

Unsupervised Transfer Learning: Both the source and target tasks are unsupervised. This could involve transferring clustering techniques from one financial dataset to another.

Practical Applications in Finance

Transfer Learning has a multitude of applications in the financial sector, where it can significantly enhance the efficiency and accuracy of predictive models.

1. Cross-Market Analysis:

One of the prominent use cases is in cross-market analysis. Financial markets exhibit certain universal patterns due to the interconnected nature of the global economy. A model trained on the US stock market can be fine-tuned to predict movements in the European stock market, accelerating the learning process and improving predictive accuracy without requiring extensive re-training.

2. Credit Scoring Across Demographics:

In credit scoring, Transfer Learning can be utilized to adapt models developed for one demographic or geographic region to another. For example, a model trained on credit data from North America can be transferred to a European dataset, adjusting for local economic conditions and consumer behavior patterns.

3. Fraud Detection in Different Financial Institutions:

Fraud patterns often share common characteristics across different financial institutions. A fraud detection model trained on data from one bank can be transferred to another bank, enabling quick adaptation to new datasets and improving detection rates.

4. Sentiment Analysis of Financial News:

Transfer Learning is also highly effective in natural language processing tasks such as sentiment analysis. A model trained on a large corpus of general news articles can be fine-tuned to analyze financial news, extracting sentiment indicators that influence market movements.

5. Economic Forecasting:

Economic indicators, while unique to each region, often follow similar trends influenced by global events. A model trained on economic data from one country can be transferred to another, enabling more accurate forecasts by leveraging shared economic patterns.

Integrating Transfer Learning with Scikit-Learn

While Scikit-Learn is not inherently designed for Transfer

Learning, it can be effectively integrated with deep learning frameworks such as TensorFlow, Keras, and PyTorch to implement transfer learning models. These integrations allow the seamless application of pre-trained models to new financial datasets.

Installation:

To begin, ensure that the necessary libraries are installed:

```bash
pip install tensorflow keras scikit-learn
```

Example: Transfer Learning for Stock Price Prediction

Let's walk through an example where we transfer a pre-trained model from the US stock market to predict stock prices in the European market.

Step 1: Load the Pre-trained Model

We first load a pre-trained model, which has been trained on the US stock market data.

```python
import tensorflow as tf

from tensorflow.keras.models import load_model

Load pre-trained model

us_stock_model = load_model('us_stock_model.h5')
```

Step 2: Prepare the European Stock Market Data

Next, we prepare the new dataset for the European market, ensuring it is in a compatible format.

```python
import pandas as pd
from sklearn.preprocessing import MinMaxScaler

Load European stock data
european_stock_data = pd.read_csv('european_stock_data.csv')

Normalize the dataset
scaler = MinMaxScaler(feature_range=(0, 1))
scaled_data = scaler.fit_transform(european_stock_data)
```

Step 3: Fine-Tune the Model

We then fine-tune the pre-trained model using the new dataset. This involves adjusting the model's weights to better fit the European market data.

```python
from tensorflow.keras.optimizers import Adam

Compile the pre-trained model
```

```
us_stock_model.compile(optimizer=Adam(lr=0.0001),
loss='mean_squared_error')

Fine-tune the model with European stock data
us_stock_model.fit(scaled_data, epochs=10, batch_size=32)
```

Step 4: Make Predictions

Finally, we use the fine-tuned model to make predictions on the European stock market.

```python
Predict stock prices
predictions = us_stock_model.predict(scaled_data)

Inverse transform the predictions to original scale
original_predictions = scaler.inverse_transform(predictions)
```

Transfer Learning holds immense potential in the financial sector, enabling models to adapt quickly to new tasks and datasets, thus saving time and computational resources. By integrating Scikit-Learn with powerful deep learning frameworks, financial professionals can harness the benefits of Transfer Learning to enhance cross-market analysis, credit scoring, fraud detection, sentiment analysis, and economic forecasting. As the financial landscape continues to evolve, embracing Transfer Learning will be crucial in maintaining a competitive edge and driving innovation in predictive modeling.

Transfer Learning is not merely a tool but a paradigm shift in how we approach machine learning in finance. It empowers us to build robust, adaptable models that can seamlessly transition across various financial domains, unlocking new possibilities and insights.

Semi-Supervised Learning for Limited Datasets

Data scarcity can be a significant hurdle. Often, while large volumes of raw data are available, labeled data—which is essential for training supervised learning models—is limited. This is where semi-supervised learning steps in, bridging the gap between supervised and unsupervised learning. By leveraging both labeled and unlabeled data, semi-supervised learning models can achieve higher accuracy and robustness, making them invaluable tools for financial analysts.

The Concept of Semi-Supervised Learning

Semi-supervised learning (SSL) lies between supervised and unsupervised learning. While supervised learning relies entirely on labeled data to make predictions, and unsupervised learning operates without any labeled data, SSL utilizes a small amount of labeled data along with a larger set of unlabeled data. This approach is particularly effective in scenarios where obtaining labeled data is expensive or time-consuming, such as in finance.

The fundamental idea is that the model learns from the labeled data and then uses the structure of the unlabeled data to improve its learning process. This way, SSL harnesses the vast amounts of available unlabeled data to enhance the model's predictive capabilities.

## Why Semi-Supervised Learning in Finance?

In the finance sector, acquiring labeled data often involves manual annotation by domain experts, which is resource-intensive. For instance, labeling data for credit scoring might require an in-depth analysis of financial histories, while fraud detection entails scrutinizing transaction details meticulously. Semi-supervised learning helps mitigate these challenges by significantly reducing the dependence on labeled data, thereby speeding up the model development process and cutting down associated costs.

Moreover, financial data typically has an underlying structure that SSL models can exploit. For example, transactions or stock price movements might exhibit patterns that the model can learn from the unlabeled data, improving its accuracy in predicting future trends or anomalies.

## Types of Semi-Supervised Learning Techniques

Several techniques and algorithms are used in semi-supervised learning, each with its unique approach to combining labeled and unlabeled data. Some of the most prominent ones include:

1. Self-Training:

In self-training, a supervised learning model is initially trained on the small labeled dataset. The model is then used to predict labels for the unlabeled data. The most confident predictions are added to the labeled dataset, and the process is repeated. This iterative approach helps the model improve over time by expanding its training set.

2. Co-Training:

Co-training involves training two different models on two different views of the data (e.g., different sets of features). Each model is initially trained on the labeled data and then predicts labels for the unlabeled data. The predictions from one model are used to expand the labeled dataset for the other model, and vice versa. This mutual learning process helps both models improve.

3. Graph-Based Methods:

Graph-based methods model the data as a graph, where nodes represent data points, and edges represent similarities between them. Labels are propagated from the labeled nodes to the unlabeled nodes based on the graph structure, leveraging the relationships between data points to improve learning.

4. Generative Models:

Generative models, such as Gaussian Mixture Models (GMMs), assume that the data is generated from a mixture of underlying distributions. These models learn the parameters of these distributions using both labeled and unlabeled data, improving their ability to classify new data points.

Here is a practical example of implementing self-training using the Scikit-Learn library:

```python
import numpy as np
from sklearn.model_selection import train_test_split
from sklearn.semi_supervised import SelfTrainingClassifier
from sklearn.ensemble import RandomForestClassifier
```

```
from sklearn.metrics import accuracy_score

Example: Financial data (features and labels)
For illustration, we use random data; replace this with actual financial data
np.random.seed(42)
X = np.random.rand(1000, 10)  1000 samples, 10 features each
y = np.random.randint(2, size=1000)  Binary labels (0 or 1)

Simulate the scenario of limited labeled data
X_labeled, X_unlabeled, y_labeled, _ = train_test_split(X, y, test_size=0.95, random_state=42)

Create a self-training classifier
base_clf = RandomForestClassifier(n_estimators=100, random_state=42)
self_training_clf = SelfTrainingClassifier(base_clf)

Train the model
self_training_clf.fit(X_labeled, y_labeled)

Predict on the entire dataset
y_pred = self_training_clf.predict(X)

Evaluate the model
accuracy = accuracy_score(y, y_pred)
print(f"Accuracy: {accuracy:.2f}")
```

In the example above, we use a self-training classifier with a RandomForestClassifier as the base model. Initially, only 5% of the data is labeled. The self-training classifier iteratively labels the unlabeled data, progressively improving its performance.

Applications in Finance

Semi-supervised learning can be applied to a variety of financial problems:

- Credit Scoring:

Financial institutions can leverage SSL to build more accurate credit scoring models with limited labeled data. By incorporating large volumes of unlabeled transaction data, the models become more effective in predicting creditworthiness.

- Fraud Detection:

In fraud detection, labeled examples of fraudulent transactions are often scarce. SSL techniques can use the vast amounts of unlabeled transaction data to identify patterns indicative of fraud, enhancing detection capabilities.

- Stock Price Prediction:

Stock prices are influenced by numerous factors, creating a rich landscape of unlabeled data. SSL models can utilize this data to improve predictions, even with a limited set of labeled historical prices.

While semi-supervised learning offers significant advantages, it also comes with challenges. The quality of the unlabeled data and the initial labeled dataset greatly impacts the model's performance. Noise and inaccuracies in unlabeled data can propagate errors, requiring careful preprocessing and validation.

Additionally, the choice of SSL technique and model hyperparameters can dramatically influence the results. It's crucial to experiment with different methods and fine-tune the models to find the optimal setup for specific financial applications.

Semi-supervised learning presents a powerful approach for tackling data scarcity in finance. By skillfully combining labeled and unlabeled data, financial analysts can build robust models that offer improved predictive power. Through techniques like self-training, co-training, and graph-based methods, SSL unlocks new possibilities in credit scoring, fraud detection, stock price prediction, and beyond.

## Natural Language Processing (NLP) in Financial News Analysis

Timely and accurate information is critical. Financial news, reports, and articles often contain valuable insights that can influence market trends, investor sentiment, and ultimately, financial decisions. Natural Language Processing (NLP) emerges as a transformative technology, enabling the extraction of actionable insights from vast streams of textual data. By leveraging NLP, financial analysts can gain a competitive edge, predicting market movements, detecting sentiment shifts, and making informed investment decisions.

### Understanding Natural Language Processing (NLP)

Natural Language Processing is an interdisciplinary field

that combines computer science, artificial intelligence, and linguistics to enable machines to understand, interpret, and generate human language. In finance, NLP techniques are used to process and analyze textual data from various sources, including news articles, social media posts, analyst reports, and regulatory filings. The goal is to convert unstructured text into structured information that can be used for predictive modeling, sentiment analysis, and risk assessment.

NLP encompasses a broad range of techniques and methods, including text preprocessing, tokenization, part-of-speech tagging, named entity recognition, sentiment analysis, and topic modeling. Each technique plays a crucial role in transforming raw text into meaningful data.

Key NLP Techniques in Financial News Analysis

1. Text Preprocessing:

Before any analysis can be performed, textual data must be preprocessed to clean and normalize it. This involves removing noise (e.g., special characters, numbers), converting text to lowercase, and eliminating stopwords (common words like "and," "the," "is" that do not carry significant meaning). Text preprocessing ensures that the data is in a suitable format for further analysis.

2. Tokenization:

Tokenization is the process of splitting text into smaller units called tokens (e.g., words or phrases). This step is essential for breaking down the text into manageable pieces that can be analyzed individually.

3. Part-of-Speech Tagging:

Part-of-speech tagging involves assigning grammatical tags (e.g., noun, verb, adjective) to each token in the text. This helps in understanding the syntactic structure of the text and identifying relationships between words.

4. Named Entity Recognition (NER):

Named entity recognition is used to identify and classify entities mentioned in the text, such as company names, stock symbols, dates, and monetary values. NER is particularly useful in financial news analysis, as it allows for the extraction of specific information about companies, events, and transactions.

5. Sentiment Analysis:

Sentiment analysis aims to determine the sentiment expressed in the text, whether it is positive, negative, or neutral. In finance, sentiment analysis can be applied to news articles and social media posts to gauge market sentiment and predict potential market movements.

6. Topic Modeling:

Topic modeling is a technique used to identify the main topics or themes present in a collection of documents. By analyzing the distribution of words across documents, topic modeling algorithms can uncover hidden patterns and trends in financial news.

Practical Example: Analyzing Financial News with NLP

Let's walk through a practical example of using NLP to analyze financial news articles and predict stock price movements. We'll use the Scikit-Learn library along with other NLP tools like NLTK and spaCy.

```python
import pandas as pd
import numpy as np
from sklearn.model_selection import train_test_split
from sklearn.feature_extraction.text import TfidfVectorizer
from sklearn.linear_model import LogisticRegression
from sklearn.metrics import accuracy_score, classification_report
from nltk.corpus import stopwords
from nltk.tokenize import word_tokenize
import spacy

Load financial news dataset (for illustration, replace with actual dataset)
data = pd.read_csv('financial_news.csv')  Assume 'text' and 'label' columns

Text preprocessing function
def preprocess_text(text):
    stop_words = set(stopwords.words('english'))
    tokens = word_tokenize(text.lower())
    filtered_tokens = [word for word in tokens if word.isalpha() and word not in stop_words]
    return ' '.join(filtered_tokens)

Apply preprocessing
data['cleaned_text'] = data['text'].apply(preprocess_text)
```

Split the data into training and test sets

X_train, X_test, y_train, y_test = train_test_split(data['cleaned_text'], data['label'], test_size=0.2, random_state=42)

Convert text to TF-IDF features

vectorizer = TfidfVectorizer()

X_train_tfidf = vectorizer.fit_transform(X_train)

X_test_tfidf = vectorizer.transform(X_test)

Train a logistic regression model

model = LogisticRegression()

model.fit(X_train_tfidf, y_train)

Predict on the test set

y_pred = model.predict(X_test_tfidf)

Evaluate the model

accuracy = accuracy_score(y_test, y_pred)

print(f"Accuracy: {accuracy:.2f}")

print(classification_report(y_test, y_pred))

Example output: Predicting stock price movements based on news sentiment

news = "Company XYZ reports record earnings for Q3, beating expectations."

cleaned_news = preprocess_text(news)

news_tfidf = vectorizer.transform([cleaned_news])

```
prediction = model.predict(news_tfidf)
print(f"Predicted stock movement: {'Up' if prediction[0] == 1 else 'Down'}")
```

In this example, we start by loading a dataset of financial news articles with corresponding labels indicating positive (1) or negative (0) stock movements. We preprocess the text data by removing stopwords and tokenizing the text. Next, we convert the cleaned text into TF-IDF features, which represent the importance of words in the documents. We then train a logistic regression model on the training data and evaluate its performance on the test set. Finally, we use the trained model to predict stock movements based on a new piece of financial news.

Applications of NLP in Finance

NLP has a wide range of applications in the financial industry:

- Market Sentiment Analysis:

By analyzing news articles, social media, and analyst reports, NLP can gauge market sentiment and predict market trends. Positive sentiment may indicate bullish market conditions, while negative sentiment may suggest bearish trends.

- Algorithmic Trading:

NLP can be used to develop trading algorithms that react to real-time news and events. By instantly analyzing news feeds, the algorithms can make buy or sell decisions based on the sentiment and content of the news.

- Risk Management:

NLP helps in identifying potential risks by analyzing regulatory filings, earnings reports, and news articles. It can detect early warning signs of financial distress, fraud, or regulatory changes.

- Event Detection:

NLP can identify significant events, such as mergers and acquisitions, earnings announcements, and product launches, from news articles and press releases. This information is valuable for making informed investment decisions.

- Credit Assessment:

By analyzing textual data from credit applications, financial statements, and news reports, NLP can assist in assessing the creditworthiness of individuals and companies.

While NLP offers powerful tools for financial news analysis, it also presents several challenges:

- Data Quality:

The accuracy of NLP models depends on the quality and relevance of the textual data. Noisy or biased data can lead to incorrect predictions and insights.

- Interpretability:

NLP models, especially complex ones like deep learning models, can be difficult to interpret. Understanding how the model arrives at its predictions is crucial for making informed decisions.

- Dynamic Nature of Language:

Financial language evolves over time, with new terms, jargon, and expressions constantly emerging. NLP models need to be regularly updated to keep up with these changes.

- Sentiment Analysis Complexity:

Financial texts often contain nuanced language, making sentiment analysis challenging. Sarcasm, idioms, and context-specific meanings can complicate the accurate determination of sentiment.

Natural Language Processing is revolutionizing the way financial analysts and institutions process and interpret textual data. By harnessing NLP techniques, professionals can unlock insights from financial news, predict market movements, and make well-informed investment decisions. From sentiment analysis to event detection, the applications of NLP in finance are vast and transformative. As the field continues to evolve, mastering NLP will become an essential skill for anyone looking to excel in the data-driven world of finance.

## Blockchain and Machine Learning Convergence

Two groundbreaking technologies have come to the forefront: blockchain and machine learning. Individually, each has had a transformative impact; blockchain has revolutionized the way we think about data integrity and decentralization, while machine learning has unlocked new avenues for predictive analytics and automation. But what happens when these two technologies converge? The intersection of blockchain and machine learning presents a unique opportunity to enhance financial systems' transparency, security, and intelligence.

Understanding Blockchain Technology

Blockchain is a decentralized, distributed ledger that records transactions across many computers so that the record cannot be altered retroactively. This ensures the integrity and transparency of data. In finance, blockchain technology underpins cryptocurrencies like Bitcoin and Ethereum, enabling secure and transparent peer-to-peer transactions without the need for a central authority. Beyond cryptocurrencies, blockchain's applications extend to smart contracts, supply chain management, and secure, immutable record-keeping.

Key Features of Blockchain:

- Immutability: Once data is recorded on a blockchain, it cannot be altered, ensuring data integrity.

- Decentralization: Transactions are verified by a network of nodes, removing the need for a central authority.

- Transparency: Every transaction is visible to all participants in the network, increasing trust and accountability.

- Security: Cryptographic techniques ensure that data is securely stored and transmitted.

Machine Learning in Finance

Machine learning, a subset of artificial intelligence, involves training algorithms to identify patterns and make predictions based on data. In finance, machine learning applications include algorithmic trading, risk management, fraud detection, and customer service automation. Techniques such as supervised learning, unsupervised learning, and reinforcement learning are used to analyze large datasets, forecast market trends, and automate decision-making processes.

The Synergy of Blockchain and Machine Learning

The convergence of blockchain and machine learning brings together the strengths of both technologies, creating a powerful synergy with far-reaching implications for the financial industry. Here are some key areas where this convergence can be leveraged:

1. Data Integrity for Machine Learning Models:

Machine learning models rely on vast amounts of high-quality data. Blockchain's immutable ledger ensures that the data fed into these models is tamper-proof and trustworthy. By storing data on a blockchain, financial institutions can maintain a verifiable audit trail, enhancing the reliability of their machine learning predictions.

2. Decentralized Machine Learning:

Traditional machine learning models are typically centralized, meaning they rely on a central repository of data. Blockchain enables decentralized machine learning, where data and model updates are distributed across multiple nodes. This approach not only enhances data privacy but also allows for collaborative model training without sharing sensitive data.

3. Smart Contracts for Automated Decision-Making:

Smart contracts, self-executing contracts with the terms of the agreement directly written into code, can be integrated with machine learning models to automate complex financial transactions. For example, a smart contract could automatically execute a trade based on real-time market predictions generated by a machine learning algorithm.

4. Enhanced Security and Fraud Detection:

Machine learning algorithms can analyze transaction data stored on a blockchain to detect fraudulent activities. Blockchain's transparent and immutable nature ensures that once a fraudulent transaction is identified, it cannot be altered or deleted, aiding in forensic investigations and enhancing overall security.

5. Tokenization and Predictive Analytics:

Asset tokenization, the process of converting physical and intangible assets into digital tokens on a blockchain, can be combined with machine learning to perform predictive analytics on tokenized assets. This can provide valuable insights into asset performance, market trends, and investment opportunities.

Practical Example: Using Blockchain and Machine Learning for Fraud Detection

Let's explore a practical example of how blockchain and machine learning can be combined to enhance fraud detection in financial transactions.

```python
import pandas as pd

import numpy as np
```

from sklearn.ensemble import RandomForestClassifier

from sklearn.model_selection import train_test_split

from sklearn.metrics import accuracy_score, classification_report

from blockchain import Blockchain Hypothetical blockchain library

Hypothetical blockchain data (for illustration, replace with actual blockchain data)

data = pd.read_csv('blockchain_transactions.csv') Assume 'features' and 'label' columns

Preprocess the data

X = data.drop('label', axis=1)

y = data['label']

Split the data into training and test sets

X_train, X_test, y_train, y_test = train_test_split(X, y, test_size=0.2, random_state=42)

Train a Random Forest classifier

model = RandomForestClassifier(n_estimators=100, random_state=42)

model.fit(X_train, y_train)

Predict on the test set

y_pred = model.predict(X_test)

Evaluate the model

accuracy = accuracy_score(y_test, y_pred)

```
print(f"Accuracy: {accuracy:.2f}")
print(classification_report(y_test, y_pred))

Integrate with a hypothetical blockchain for transaction validation
blockchain = Blockchain()

def validate_transaction(transaction):
     Extract features from the transaction
    features = extract_features(transaction)
     Predict fraud likelihood
    is_fraud = model.predict([features])[0]
    return is_fraud

Example transaction validation
transaction = {
    'sender': 'Alice',
    'receiver': 'Bob',
    'amount': 1000,
    'timestamp': '2023-10-01T12:00:00Z'
}
is_fraud = validate_transaction(transaction)
print(f"Transaction is {'fraudulent' if is_fraud else 'legitimate'}.")
```

In this example, we start by loading a dataset of blockchain transactions labeled as either fraudulent or legitimate. We preprocess the data and train a Random Forest classifier to predict fraudulent transactions. Using a hypothetical blockchain library, we then integrate the trained model with the blockchain to validate new transactions in real-time, flagging any that are likely to be fraudulent.

Challenges and Future Directions

While the convergence of blockchain and machine learning holds immense potential, it also presents several challenges:

- Scalability: Both blockchain and machine learning require significant computational resources. Ensuring scalability while maintaining performance is a critical challenge.
- Data Privacy: Balancing the need for data transparency on the blockchain with the privacy concerns of sensitive financial information is complex.
- Interoperability: Integrating blockchain with existing financial systems and machine learning frameworks requires standardization and interoperability.

Future research and development in this field will likely focus on addressing these challenges, exploring new use cases, and enhancing the synergy between blockchain and machine learning. As both technologies continue to evolve, their combined impact on the financial industry is poised to be transformative.

The convergence of blockchain and machine learning is revolutionizing the financial industry, offering new levels of transparency, security, and intelligence. From enhancing data integrity and enabling decentralized machine learning to automating decision-making with smart contracts and improving fraud detection, the synergy of these technologies is unlocking unprecedented opportunities. As we continue to explore and innovate at this intersection, mastering the integration of blockchain and machine learning will be essential for staying ahead in the data-driven world of finance.

## Ethical Considerations in Financial Machine Learning

### 1. Bias and Fairness

One of the most critical ethical concerns in financial machine learning is bias. Machine learning models are trained on historical data, and if this data contains biases, the models will inevitably learn and perpetuate these biases. In finance, this can manifest in various ways, such as discriminatory lending practices, biased credit scoring, and unequal access to financial services.

Example:

Consider a credit scoring model that disproportionately assigns lower scores to certain demographic groups due to historical disparities in economic opportunities. If left unchecked, such a model can exacerbate existing inequalities.

Addressing Bias:

- Diverse Data: Ensure the training data is representative of all demographic groups.

- Bias Detection: Implement techniques to detect and quantify bias in models. This can include fairness-aware algorithms that adjust predictions to mitigate bias.

- Transparency: Maintain transparency in model decisions and provide clear explanations for outcomes, making it easier to identify and correct biases.

2. Privacy and Data Security

Financial data is highly sensitive, encompassing personal information, transaction history, and financial behaviors. The use of machine learning in finance raises significant concerns about privacy and data security. Unauthorized access, data breaches, and misuse of personal information can have severe consequences for individuals and institutions.

Example:

A machine learning model predicting investment behaviors might access and process individual transaction histories. Without robust security measures, this data could be vulnerable to breaches.

Ensuring Privacy and Security:

- Data Encryption: Use advanced encryption techniques to protect data at rest and in transit.

- Anonymization: Anonymize personal information to prevent identification of individuals in datasets.

- Access Controls: Implement strict access controls to limit data access to authorized personnel only.

- Regulatory Compliance: Adhere to data protection regulations such as GDPR, ensuring that data handling practices are compliant with legal requirements.

3. Transparency and Explainability

Machine learning models, especially those based on deep learning, are often considered "black boxes" due to their complexity and lack of interpretability. In finance, where decisions can have profound impacts on individuals and markets, it is essential that models are transparent and their decisions explainable.

Example:

A loan approval model that denies an application without providing a clear explanation can erode trust and provoke legal challenges.

Enhancing Transparency and Explainability:

- Model Interpretation: Use techniques such as LIME (Local Interpretable Model-agnostic Explanations) and SHAP (SHapley Additive exPlanations) to interpret model predictions.
- Documentation: Maintain comprehensive documentation of model development, including data sources, feature selection, and decision criteria.
- Stakeholder Communication: Clearly communicate model purposes, limitations, and outcomes to stakeholders, ensuring they understand how and why decisions are made.

4. Accountability and Governance

The deployment of machine learning models in finance requires robust accountability and governance frameworks to ensure ethical standards are upheld. This involves clearly defining responsibilities, monitoring model performance, and establishing protocols for addressing ethical issues.

Example:

An investment firm using algorithmic trading models must have governance structures in place to monitor model behavior, ensuring it does not engage in manipulative trading practices.

Establishing Accountability and Governance:

- Ethics Committees: Form ethics committees to oversee model development and deployment, ensuring ethical considerations are prioritized.
- Auditing: Regularly audit models to assess their performance, fairness, and compliance with ethical guidelines.
- Incident Management: Develop protocols for managing and rectifying ethical issues, including mechanisms for reporting and addressing grievances.

5. Societal Impact

The societal impact of financial machine learning extends beyond individual users to broader economic systems and communities. Ethical considerations must account for the potential consequences of model deployment on economic stability, market fairness, and social welfare.

Example:

High-frequency trading algorithms can exacerbate market volatility, potentially destabilizing financial markets and affecting economic stability.

Mitigating Societal Impact:

- Impact Assessment: Conduct thorough impact assessments to evaluate the potential societal effects of machine learning models.
- Ethical Design: Design models with ethical considerations in

mind, prioritizing societal welfare and minimizing negative externalities.

- Stakeholder Engagement: Engage with a diverse range of stakeholders, including regulators, advocacy groups, and affected communities, to understand and address societal concerns.

Case Study: Ethical Challenge in Credit Scoring

Let's consider a case study involving a credit scoring model to illustrate the ethical challenges and potential solutions.

Scenario:

A financial institution deploys a machine learning model to assess creditworthiness. Over time, it becomes apparent that the model disproportionately denies credit to applicants from certain minority groups.

Challenges:

- Bias: The model perpetuates existing biases present in historical lending data.

- Lack of Transparency: Applicants receive no clear explanation for credit denials, eroding trust in the institution.

- Privacy Concerns: The model processes sensitive personal data, raising privacy issues.

Solutions:

1. Bias Mitigation:

   - Retrain the model using a more diverse and representative dataset.

   - Implement fairness-aware algorithms to adjust predictions

and reduce bias.

2. Transparency:

- Use explainability techniques such as LIME to provide clear explanations for credit decisions.

- Communicate decision criteria to applicants, enhancing transparency.

3. Privacy Protection:

- Anonymize data to protect individual identities.

- Implement robust encryption and access controls to secure sensitive information.

Addressing these ethical challenges, the financial institution can ensure its credit scoring model is fair, transparent, and respectful of privacy, thereby fostering trust and promoting financial inclusion.

As machine learning continues to revolutionize the financial industry, ethical considerations must remain at the forefront of innovation. Addressing bias, ensuring privacy, enhancing transparency, establishing accountability, and mitigating societal impact are essential for the responsible and ethical deployment of machine learning in finance.

Future Trends: Quantum Computing and Finance

To grasp the implications of quantum computing in finance, it's essential to understand its foundational principles. Traditional computers operate on bits—binary digits that represent 0s and 1s. In contrast, quantum computers use quantum bits or qubits, which can exist in multiple states simultaneously due to the principles of superposition and entanglement. This unique capability allows quantum computers to process vast amounts of information at unprecedented speeds, making them exceptionally powerful for certain types of computations.

Example:

Consider the problem of optimizing a large portfolio. Traditional computers may require significant time to evaluate numerous asset combinations. Quantum computers, leveraging their parallel processing capabilities, can evaluate multiple combinations simultaneously, drastically reducing computation time.

Applications of Quantum Computing in Finance

Quantum computing has the potential to address several pressing challenges in finance, offering solutions that are currently infeasible with classical computing. Here are some key applications:

1. Portfolio Optimization

Portfolio optimization involves selecting the best mix of assets to maximize returns while minimizing risk. This problem is inherently complex due to the vast number of possible asset combinations and the need to balance various constraints.

Quantum Approach:

Quantum algorithms, such as the Quantum Approximate Optimization Algorithm (QAOA), can tackle this problem more efficiently by exploring multiple potential solutions simultaneously. This allows for faster and more accurate optimization, enabling investors to make better-informed decisions.

2. Risk Management

Effective risk management requires accurately assessing and mitigating potential financial risks. Traditional methods often rely on approximations and can be computationally intensive.

Quantum Approach:
Quantum computing can enhance risk management by improving the precision and speed of simulations used to assess risk. For instance, quantum Monte Carlo simulations can provide more accurate risk estimations for complex financial instruments.

3. Fraud Detection

Detecting fraudulent transactions involves analyzing vast amounts of data to identify patterns and anomalies. This process can be time-consuming and may miss subtle fraud indicators.

Quantum Approach:
Quantum machine learning algorithms can analyze large datasets more efficiently, improving the accuracy and speed of fraud detection. Quantum computers can process and correlate data points in ways that classical computers cannot, uncovering hidden patterns indicative of fraudulent activity.

4. Pricing Derivatives

Pricing complex financial derivatives, such as options and futures, involves solving mathematical models. Traditional methods, like the Black-Scholes model, have limitations and can be computationally expensive for high-dimensional problems.

Quantum Approach:

Quantum algorithms can solve these models more efficiently, providing faster and more accurate pricing of derivatives. This can lead to better risk assessment and more effective trading strategies.

While the potential of quantum computing in finance is immense, several challenges must be addressed before it can be fully realized.

1. Technological Maturity

Quantum computing is still in its nascent stages, with many practical and technical hurdles to overcome. Current quantum computers, known as Noisy Intermediate-Scale Quantum (NISQ) devices, are prone to errors and have limited qubit counts.

Consideration:

Continued advancements in quantum hardware and error-correction techniques are essential for realizing the full potential of quantum computing in finance.

2. Integration with Classical Systems

Integrating quantum computing with existing classical systems presents significant challenges. Financial institutions must develop hybrid approaches that leverage the strengths of both quantum and classical computing.

Consideration:

Developing algorithms and frameworks that seamlessly integrate quantum and classical computations will be crucial for practical applications in finance.

3. Regulatory and Ethical Considerations

The adoption of quantum computing in finance raises important regulatory and ethical questions. Ensuring compliance with financial regulations and addressing ethical concerns, such as data privacy, will be vital.

Consideration:

Establishing clear guidelines and regulatory frameworks for the use of quantum computing in finance will help mitigate risks and ensure responsible adoption.

Future Prospects and Research Directions

The future of quantum computing in finance is promising, with ongoing research and development paving the way for transformative applications. Here are some key areas of focus:

1. Quantum Machine Learning

Quantum machine learning combines the power of quantum

computing with advanced machine learning techniques. This field holds significant potential for improving predictive models, enhancing data analysis, and optimizing trading strategies.

Research Direction:

Developing quantum algorithms for machine learning tasks, such as clustering, classification, and regression, will be a major area of focus. These algorithms can provide more accurate and efficient solutions for financial applications.

2. Quantum Cryptography

Quantum cryptography leverages the principles of quantum mechanics to create secure communication channels. This technology can enhance the security of financial transactions and protect sensitive information from cyber threats.

Research Direction:

Exploring quantum key distribution (QKD) and other quantum cryptographic techniques will be crucial for developing secure financial systems.

3. Quantum Optimization

Optimization problems are central to many financial applications, from portfolio management to trading strategies. Quantum optimization algorithms can provide faster and more precise solutions to these complex problems.

Research Direction:

Advancing quantum optimization techniques, such as the

Quantum Approximate Optimization Algorithm (QAOA) and Variational Quantum Eigensolver (VQE), will drive the development of practical applications in finance.

Quantum computing represents a paradigm shift in the way financial problems are approached and solved. Its potential to revolutionize portfolio optimization, risk management, fraud detection, and derivative pricing is immense. However, realizing this potential requires overcoming significant technological, integration, and regulatory challenges.

Integration with Other Libraries and Frameworks (TensorFlow, PyTorch)

Before diving into integration specifics, it's essential to understand why TensorFlow and PyTorch are game-changers in the landscape of machine learning and finance.

TensorFlow: Developed by Google Brain, TensorFlow is an open-source deep learning library known for its flexibility and scalability. It excels in building and deploying advanced neural network models, making it invaluable for tasks requiring complex computations and large-scale data processing.

PyTorch: Created by Facebook's AI Research lab, PyTorch is another open-source deep learning framework. It stands out for its dynamic computational graph and ease of use, which facilitate rapid prototyping and experimentation. PyTorch is particularly favored in the research community and is increasingly used in production environments.

Why Integrate with Scikit-Learn?

Scikit-Learn, though powerful, is fundamentally designed for traditional machine learning tasks. Integrating it with TensorFlow and PyTorch allows you to leverage the best of both worlds: the simplicity and efficiency of Scikit-Learn with the advanced, high-performance capabilities of deep learning frameworks.

1. Enhanced Model Flexibility

Integrating these libraries facilitates the construction of more sophisticated models. For instance, while Scikit-Learn might handle the data preprocessing and feature engineering, TensorFlow or PyTorch can build and train deep neural networks for complex tasks like high-frequency trading or sentiment analysis from financial news.

2. Improved Computational Performance

Deep learning libraries are optimized for parallel processing on GPUs, significantly speeding up training times for large datasets. This computational prowess is critical for financial applications, where timely insights can lead to substantial economic advantages.

3. Comprehensive Ecosystem

Both TensorFlow and PyTorch come with extensive ecosystems that include tools for data visualization, deployment, and optimization. These ecosystems complement Scikit-Learn's suite of tools, providing a holistic environment for machine learning in finance.

Practical Implementation

Let's explore how to integrate Scikit-Learn with TensorFlow and PyTorch through a practical example: predicting stock prices using a neural network.

Data Preprocessing with Scikit-Learn

First, we use Scikit-Learn to preprocess financial data. Assume we have a dataset of historical stock prices.

```python
import pandas as pd
from sklearn.preprocessing import StandardScaler
from sklearn.model_selection import train_test_split

Load dataset
data = pd.read_csv('historical_stock_prices.csv')

Feature selection and scaling
features = data[['open', 'high', 'low', 'volume']]
target = data['close']
scaler = StandardScaler()
scaled_features = scaler.fit_transform(features)

Train-test split
X_train, X_test, y_train, y_test = train_test_split(scaled_features, target, test_size=0.2, random_state=42)
```

## Building and Training a Neural Network with TensorFlow

Next, we build and train a neural network using TensorFlow.

```python
import tensorflow as tf
from tensorflow.keras.models import Sequential
from tensorflow.keras.layers import Dense

Define the model
model = Sequential([
    Dense(128, activation='relu', input_shape=(X_train.shape[1],)),
    Dense(64, activation='relu'),
    Dense(1)
])

Compile the model
model.compile(optimizer='adam', loss='mean_squared_error')

Train the model
model.fit(X_train, y_train, epochs=50, batch_size=32, validation_split=0.2)
```

## Using PyTorch for Training

Alternatively, we can use PyTorch to achieve similar outcomes.

```python
import torch
import torch.nn as nn
import torch.optim as optim
from torch.utils.data import DataLoader, TensorDataset

Convert data to PyTorch tensors
X_train_tensor = torch.tensor(X_train, dtype=torch.float32)
y_train_tensor = torch.tensor(y_train.values, dtype=torch.float32).view(-1, 1)
train_dataset = TensorDataset(X_train_tensor, y_train_tensor)
train_loader = DataLoader(train_dataset, batch_size=32, shuffle=True)

Define the model
class StockPredictor(nn.Module):
    def __init__(self):
        super(StockPredictor, self).__init__()
        self.fc1 = nn.Linear(X_train.shape[1], 128)
        self.fc2 = nn.Linear(128, 64)
        self.fc3 = nn.Linear(64, 1)

    def forward(self, x):
        x = torch.relu(self.fc1(x))
        x = torch.relu(self.fc2(x))
        x = self.fc3(x)
```

```
        return x

model = StockPredictor()

Define loss and optimizer
criterion = nn.MSELoss()
optimizer = optim.Adam(model.parameters(), lr=0.001)

Train the model
for epoch in range(50):
    for X_batch, y_batch in train_loader:
        optimizer.zero_grad()
        predictions = model(X_batch)
        loss = criterion(predictions, y_batch)
        loss.backward()
        optimizer.step()
```

Combining Results

After training, we can combine the results from TensorFlow or PyTorch models with Scikit-Learn's evaluation metrics.

```python
from sklearn.metrics import mean_squared_error

TensorFlow predictions
tf_predictions = model.predict(X_test)
tf_mse = mean_squared_error(y_test, tf_predictions)
```

```
PyTorch predictions
model.eval()
with torch.no_grad():
    X_test_tensor = torch.tensor(X_test, dtype=torch.float32)
    pytorch_predictions = model(X_test_tensor).numpy()
pytorch_mse = mean_squared_error(y_test, pytorch_predictions)

print(f'TensorFlow MSE: {tf_mse}')
print(f'PyTorch MSE: {pytorch_mse}')
```

Integrating these libraries isn't without its challenges. Here are a few considerations:

1. Compatibility Issues

Ensure compatibility between different library versions. TensorFlow and PyTorch frequently update, and changes can sometimes break existing code. Always check compatibility when integrating these tools into your workflow.

2. Learning Curve

While Scikit-Learn is user-friendly, TensorFlow and PyTorch require a deeper understanding of neural networks and machine learning principles. Time investment in learning these frameworks is essential for effective integration.

3. Computational Resources

Deep learning models can be resource-intensive, requiring powerful GPUs for efficient training. Ensure you have the necessary computational resources or consider using cloud services for scalable solutions.

Future Directions

The future of integrating Scikit-Learn with TensorFlow and PyTorch is promising. As both libraries continue to evolve, their synergy will likely become more seamless and powerful. Future advancements may bring enhanced tools for:

1. Automated Machine Learning (AutoML)

AutoML frameworks are becoming more prevalent, offering automated pipeline creation and hyperparameter tuning. Integrating Scikit-Learn's simplicity with TensorFlow and PyTorch's capabilities in AutoML frameworks will streamline model development.

2. Transfer Learning

Leveraging pre-trained models from TensorFlow and PyTorch can significantly reduce the training time and improve performance. Combining these models with Scikit-Learn's preprocessing and feature engineering capabilities will be a powerful approach for financial applications.

3. Federated Learning

As data privacy concerns grow, federated learning—training models across decentralized devices without centralizing data—will become crucial. Integrating Scikit-Learn with TensorFlow and PyTorch in federated learning frameworks will enhance secure and efficient financial modeling.

Integrating Scikit-Learn with TensorFlow and PyTorch is not just a technical enhancement but a strategic necessity for staying ahead in the competitive financial landscape. By harnessing the strengths of these powerful libraries, you can build more sophisticated, accurate, and efficient models, driving innovation and success in your financial endeavors.

## Practical Project: Building a Comprehensive Financial Prediction System

### Step 1: Defining the Problem

The first step in building any prediction system is to define the problem clearly. For this project, let's focus on predicting stock prices. Our goal is to forecast the closing price of a stock based on historical data, incorporating various features such as open price, high price, low price, volume, and other relevant indicators.

### Step 2: Data Collection and Preprocessing

Data is the backbone of any machine learning project. We will use a historical stock price dataset, which can be sourced from financial APIs like Alpha Vantage, Yahoo Finance, or local exchanges.

```python
import pandas as pd
from alpha_vantage.timeseries import TimeSeries

Fetching data from Alpha Vantage
api_key = 'YOUR_ALPHA_VANTAGE_API_KEY'
ts = TimeSeries(key=api_key, output_format='pandas')
data, meta_data = ts.get_daily(symbol='AAPL', outputsize='full')

Selecting relevant columns
data = data[['1. open', '2. high', '3. low', '4. close', '5. volume']]
data.columns = ['open', 'high', 'low', 'close', 'volume']
```

Next, we preprocess the data to handle missing values, scale features, and split the dataset into training and testing sets.

```python
from sklearn.preprocessing import StandardScaler
from sklearn.model_selection import train_test_split

Handling missing values
data.dropna(inplace=True)

Feature scaling
scaler = StandardScaler()
```

scaled_data = scaler.fit_transform(data)

Splitting the data

X = scaled_data[:, :-1]  Features: open, high, low, volume

y = scaled_data[:, -1]  Target: close price

X_train, X_test, y_train, y_test = train_test_split(X, y, test_size=0.2, random_state=42)

```

Step 3: Feature Engineering

Feature engineering involves creating new features that can improve the model's predictive power. For instance, we can include technical indicators like moving averages, Relative Strength Index (RSI), and Bollinger Bands.

```python
import ta  Technical Analysis library

Adding technical indicators
data['MA20'] = data['close'].rolling(window=20).mean()
data['RSI'] = ta.momentum.RSIIndicator(data['close']).rsi()
data['Bollinger_Upper'] = ta.volatility.BollingerBands(data['close']).bollinger_hband()
data['Bollinger_Lower'] = ta.volatility.BollingerBands(data['close']).bollinger_lband()

Dropping NaN values created by rolling calculations
data.dropna(inplace=True)
```
```

Re-scaling and re-splitting data

scaled_data = scaler.fit_transform(data)

X = scaled_data[:, :-1]

y = scaled_data[:, -1]

X_train, X_test, y_train, y_test = train_test_split(X, y, test_size=0.2, random_state=42)

```

Step 4: Model Selection and Training

We will use an ensemble approach, combining multiple models to improve accuracy. For this project, let's use a Random Forest Regressor and a Gradient Boosting Regressor.

```python
from sklearn.ensemble import RandomForestRegressor, GradientBoostingRegressor

from sklearn.metrics import mean_squared_error

Initializing the models

rf_model = RandomForestRegressor(n_estimators=100, random_state=42)

gb_model = GradientBoostingRegressor(n_estimators=100, learning_rate=0.1, random_state=42)

Training the models

rf_model.fit(X_train, y_train)

gb_model.fit(X_train, y_train)
```
```

```
Making predictions
rf_predictions = rf_model.predict(X_test)
gb_predictions = gb_model.predict(X_test)

Evaluating the models
rf_mse = mean_squared_error(y_test, rf_predictions)
gb_mse = mean_squared_error(y_test, gb_predictions)

print(f'Random Forest MSE: {rf_mse}')
print(f'Gradient Boosting MSE: {gb_mse}')
```

Step 5: Model Validation and Hyperparameter Tuning

To ensure our model's reliability, we will validate it using cross-validation and optimize its hyperparameters using GridSearchCV.

```python
from sklearn.model_selection import GridSearchCV

Defining the parameter grid for Random Forest
rf_param_grid = {
    'n_estimators': [50, 100, 200],
    'max_features': ['auto', 'sqrt', 'log2'],
    'max_depth': [None, 10, 20, 30]
}
```

```
Defining the parameter grid for Gradient Boosting
gb_param_grid = {
    'n_estimators': [50, 100, 200],
    'learning_rate': [0.01, 0.1, 0.2],
    'max_depth': [3, 5, 7]
}

Initializing GridSearchCV for Random Forest
rf_grid_search = GridSearchCV(estimator=rf_model, param_grid=rf_param_grid, cv=5, scoring='neg_mean_squared_error', n_jobs=-1)
rf_grid_search.fit(X_train, y_train)

 Initializing GridSearchCV for Gradient Boosting
gb_grid_search = GridSearchCV(estimator=gb_model, param_grid=gb_param_grid, cv=5, scoring='neg_mean_squared_error', n_jobs=-1)
gb_grid_search.fit(X_train, y_train)

 Best parameters and scores
print(f'Best RF Parameters: {rf_grid_search.best_params_}')
print(f'Best GB Parameters: {gb_grid_search.best_params_}')
```

Step 6: Integration with External Libraries

To further enhance our prediction system, we integrate TensorFlow for building a deep learning model.

```python
import tensorflow as tf
from tensorflow.keras.models import Sequential
from tensorflow.keras.layers import Dense, LSTM

Defining the LSTM model
model = Sequential([
    LSTM(50, return_sequences=True, input_shape=(X_train.shape[1], 1)),
    LSTM(50, return_sequences=False),
    Dense(25),
    Dense(1)
])

Compiling the model
model.compile(optimizer='adam', loss='mean_squared_error')

Reshaping data for LSTM
X_train_lstm = X_train.reshape((X_train.shape[0], X_train.shape[1], 1))
X_test_lstm = X_test.reshape((X_test.shape[0], X_test.shape[1], 1))

Training the LSTM model
model.fit(X_train_lstm, y_train, batch_size=32, epochs=50, validation_split=0.2)

Making predictions with LSTM
```

```
lstm_predictions = model.predict(X_test_lstm)
lstm_mse = mean_squared_error(y_test, lstm_predictions)

print(f'LSTM MSE: {lstm_mse}')
```

Step 7: Deployment and Monitoring

Finally, deploying the model ensures it can be used in real-time trading systems or financial decision-making platforms. Using cloud services like AWS, Azure, or Google Cloud can facilitate deployment and monitoring.

```python
Example of saving the model
rf_model.save('random_forest_model.pkl')
model.save('lstm_model.h5')

Example of loading the model for future predictions
loaded_rf_model = pd.read_pickle('random_forest_model.pkl')
loaded_lstm_model =
tf.keras.models.load_model('lstm_model.h5')

Making predictions with loaded models
new_rf_predictions = loaded_rf_model.predict(X_test)
new_lstm_predictions =
loaded_lstm_model.predict(X_test_lstm)
```

Building a comprehensive financial prediction system involves meticulous steps—from data preprocessing and feature engineering to model selection, validation, and deployment. By integrating Scikit-Learn with advanced libraries like TensorFlow and PyTorch, you can harness the full power of machine learning and deep learning, delivering precise and reliable financial predictions. This practical project serves as a blueprint, empowering you to innovate and excel in the ever-competitive financial sector. Dive in, experiment, and refine—your journey into the world of financial prediction is just beginning.

www.ingramcontent.com/pod-product-compliance
Lightning Source LLC
LaVergne TN
LVHW051219050326
832903LV00028B/2171

*9798327625259*